EXEGETICAL ANALYSIS

A PRACTICAL GUIDE FOR APPLYING BIBLICAL RESEARCH TO THE SOCIAL SCIENCES

Foreword by Corné J. Bekker

JOSHUA D. HENSON, Ph.D.
Regent University

STEVEN S. CROWTHER, Ph.D.
Grace College of Divinity

RUSSELL L. HUIZING, Ph.D.
Toccoa Falls College

Kendall Hunt
publishing company

Cover image: © Shutterstock.com

ESV: Scripture quotations are from the ESV® Bible (The Holy Bible, English Standard Version®), copyright © 2001 by Crossway Bibles, a publishing ministry of Good News Publishers. Used by permission. All rights reserved.

www.kendallhunt.com
Send all inquiries to:
4050 Westmark Drive
Dubuque, IA 52004-1840

Copyright © 2020 by Kendall Hunt Publishing Company

ISBN 978-1-7924-1217-2

All rights reserved. No part of this publication may be reproduced, stored in a retrieval system, or transmitted, in any form or by any means, electronic, mechanical, photocopying, recording, or otherwise, without the prior written permission of the copyright owner.

Published in the United States of America

*To Dina, Makenzie, and AJ. You are my home and my reason for being.
I love you more than words can express.*

Joshua D. Henson

*To Terri, my love and my children: Jason, Justin, Timothy, and Stefanie.
You are my inspiration and my foundation for teaching others.*

Steven S. Crowther

*To Margaret, Noah, Joshua, Nathan, and Andrew . . . I teach
because of what you have taught me. I love you all.*

Russell L. Huizing

Contents

Foreword xi
Introduction xv

Part 1 Knowing the "Whys" 1

Chapter 1 Exegetical Analysis and the Holy Scriptures 3
Why We Study the Holy Scriptures 3
Exegetical Analysis Is Scientific 4
Exegetical Analysis Is Spiritual 7
Exegetical Analysis Is Applicable 8
Conclusion 9
Chapter One Reflective Exercises 10

Part 2 Discovering the "Whats" 11

Chapter 2 Choosing What to Study 13
Starting with a Topic 14
Choosing the Right Sources 14
Reviewing the Literature 15
Selecting the Right Pericope 18
Writing the Introduction 22
Constructing the Proper Research Question(s) 25
Conclusion 27
Chapter Two Reflective Exercises 28

Part 3 Answering the "Hows" 29

Chapter 3 The Various Approaches to "How" 31
Grammatical–Historical Interpretation 31
Textual Criticism 35

v

Inductive Biblical Analysis	36
The Interpretive Journey	46
Genre Analysis	48
Conclusion	59
Chapter Three Reflective Exercises	59

Chapter 4 Timing Matters—Dealing with Authorship and Dating 61

Determining the Author	62
Determining the Audience	65
Determining the Date	67
Determining the Purpose	68
Conclusion	69
Chapter Four Reflective Exercises	70

Chapter 5 Why Socio-Rhetorical Analysis? 71

It Is Scientific	73
It Is Systematic	76
It Is Holistic	78
Conclusion	80
Chapter Five Reflective Exercises	81

Chapter 6 Working Through Socio-Rhetorical Analysis—Inner Texture 83

Textual Units	84
Repetitive Patterns	85
Progressive Patterns	89
Opening-Middle-Closing Patterns	92
Argumentative Patterns	93
Sensory-Aesthetic Patterns	94
An Example from John 21	96
Conclusion	102
Chapter Six Reflective Exercises	102

Chapter 7 Working Through Socio-Rhetorical Analysis—Intertexture 105

Oral-Scribal Intertexture	107
Cultural Intertexture	114

Social Intertexture 117
Historical Intertexture 119
Reciprocal Intertexture 120
Conclusion 121
Chapter Seven Reflective Exercises................................. 121

Chapter 8 **Working Through Socio-Rhetorical Analysis— Social and Cultural Texture 123**
Social and Cultural Texture Method 124
Specific Social Topics (Worldview—From Conversionist to Utopian) 126
Interpretation 134
Application.. 136
Example 137
Common Social and Cultural Topics 140
Final Cultural Categories 149
Application.. 153
Conclusion 158
Chapter Eight Reflective Exercises 159

Chapter 9 **Working Through Socio-Rhetorical Analysis— Ideological Texture 161**
Individual Locations 161
Relation to Groups 162
Modes of Intellectual Discourse 165
Spheres of Ideology... 167
Seeing the Picture 168
What Is Love? An Analysis of 1 Corinthians 13........... 169
Conclusion 173
Chapter Nine Reflective Exercises................................. 174

Chapter 10 **Working Through Socio-Rhetorical Analysis— Sacred Texture 175**
Deity 176
Holy Person 177
Spirit Being.. 179
Divine History or Eschatology...................................... 180
Human Redemption.. 182

Human Commitment 183
Religious Community 183
Ethics 185
Application 186
Conclusion 186
Chapter Ten Reflective Exercises 189

Chapter 11 **Treating the Text as a Data Source** **191**
The Use of Qualitative Analysis 192
Types of Qualitative Analysis 192
Results of Qualitative Analysis 194
The Holy Spirit in Interpretation 196
Interpretation's Effect on the Interpreter 198
Conclusion 199
Chapter Eleven Reflective Exercises 200

Part 4 Addressing the "So Whats" 201

Chapter 12 **Moving from Interpretation to Application** **203**
Revisiting the Research Question(s) 204
Recognizing Our Own Biases 206
Applying the Text to the Context 209
Conclusion 212
Chapter Twelve Reflective Exercises 213

Part 5 Ending with the "Now Whats" 215

Chapter 13 **The Potential for Future Research to Bridge Theory and Practice** **217**
Theory and Theology 218
The Chicken or the Egg? 218
Conclusion 223
Chapter Thirteen Reflective Exercises 224

Appendices 225
Appendix A Choosing What to Study 227
Appendix B Example of Inductive Bible Analysis 231

Definition of Terms *237*
Resources for Further Study *245*
List of References *249*
List of Scripture References *261*
About the Authors *265*

Foreword

This is a welcome text. I applaud Joshua Henson, Steven Crowther, and Russell Huizing for boldly taking a stand and declaring what Hebrew and Christian believers have known for thousands of years: The Holy Scriptures is the source for understanding our world and our place in it. There was a time when theology was considered the queen of the sciences. But at most places of learning today, this throne stands empty. The reformer, Martin Luther, laments the loss of theology at institutions of higher learning in a letter he wrote in the 16th century:

> I am much afraid that the universities will prove to be the great gates of hell, unless they diligently labor in explaining the Holy Scriptures, and engraving them in the hearts of youth. I advise no one to place his child where the Scriptures do not reign paramount. Every institution in which men are not unceasingly occupied with the Word of God must become corrupt (*Es muss verderben, alles was nicht Gottes Wort ohn Unterlass treibt*, 486).

Not much has changed since the days of Luther. Researchers in the social sciences that return to the Scriptures as a valid avenue of research might often feel that they are on a lonely pilgrimage.

The image of a pilgrimage is one that has been used in the Scriptures (Ps. 84:5; Heb. 11:9) and in the history of Christianity to describe the call to a spiritual life. Early Christians taught that life is like a journey, that this world is not our ultimate destination, and that we are all on our way back to God who is our truest home (cf. Heb 11:13). Scaperlanda and Scaperlanda (2004, p. 7) describe a pilgrimage as: ". . . the journey of those who, deliberately seek answers to the questions of meaning, purpose, and eternity. Instead of seeking fulfillment in things that will never satisfy, the sacred pilgrim sets out to find that which the heart truly desires: God's very presence."

This erudite description of a "sacred pilgrim" is appropriate in our quest to not only discover the story of God's people in history but also to become aware of our journey as those who intend to seek diligently "answers to the questions of meaning, purpose, and eternity" in our respective contexts. If we, who desire to be formed in God's image through God's Spirit (2 Cor 3:18), are then indeed pilgrims on the way of truth, what tools must we carry on this adventure of (re)discovery?

A story is told about the 20th-century pilgrim, William McElwee Miller, which highlights the travel necessities required in our journey of becoming:

> While travelling along the border of Iran and Afghanistan, Dr. Miller had encountered a Muslim sage. Together the missionary and the mullah rode along the narrow path. In the course of their conversion the Persian asked the Presbyterian, "What is Christianity?" Dr. Miller said, "It is like a journey. For that trip I need four things—bread, for nourishment; water, for refreshment; a book, for direction; and opportunity, for service. These are my pilgrim fare. Jesus provided me with these things. I trust Him on my way. That is Christianity" (Arnold & George Fry, 1988).

This book that we have been given on our journey for direction is the collection of sacred Hebrew and Christian Scriptures, the Bible; through which we are invited to respond to the reality of our Creator and omnipresent God with a love and devotion that includes not only our body and heart, but also our critical faculties (cf. Jesus' use of the great *Shema* of Deut. 6:5 appearing in Matt. 22:37). It is a book offering an invitation to see ourselves in the narratives of the people of the Book (past, present, and future). We read the Scriptures with those who lived these realities, we are part of the construction of these inspired texts and received them through the centuries. We are not on this pilgrimage alone. We travel with all of God's people who have read and wrestled with these texts throughout the centuries. We learn from their methods, their victories, and their failures. We journey to our common goal of being transformed into His image (Ro 8:26–30).

Exegesis is the interpretative process of finding, seeing, and hearing God in the Sacred Scriptures (Deist, 1992), the collective history of those faithful pilgrims that have come before us in the journey. In his recent book on reading the Bible for spiritual formation, paleo-orthodox thinker and theologian Richard Foster (2008) proposes four simplified and practical steps for reading the Scriptures in communal ways. Each step has equal value (Foster):

1. **Read the Scriptures literally.** We use all the tools of linguistic, rhetorical, and communication analyses to enter into the words of the sacred texts. We take the original languages, literature, and communication styles of the first authors and readers seriously. We aim to immerse ourselves in the linguistic and artistic worlds of these first people of the text.
2. **Read the Scriptures in its historic and social contexts.** We actively avoid anachronistic and ethnocentric readings of the sacred texts by utilizing the disciplines of history, sociology, and anthropology to enter into the worlds of the people of the Bible. We do not think of the first contexts of the sacred as merely incidental to the meaning of the texts, but rather consider these contexts are central in the process of unlocking the meaning of the texts.

3. **Read the Scriptures in conversation with itself.** We proactively allow Scripture to interpret Scripture and form conclusions and interpretations based on rigorous synthesis, so as to enter the larger message of these sacred texts. We aim to uncover the larger narrative of God's people and see ourselves as part of this Biblical larger story.
4. **Read the Scriptures in conversation with the historic witness of the People of God.** We join the theological, philosophical, and formational discussions of all of God's people in history in a continued quest to enter into the truths of the sacred texts and its implications for our world.

We are a pilgrim people on a sacred journey in a quest to "incarnate" God's truths in our world. We do not walk blindly, and we do not walk alone. We have been given a book for our journey, a sacred book that is God-breathed, infused by God's Spirit, and is "profitable for teaching, for reproof, for correction, and for training in righteousness" (2 Tim. 3:16, ESV)—a book that provides direction for pilgrims on the way of truth. In addition, we also read this book together with all of those that we have come before us, shaped, and formed through God's Spirit by their witness and engagement with the text. Eugene Peterson (2009) illustrates how this kind of reading can be transformative and translate into missional orientations:

> Christians feed on Scripture. Holy Scripture nurtures the holy community as food nurtures the human body. Christians don't simply learn or study or use Scripture; we assimilate it, take it into our lives in such ways that it gets metabolized into acts of love, cups of cold water, missions into all the world, healing and evangelism and justice in Jesus' name, hands raised in adoration of the Father, feet washed in company with the Son (p. 84).

Louise Kretzschmar (2002), a South African Baptist scholar, in attempt to discover a way of reading the Scriptures that results in ethical and moral formation, proposes a process of conversions in our engagement with the Scriptures. Kretzschmar's (2007) proposals take its cue from the theology, spirituality, and leadership praxis of the Medieval Christian leader, Francis of Assisi (1181-1226 AD). Kretzschmar, as a Protestant, reads the Scriptures together with a Medieval Catholic figure and in doing so constructs a process description of formation that could positively contribute to the rebuilding of Kretzschmar's homeland of South Africa.

The radical and immediate exegetical practice of Francis, although removed in location and time, serves as an interlocutor with Kretzschmar's own ethical and contextual theology and thus provides a new way forward. Kretzschmar (2007) proposes that a series of conversions need to take place as we wrestle with the meaning and imperatives of the Scriptures (pp. 18–36). This wrestling with the text in the quest for meaning are all mediated by the Spirit of God who bridges time and place. According to Kretzschmar, as we read the Scriptures in community, we encounter five "conversions" (pp. 25–36):

1. **Intellectual conversion.** As we read the Scriptures in community, we submit to the presence of the Spirit, as we constantly rethink or evaluate our own and others' moral framework. This involves the disciplines of self-awareness and critique in order to develop the virtue of prudence (correct judgment) in both thought and action.
2. **Affective conversion.** As we read the Scriptures in community, we value *orthokardia* (right heartedness toward God). Empowered by the Spirit and the examples of those that have come before us, we consider the ultimate location of our affections and adopt biblical, historic, and ascetic disciplines in service to the world.
3. **Volitional conversion.** As we read the Scriptures in community and inspired by the Spirit, we seek to have a redeemed human will that moves from willfulness (identified as arrogant self-sufficiency) to willingness (described as flexible receptivity) in quest to be formed and to serve.
4. **Relational conversion.** As we read the Scriptures in community, we seek to have our moral conscience to be formed and challenged by the Spirit in community (past and present). In response, we engage in moral relational power that brings personal and communal transformation to perceptions and applications of service.
5. **Moral action**. The intellectual, affective, volitional, and relational conversions that result from reading the Scriptures in community then motivate moral action that facilitates the wider conversion of the contexts in which we live and serve.

The reintroduction of disciplines of receiving the Scriptures that are thoroughly engaged with the historic practice of the faithful traditions of Christianity and communal in nature can not only reenergize and revitalize our understanding of spiritual and human formation, but also result in a renewed experience of the Holy Spirit. Francis of Assisi (1181–1226 AD), in a concluding prayer in a letter to his entire order says it best: "Inwardly cleansed, interiorly enlightened and inflamed by the fire of the Holy Spirit, may we be able to follow in the footsteps of your beloved Son" (*Epistula Toti Ordini Missa*).

May this important text forge the way forward for all who in their respectful fields seek to be cleansed, enlightened, and inflamed—so that our world might be changed for the glory of Christ.

Corné J. Bekker, D. Litt. et Phil.
Dean & Professor
Regent University School of Divinity
October 2019

Introduction

As technology continues to evolve, the social and cultural constructs of our society are changing rapidly. The shifting landscape of information and communication is transforming every facet of society—for the good and for the bad. Leaders from every arena of life are grappling with the new realities created by social interactions that question the very institutional foundations upon which civilization is built. As a result, our social contexts have become skewed in a way that traditional institutions, such as religion, have been cast to the peripheral of human thought. Yet, even in the midst of the changing tides that govern contemporary society, there is increased interest in the role of faith and spirituality. For Christians, at the heart of faith and spirituality is the Bible.

There is arguably no document in human history more influential than the Holy Bible. The principles derived from Scripture have guided the lives of its adherents for millennia. So, as our society embarks upon an unknown future, scholars from various fields have returned to ancient documents for answers. Many of these scholars are not trained in biblical languages nor are they versed in the various methodologies of biblical hermeneutics. Yet, the desire to better understand the truths of Scripture exists. Equipped with modern English translations, scholarly commentaries, lexicons, and other Greek/Hebrew language tools, social scientists are discovering the Bible anew. As sociological and anthropological principles are being applied to the Scriptures, there is a need to better understand how to apply biblical principles to contemporary contexts while also honoring original intent.

The interdisciplinary nature of the social sciences requires an interdisciplinary hermeneutical methodology. The problem, however, is that the various hermeneutical practices are often walled off from one another such that the lessons gleaned from one methodology do not necessary inform the lessons of other methodologies. Given this, Vernon Robbins and associates undertook the task of developing a methodology that was interdisciplinary by nature; bringing together the traditional hermeneutics and social scientific principles. By viewing a text as an interaction between written and oral traditions and the social and cultural contexts of the people represented by a text, the interpretative depth, or texture, within a text can be revealed.

While honoring the work of Robbins and associates, and also being cognizant the significant debate regarding the nature and limitations of socio-rhetorical criticism, we recognized a need for a book that would provide researchers with a methodological guide to biblical research from choosing a topic to considering the implications of future research. In this book, we endeavor to demonstrate that biblical research can be both spiritual and scientific. With a high view of Scripture and its power to transform the human heart, we set out to provide a systematic approach to exegesis that leaves space for the leading of the Holy Spirit.

We openly recognize the ongoing debate regarding the best practices of hermeneutics, and do not seek to engage this too heavily. It is our expressed purpose that we will remain true to the *practical* in *Exegetical Analysis: A Practical Guide for Applying Biblical Research to the Social Sciences*. Given this, it is necessary for us to consider what this book *is* and what this book *is not*.

1. This book is designed for the Christian researcher. It is not written for the atheist or the agnostic scholar. We take a strong position that we believe that the Bible is first and foremost a spiritual document and must be studied spiritually. To come to the hermeneutical process without fully understanding the nature of Scripture as God's divine revelation to humanity will severely limit one's ability to effectively exegete biblical passages.
2. This book is written for social-scientific researchers who may or may not have formal training in biblical languages and hermeneutics. We apply principles of qualitative data analysis to the exegetical process. Given this, while hermeneutics is often only thought of as a means to an end—the goal being a sermon or lesson to be taught—the goal of this book is to help researchers write sound exegetical research papers in the various social-scientific fields in which they work. We believe biblical truths are available to all people regardless of their familiarity with biblical languages. Thus, this book is rudimentary enough for novice researchers while also being extensive enough for seasoned scholars.
3. This book is not an in-depth exploration of all available options for biblical interpretation. Further, while we will cover many approaches to biblical interpretation, this book is not an *equally* in-depth examination of all of the mentioned methods of biblical interpretation. It is an examination of several effective current methods of biblical interpretation with an in-depth look at socio-rhetorical analysis (SRA). It is not a historical examination of the development of biblical interpretation nor is it a look at Patristic, Medieval, or Reformation hermeneutics and interpretation.
4. This book is designed specifically for biblical research. While SRA can be utilized with a variety of texts, this book focuses primarily on the how to apply SRA methodology to the Scriptures: exploring in-depth the five textures of SRA and providing examples of each method in practice.

Chapter One provides a definition and overview of exegetical analysis. The chapter discusses why it is beneficial to study the Holy Scriptures. By comparing and contrasting quantitative and qualitative research methodologies, exegetical analysis is shown to be a scientific or systematic approach to analysis. Further, it is asserted that the Bible is both a spiritual document and applicable to contemporary society.

Chapter Two utilizes qualitative methodological principles to explore effective strategies for choosing a topic, conducting a literature review, and constructing research questions. This chapter demonstrates how to narrow a topic down to a stated problem and how to choose the proper biblical pericope. Moving from research to writing, there is a detailed discussion of how to write a strong introduction and purpose statement.

Chapter Three is an examination of several different methods or concepts of biblical interpretation that are widely used for research. The foundational method for research is grammatical–historical interpretation that focuses on the analysis of words and grammar using the study of languages as a key component for interpretation. Inductive Biblical Analysis is a method that focuses on an inductive analysis of the text of Scripture with a close reading of the pericope yielding observations that lead to interpretation. The Interpretive Journey provides a five-step methodology that seeks to bridge ancient contexts embedded in the text to contemporary applications through transhistorical principles. Genre analysis builds on established hermeneutical principles of literature analysis to identify the specific genres of Scripture and the unique interpretive principles for each. Textual criticism is concerned with ensuring the accuracy of biblical translations in comparison to its original manuscripts.

Chapter Four deals with matters concerning the authorship, audience, dating, and purpose of biblical pericopae. The chapter offers strategies for determining each of these in both the Old and New Testaments. Further, we discuss the importance of authorship, audience, date, and purpose to the interpretative process.

Chapter Five is an in-depth exploration of socio-rhetorical analysis from the perspective of why this method is used in biblical interpretation. This is an effective method for several reasons but many of these can be divided into three categories. First, SRA is systematic in that it develops a plan for the research process. Second, SRA is scientific in that it uses proven methods in the research that come from several different fields of study. Last, SRA is holistic in that it views the text from several perspectives. Together these aspects of research form a solid research agenda with a thick description of the text yielding a finely nuanced interpretation.

Chapter Six reviews what is commonly the first step in most exegetical analysis—inner texture—finding meaning in specific words and phrases within the text. While this cannot be fully completed without insights from the other textures, this focus is designed to allow the text to speak in its own right before moving on to how it is influenced by other factors that reside outside the text. Thus, the structure, patterns, and rhetoric of the passage are considered within the analysis of a text.

Chapter Seven explores the relationship of a text with the world outside the text through intertexture analysis. Intertexture analysis considers how an author configures outside sources or traditions to evoke meaning. Intertexture is explored through five subtextures: oral-scribal, cultural, social, historical, and reciprocal intertexture.

Chapter Eight is an examination of social and cultural texture, which is a clearly distinct aspect of research different than social or cultural intertexture. This research examines the person or groups of a text and their social and cultural perspectives that would impact the understanding of the text. This texture is divided into three distinct categories that examine religious worldviews, common topics that were known to the people of the time of the text that may be foreign to others and finally there is a consideration of cultural locations. These aspects help the researcher determine the kind of the person involved in a text and the implications for understanding the message.

Chapter Nine is a discussion of ideological texture through which the researcher seeks to understand the various perspectives that have viewed the text and the unique preconceptions that those different views bring to the text. Following steps to identify the locations of the author, audience, historical interpretation, and the contemporary writer, this methodology allows the researcher to determine not only how closely these perspectives align but also to decide which perspective should be the controlling perspective for interpretation.

Chapter Ten provides a robust exploration of Sacred Texture; addressing the aspect of a text that involves divine issues or theology. This is the study of God and His connections to people. Sacred Texture is the examination of these divine issues from several aspects of God; concerning who He is, how He works in history, how He works through redemption, and the human response to God in areas like community, commitment, and ethics. Together these different aspects of research into the divine and divine intention create a holistic and nuanced understanding of God and His ways as found in the text.

Chapter Eleven discusses the role of Scripture as a data source. Approaching an artifact as sacred as Scripture and treating it like data might seem profane to some. However, this chapter reviews the qualitative analysis methodology and shows that Scripture will be interpreted as data whether done explicitly or implicitly. Additionally, from a Christian perspective, there is the possibility of illumination from the Holy Spirit who can provide guidance in the interpretive process.

Chapter Twelve explains issues found toward the end of the research process as a study moves from the interpretive phase to the application phase. The first step on this later process is to go back to the research question to ensure that the results are on track to answer the question and possibly find new ways in the text to answer contemporary issues. The researcher should then address his or her own sets of biases as the study moves into the application phase. The researcher then moves the message from interpretation to application by recontextualizing the intended message of the text into a contemporary setting.

Chapter Thirteen seeks to point a road forward for exegetical study. While most exegetical analysis is going to result in theoretical principles of Christian leadership, the pursuit of practical application that can be researched both qualitatively and quantitatively must be developed. This will allow for the theory to be refined and new insights to be developed.

Exegetical Analysis: A Practical Guide for Applying Biblical Research to the Social Sciences is designed with the expressed goal of equipping Christian researchers with the tools necessary to accurately and effectively interpret the Bible. Therefore, the purpose of this book is to *provide Christian researchers with a practical methodology for biblical research that guides the researcher in selecting a general topic, choosing a biblical pericope, scientifically and spiritually interpreting the pericope, and accurately applying its biblical principles to contemporary contexts.*

Part 1
Knowing the "Whys"

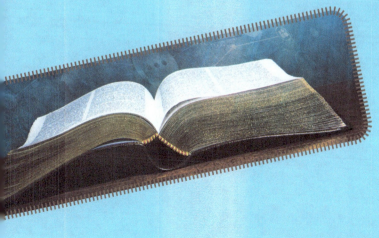

Chapter 1

Exegetical Analysis and the Holy Scriptures

Pilate said to him, "What is truth?" (John 18:38, ESV)

Contemporary century scholars and researchers, like their predecessors, wrestle with a question that both influences their research and challenges their thinking: What is truth? For Christians, this truth is found in the sacred text of the Holy Bible. Yet, there is a tendency to view the Scriptures as though there is a rigid dichotomy between scientific research and that of biblical studies. This could not be further from the truth. In what is generally coined as *all truth is God's truth*, St. Augustine of Hippo once wrote: "let every good and true Christian understand that wherever truth may be found, it belongs to his Master" (Augustine, n.d., II.72). Rather than viewing science and Scripture as *contradictory*, we believe that they are *complementary*.

As the various fields of social science continue to expand, there is a place for the exploration of these contexts from the Christian worldview, and thus, the need for the scientific study of Scripture. While, as Christians, we believe that our knowledge comes from God and the Bible, we also recognize the need to research and integrate biblical principles and scientific research. If truth is to be found, it is both already known to God and available to us. So then, we approach the sacred Scriptures with a reverent desire to discover the truth that God has made available to us and apply it into our contemporary social scientific contexts.

Why We Study the Holy Scriptures

Christianity was designed to operate in the marketplace and in the workplace: the early Christians existed in every sphere of society (Moynagh, 2018). While the Church increasingly disengaged over the centuries, fundamental shifts in modern society have caused the Church to reconsider once again the need to find its place in the communities in which believers socialize. Given this, there is increased interest in Christian spirituality in a variety of social scientific contexts.

There is much debate over the role of the Bible in contemporary social contexts (Bray, 1996). This area of study exists in the tension between two general fields of study: biblical studies and the social sciences. There are those from both camps who challenge the applicability of biblical interpretation in the social sciences. We recognize this tension; however, we accept the challenge to simultaneously exegete the original meaning of the Bible and faithfully apply it to modern social constructs. The message of Scripture is neither so distant that it cannot be discerned nor is its meaning malleable to the whims of modern thought. The Word of God, as the Divine revelation of God's plan of salvation, is both applicable and unchangeable. It is the responsibility of those who desire to understand its truth to approach the Scriptures with humility and reverence.

There are those who would shy away from biblical exploration in their scientific pursuits; however, there is danger in conducting research that either excludes God or stands in contradiction to His Word (Linnemann, 1990). Christian research should always seek a deeper understanding of God's truth: "Christian research, in contrast [*to secular research*], strives to depend on God in the selection of the object of study, in the means adopted for study, and in the motives for study. It attempts to rely on God at every step" (p. 41). Further, González (1971) asserted: "It is rather that God the Word places in the human mind the knowledge of ideas that exist eternally in God" (p. 36). Thus, it is through the illumination of the Word of God that we are able to transform our contemporary contexts. It is for this reason that we study the Holy Scriptures and hope to inspire and empower others to do so as well.

Exegetical Analysis Is Scientific

Faithfully interpreting the Bible is an arduous and complex task (Klein, Blomberg, & Hubbard, 2017). There are many different methods of exegeting the Scriptures (Vyhmeister & Robertson, 2014). Stone and Duke (2013) call us to *responsible interpretation*: "the biblical text does not speak for itself; every reading is someone's interpretation of it" (p. 49). It is of paramount importance that we systematically approach the interpretative process. Therefore, in this sense exegetical analysis is scientific. We use *scientific* loosely here; preferring the informal definition of systematic or methodological. Thus, we assert that *exegetical analysis* is a scientific, or systematic, approach to the Scriptures with the interpretative intent of exploring biblical texts in their original context for application to contemporary society.

It is from the belief that biblical interpretation can be conducted in a systematic fashion that both preserves original meaning while being applicable to contemporary society that we use the term *exegetical analysis*. Here, it may be important to define key words that will be used throughout the remaining chapters. We begin by deconstructing the term *exegetical analysis* and defining each part (Figure 1.1).

Exegetical Analysis

definition of exegetical

[1] relating to exegesis

[2] comes from the Greek word *to interpret*

[3] to *pull out* meaning

exegesis - exegete

definition of analysis

[1] the act of analyzing something

[2] a detailed examination of anything complex in order to understand its nature

[3] a thorough study of

analyze - analyses

Figure 1.1 Defining Exegetical Analysis
Source: Joshua Henson

Exegesis is derived from the Greek word meaning to interpret. In contrast to the word *eisegesis,* which means to "read into," *exegesis* means to "pull out of" a text (Osborne, 2006, p. 57). While there is always the potential for *eisegesis* to some extent, at its core, *exegesis* "keeps Scripture uppermost" (Vyhmeister & Robertson, 2014, p. 12). Another term that is often used synonymously with exegesis is *hermeneutics*. While, like exegesis, *hermeneutics,* is derived from a Greek word meaning "to interpret," hermeneutics is the overall term for interpreting an author's meaning: exegesis and contextualization are two aspects of the larger hermeneutical task (Klein et al., 2017; Osborne, 2006, p. 21). So then, we exegete a biblical text with the purpose of properly contextualizing it: "true interpretation of the Bible combines both an exercise in ancient history and a grappling with its impact on our lives" (Klein et al., 2017, p. 19). The question still remains: How do we apply the Scriptures to our lives without compromising its original meaning?

In the field of biblical studies, you will often hear the words *criticism* or *interpretation.* While *interpretation* is obvious at this point, *criticism* is generally understood as the science of studying Scripture with the intent of uncovering the truth of its development and evolution. There are so many methods of criticism that it would be impractical to mention them all here. We will, however, in later chapters explore one in detail: socio-rhetorical criticism or socio-rhetorical interpretation. Like all forms of criticism, the name describes the intention of the methodology: exploring the sociological and rhetorical elements of Scripture (Robbins, 1996).

Rather than using the terms *criticism* or *interpretation*, we choose to use the term *analysis*. We do this, not to distance ourselves from the methodologies of biblical studies, but to find common language between that of biblical studies and that of the social sciences. There are two basic types of scientific research: quantitative research and qualitative research; requiring quantitative data analysis and qualitative data analysis, respectively. Echoing the language of social scientific research, exegetical research, as a subcategory and form of qualitative research, requires *exegetical analysis*. While the following statements do not account for every possible research design or sample, they offer a general perspective of the differentiating points of quantitative, qualitative, and exegetical research (Figure 1.2).

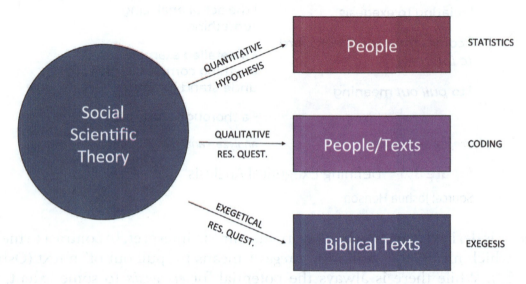

Figure 1.2 Differentiating the Types of Analysis in the Social Sciences
Source: Joshua Henson

- *Quantitative Research* seeks to quantify a problem by establishing hypotheses based on the literature and then statistically testing the hypotheses with data collected from a sample of people, or a relevant sample, through proven methodologies of *quantitative data analysis*.
- *Qualitative Research* is a method of inquiry that extracts research questions from the literature and then seeks to answer the research questions through direct observation and interviews and/or the content analysis of texts through proven methodologies of *qualitative data analysis*.
- *Exegetical Research* is a method of biblical inquiry that constructs research questions based upon the theoretical relationships between the literature and biblical texts and then seeks to answer the research questions through robust hermeneutical engagement with biblical texts through proven methodologies of *exegetical data analysis*.

Similar to quantitative and qualitative research, exegetical research, especially in the social scientific context, carries with it significant concerns regarding research bias. Even among social–rhetorical scholars like Witherington, deSilva, and Robbins, there is considerable debate regarding the nature, limits, and methodological implications of socio-rhetorical analysis. Our vision for *exegetical analysis*, and our conceptualization of socio-rhetorical analysis, is one that seeks to remain true to the original meaning of biblical texts while holding the conviction that the Bible is applicable for today. Thus, the task of socio-rhetorical analysis is to "avoid anachronism like the plague": ensuring that we always place the Scriptures in their proper historical context before attempting to apply it to ours (Witherington, 2009, p. 2). Therefore, exegetical research is the scientific study of sacred texts for the purpose of interpreting the author's original meaning and its contemporary application. However, while exegetical research is *scientific*, it is also *spiritual*.

Exegetical Analysis Is Spiritual

The study of Scripture is spiritual work. Hermeneutics should be guided by the following warning: "there are spiritual forces at work which will seek to pervert the truth, and so it is only as we reform our own opinions according to the collective witness that we will be preserved from error" (Bray, 1996, p. 15). Further, Osborne (2006) wrote that hermeneutics is: "a science . . . an art . . . and most important, hermeneutics when utilized to interpret Scripture is a spiritual act" (pp. 21–22). While we espouse the position that socio-rhetorical analysis, methodologically speaking, has the depth to adequately engage the Scriptures, there is concern that the methodology has partial roots in social-scientific criticism. Elliot (1993) wrote of social-scientific criticism: "In using the social sciences, exegetes, like sociologists, of necessity must bracket and exclude 'the God hypothesis.' The exegetical task will then become agnostic if not atheistic" (p. 89). Here, we join Christian sociologists and the litany of social scientific research from a Christian worldview and offer a full-throated rejection of such assertions. Any exegesis that removes God from its methodology fails to understand the true nature of the Bible.

While the scientific study of Scripture requires us to understand the Bible as a historical document, a religious document, and a social document, we would be remiss if we did not emphasize that the Word of God is first and foremost a *spiritual document*. The Scriptures themselves bear witness to the spiritual nature of the Bible: "All Scripture is breathed out by God and profitable for teaching, for reproof, for correction, and for training in righteousness, that the man of God may be complete, equipped for every good work" (2 Tim. 3:16–17, ESV).

Thus, the accurate interpretation of Scripture requires a truthful understanding of the nature of Scripture. For centuries, the Bible has been studied in a purely academic sense, and those who studied it, failed to comprehend the magnitude of its meaning. There are those who spend their lives dedicated to discovering *how* the Bible came to be, but never consider *why* it came to be. The Bible, being more than a historical document or scientific textbook, has the ability to "*speak* to the human heart in ways that *defy* logic, but which *transform* people's lives" (Bray, 2006, p. 250). Gonzalez (1971) offers this Augustinian perspective; "although the human mind is incapable of knowing eternal truths, be it by its own powers or through the data of the sense, it received the knowledge by a direct illumination from God" (p. 36). Therefore, to study the Scriptures scientifically without studying them spiritually will limit our understanding of the spiritual truths being conveyed by them. Linnemann (1990) provides the following insight:

> We are accustomed to regarding thought that is disciplined and regulated by scientific principles as reliable. Further, we are accustomed, not only to distinguishing between faith and thought, but also separating them from each

other, so that faith is banned from the realm of thought, and thought deems itself to be excluded from the realm of faith. Both of these customary viewpoints which have been thoroughly accepted are highly deceptive (p. 64).

It is through faith that we create space in our thinking for the scientific exploration of the limitless, eternal, and timeless truths of God's Word. Beale (2011) poses: "if one acknowledges that Scripture is God's living and written word, then one must leave room for the Spirit to break through our socially constructed knowledge" and thus find God's intended meaning of Scripture (p. 167). Jesus, as the incarnate Word, connected the pursuit of truth with the person and work of the Holy Spirit: "But the Helper, the Holy Spirit, whom the Father will send in my name, he will teach you all things and bring to your remembrance all that I have said to you" (Joh. 14:26, ESV) and the "Spirit of truth, who proceeds from the Father, he will bear witness of me" (Joh. 15:26, ESV).

So then, there should be a successful marriage of two seemingly conflicting concepts: science and spirituality. Yet, when considered in the light of what we have just discussed, science and spirituality are not in conflict. Rather, there exists a natural friction that is produced by their interaction as mortal man tries to comprehend the eternal truths of God. We end with the wisdom of John Calvin (Calvin n.d./2008):

> At the same time, we deny not that it is the office of faith to assent to the truth of God whenever, wherever, and in whatever way he speaks: we are only inquiring what faith can find in the Word of God to lean and rest upon . . . But faith ought to seek God, not shun him. It is evident, therefore, that we have not yet obtained a full definition of faith, it being impossible to give the name to every kind of knowledge of the divine will. (p. 359)

Though the limitless knowledge of God's truth boggles human understanding, those who seek truth, and do so scientifically and spiritually, recognize the necessity of the illumination of the Holy Spirit (Williams, 1996). And thus, we employ an exegetical process that makes room for divine revelation.

Exegetical Analysis Is Applicable

Exegetical analysis is scientific. It is spiritual. It is applicable. There are those who question the applicability of Scripture to contemporary contexts. Centuries of increasingly secular exploration of the historical origins of Scripture have some questioning the relevance of Scripture to modern society (Bray, 1996); however, "because God's character and human nature do not change, his Word remains relevant" (Duvall & Hays, 2005, p. 222).

Jesus' High Priestly prayer highlights the necessity of a robust and spiritual understanding of Scripture and its applications to contemporary society:

> I have given them your word, and the world has hated them because they are not of the world, just as I am not of the world. I do not ask that you take them out of the world, but that you keep them from the evil one. They are not of the world, just as I am not of the world. Sanctify them in the truth; your word is truth (Joh. 17:14–17, ESV).

As long as the Church remains part of society and as long as there is a call for believers to live-out their faith in the home, the marketplace and the workplace, then there will be a need for the Word of God to inspire, convict, and transform. The Psalmist wrote: "I have stored up your word in my heart, that I might not sin against you" (Psa. 119:11, ESV). Jesus echoed the sentiments: "it is not what goes into the mouth that defiles a person, but what comes out of the mouth; this defiles a person" (Mat. 15:11, ESV). Therefore, it is through the transformation of the heart (Bray, 2006) and the illumination of the mind (Williams, 1996), that the Christian is equipped to put faith into practice. "We face the challenge to become *biblical* Christians: Christians who learn what God's Word says, and who humbly, obediently, put it into practice" (Klein et al., 2017, p. xxv).

Linnemann (1990) wrote that the Bible is "sufficient for every person, for every age, for every situation" as it mirrors the heart of God (p. 155). What a powerful statement! So then, the Bible is a sufficient source of data for applying biblical principles to social scientific contexts. The Bible, though ancient, contains principles that are as applicable today as the day they were written. To have the Scriptures illuminated by the Holy Spirit is to see God's character, His personality, and His plan for humanity.

The emergence of modern sociological methods of biblical interpretation is fueled by a desire to see the Bible come alive again: to better know the people and cultures of Scripture. Bray (1996) asked the question: "Is it possible to use an ancient text to solve current social, economic, and political problems?" The short answer is yes. While sound hermeneutics will not solve the problem of the human condition, it will provide Christian researchers and practitioners with lessons from history, spiritual truths, and divine revelation. And, it is from this foundation, that Christian researchers can explore the role of faith and Christian spirituality in contemporary society.

Conclusion

Coming to the Scriptures with a strong understanding of its nature is essential to the interpretative process. The Scriptures teach us that it is fully possible to study the Word of God without ever fully grasping its knowledge and truth (2 Tim. 3:7). This is both a sobering reality and a challenge to researchers. Sadly, there are those who have studied the Bible for their entire professional life and are no closer to the truth than when they began. Why? Because they failed to consider the nature of the Bible. As we have discovered here, an effective interpretative process requires both science and Spirit. Thus, when we understand that the Word of God is a divine revelation, and when we treat it as such, we will enter into the interpretative process with humility and reverence.

Exegetical analysis is the scientific study of sacred texts for the purpose of interpreting the author's original meaning and its contemporary application. Biblical texts should be approached with reverence and out of an honest quest for truth. The interpretative process is a systematic exploration of biblical texts and the world of a text through rigorous time-tested practices.

Exegetical analysis involves the spiritual illumination of the mind and heart of the interpreter through the work of the Holy Spirit. The Bible is first and foremost a spiritual document: the divine revelation of God. Interpreting the Word of God requires anointed eyes (Rev. 3:18), spiritual ears (Rev. 2:29), and a teachable heart (1 Cor. 2:13–14).

Exegetical analysis applies biblical principles to contemporary contexts. The Bible is relevant for every generation. The dynamic complexities of ancient society and God's dealings with humanity provide principles that are applicable even in modern society. The Bible mirrors the heart of God, and God never changes (Heb. 13:8; Jam. 1:17). Therefore, the same truths that were available and applicable to ancient times are still available and applicable to us.

Chapter One Reflective Exercises

1. What is the role of the Christian researcher in discovering the truth? From where does truth come, and how do researchers discover it? What is the value of researching the Holy Scriptures in the context of contemporary social sciences?
2. How does a Christian researcher find balance between science and spirituality? How can the interpretative process be scientifically rigorous without ignoring the leading of the Holy Spirit? How can the interpretative process be spiritually illuminating without compromising scientific rigor?
3. What is the role of the Holy Spirit in biblical interpretation? What is the role of the researcher in relation to the Holy Spirit in the interpretive process?
4. What is the difference between *exegesis* and *eisegesis*, and how do researchers address *eisegesis* in the interpretative process?
5. As you survey the field of biblical studies, both academic and practical—the university and the church—what are some of the trends, positive and negative, of how individuals communicate *about* the Bible? What is the role of Scripture in the life of those in contemporary society? How can learning to effectively *exegete* biblical texts help to address these trends?

Part 2
Discovering the "Whats"

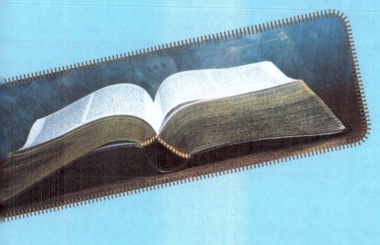

Chapter 2

Choosing What to Study

Getting started is never easy. The majority of those reading this book are likely students who have been assigned the task a writing an exegetical paper, dissertation candidates seeking to apply biblical texts in contemporary contexts, or scholars researching biblical passages in social scientific contexts. For some, there is a specific passage of Scripture that they desire to explore. For others, there is a theoretical construct that has scarcely been studied from a biblical perspective. In both cases, the struggle lies with attempting to align biblical passages and theoretical constructs. While we wholeheartedly subscribe to the idea that the Holy Scriptures, as a whole, can speak to the multitudinous sociological and anthropological facets of human interaction, we also recognize certain passages may be more closely aligned to specific constructs than others. There are few things more frustrating for a researcher than realizing, after the fact, that the sample does not yield enough data to reach conclusions. Both qualitative and quantitative research methodologies take considerable care to ensure that the researcher considers the source of data, or sample, prior to engaging in data collection and analysis. The same is true with exegetical analysis: choosing the right passage will make a world of difference in your study. So, we begin by offering this advice: *the only thing more difficult than getting started is starting off wrong.*

In this chapter, we will discuss issues of concern when selecting a research topic and a related biblical passage. Long before typing the first word of a manuscript, researchers make a series of decisions that directly impact the final product. Often, researchers spend countless hours thinking and researching only to write a few sentences. Following a sound research process will lead to an effective final product. So, let us explore how to start off right.

Starting with a Topic

Generally, all research begins with a broad topic of interest (Kibbe, 2016). This broad topic of interest can come in many forms: (a) a theoretical construct in which one is interested; (b) a biblical pericope that one would like research; or (c) a specific topic that transcends constructs yet has biblical implications. Given this, some will begin with a topic and work their way toward a biblical text while others will begin with a biblical text and work their way toward a theoretical construct.

One of the fundamental errors in research is the failure to distinguish between *opinion* and *argument*. Given the theological nature of exegetical analysis, researchers often come to the interpretive process with an *embedded theology* through which they view Scripture (Stone & Duke, 2013). Because of this, it is all the more important to distinguish opinion from argument: "an opinion is an unsupported claim; an argument is a supported claim" (Damer, 2009, p. 15). Damer defines an argument as being "constituted by two or more explicit and/or implicit claims, one or more of which support or provides evidence for the truth or merit of another claim, the conclusion" (p. 14). Therefore, the initial stages of exegetical research centers on developing a theoretical connection, or argument, that links a theoretical construct and a biblical pericope. This begins with reviewing the existing body of knowledge on a selected topic (Figure 2.1).

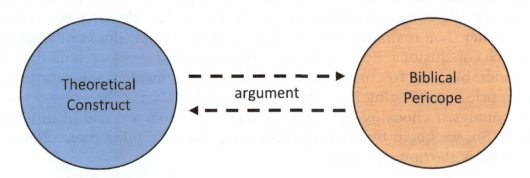

Figure 2.1 The Logical Flow of Thought
Source: Joshua Henson

Choosing the Right Sources

Before a discussion can be had on effective strategies for engaging the literature, it is necessary to consider sources. Sources will vary in type and quality. Like the ingredients of a fine dish, the quality of the research is first judged based on the quality of the sources it utilizes. The strength of an argument comes from the value that a reader places in its evidentiary support. Therefore, it essential that researchers carefully select the sources from which their theoretical arguments are made. Exegetical analysis is unique in that the research occurs in multiple unique academic arenas: social sciences, biblical studies, theology, and religion (just to name a few). While the quality of sources is essential to all rigorous research, in historical research, such as biblical and theological studies, it is necessary to distinguish between primary, secondary, and tertiary sources (Bradley & Muller, 1995; Taylor, Bogdan, & DeVault, 2016).

- **Primary Sources,** from a historical research perspective, are first-hand accounts, artifacts, and original works. From a social scientific perspective, primary sources are typically found in the form of empirical research or original theoretical works.
- **Secondary Sources** are those whose author offers a *once-removed* account of an event or comments upon, analyzes, or interprets information from a primary source. Examples of secondary sources include scholarly literature reviews of primary sources on a theoretical construct, scholarly articles or books engaging a highly specific topic, and biblical commentaries that offer an in-depth exploration of the original language and context of a text. The key characteristic of secondary sources is their dependence upon primary sources.
- **Tertiary Sources** are distinguished from primary and secondary sources in that they tend to provide an overview of a topic or rely heavily upon secondary sources. Generally, tertiary sources analyze, synthesize, and/or summarize any given topic in a user-friendly fashion. Textbooks, commentaries of the entire Bible, and encyclopedias are good examples of tertiary sources as their goal is to provide an overview of a broad topic.

Quality research seeks to establish arguments based on sound evidence, and an "initial criterion" used in assessing research is the quality of a source (Bradley & Muller, 1995, p. 30). Further, Bradley and Muller offer the following rule for scholarly research: "secondary and tertiary sources must not be used to fill gaps in one's knowledge of the primary sources" (p. 41). However, tertiary sources offer a good starting point for choosing a topic of study. There are two benefits of beginning your research by reviewing tertiary sources such as textbooks, books, or encyclopedias. First, these sources provide the researcher with the *lay-of-the-land* of a theoretical construct. This aerial view provides the researcher with perspective. Serving the purpose of summarizing a broad topic, a tertiary source offers the researcher with information related to major authors, theoretical components, practical implications, and a general theoretical frame of reference for future research. Secondly, tertiary sources offer a bibliography. Depending on the nature and the depth of research of a tertiary source, sources such as these can be a treasure-trove of primary and secondary resources. It is at this point that the literature review process can begin.

Reviewing the Literature

Now that a broad research topic has been chosen, and the general conceptual framework is understood, researchers begin the process of narrowing the topic. No single dissertation or research paper will ever be able to explore a topic in its totality.

A familiar cliché rings true here: *we are standing on the shoulders of giants*. The academic community functions in a way that allows for researchers to recontextualize, expand, challenge, and deepen the existing body of knowledge. No research exists on an island to itself. Scientific research requires researchers to establish a sound theoretical, evidence-based foundation for their research.

A literature review is typically used in all qualitative studies and frames the problem that the study seeks to research (Creswell & Creswell, 2018). The process of identifying a potential problem, gap, or opportunity to extend an existing body of knowledge on any given topic, requires funneling the literature from a broad topic to a specific, narrow problem (Figure 2.2). The starting point may be different based upon one's level of expertise in a given field; however, the earliest exploration of any theoretical construct usually begins with tertiary sources. While tertiary sources provide a general theoretical framework, their greatest value lies in their bibliography. By identifying the sources from which a tertiary source draws its information, a researcher is able to locate the secondary sources, and hopefully primary sources, of a theoretical construct. A researcher should never rely too heavily upon tertiary sources; depth of research and mastery of the literature is evidenced through the utilization of primary sources.

Now that secondary sources are identified, the literature review moves to the next phase. As with tertiary sources, secondary sources are a treasure of bibliographic material. By reviewing the bibliography of secondary sources, the researcher is most likely to find the essential empirical and theoretical studies through which a construct has been developed. Secondary resources may offer another resource: their recommendations for future research. Depending upon the type of research conducted, secondary sources not only contain an in-depth examination of the theoretical development of a construct but often give insight to the future direction of research. From this, the researcher is able to not only know where the research has been but

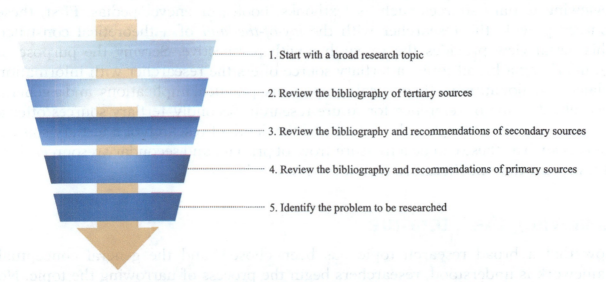

Figure 2.2 Narrowing the Literature

Source: Joshua Henson

also where it is going. Potential problems or gaps can be identified based upon this information; however, researchers should continue their review to the next phase of the process: primary sources.

Primary sources are the core of all theoretical constructs as they represent the empirical and theoretical *heart-and-soul* of a construct. It is by delving into these sources that the researcher is able to develop a keen understanding of the rationale that drives the research, corollary theoretical constructs, and evidence-based research of the theory. Once more, primary sources offer recommendations for future research; further providing researchers with potential problems and new contexts available for exploration.

At this point, the researcher has a fairly good idea of a potential direction for their research. However, how do we know if we have done our due diligence? When do we know that we have conducted an extensive literature review? We know that the review is exhaustive when we reach *bibliographical saturation*. Simply put, *bibliographical saturation* occurs when a researcher reviews the bibliographies of primary sources and no new, or relevant, sources are present. We qualify this discussion of *saturation* with the term bibliographical, because saturation is a topic of interest in qualitative research as a whole, and, specifically, in grounded theory research. Glaser and Straus (1967/1999), in their discussion of grounded theory, state that *theoretical saturation* occurs at a point to where "what has been missed will probably have little modifying effect on the theory" (p. 112). Huberman and Miles (2002) offer a pragmatic consideration: there will be a point when time, money, and resources dictate the end of data collection. Applying the above principles to the literature review, *bibliographical saturation* occurs at a point in the review process that the researcher feels that any missing sources will have minimal effect upon what is known of a theoretical construct, *or*, the researcher has exhausted the requisite resources to continue the literature review. It is necessary to state unequivocally that under no circumstances should sources be cited that have not actually been researched. Never cite a source that is located within another source and treat it as though you have researched it personally. This is tantamount to misrepresentation of data and potentially falls in the category of plagiarism. We recommend that you always follow this basic rule of research: only cite sources that you have personally researched and have a full understanding of the author's intentions.

At the end of an exhaustive literature review, researchers should have the perspective necessary to identify the problem to be researched. As we explore the literature pertaining to a theoretical construct, it is important to identify the problems, gaps, and recommendations offered by the various sources. Here, however, there is always the potential of missing the *proverbial forest for the trees*: information overload. We have reviewed the literature. We have done our due diligence. How do we identify the problem that we want to research? Creswell and Creswell (2018) suggest the use of a *literature map*: a visual representation of the literature review (Figure 2.3). Further, Creswell and Creswell also recommend, based on the level of research, that we consider building a preliminary map of 25 sources. From here we can build a full literature

18 Part 2: Discovering the "Whats"

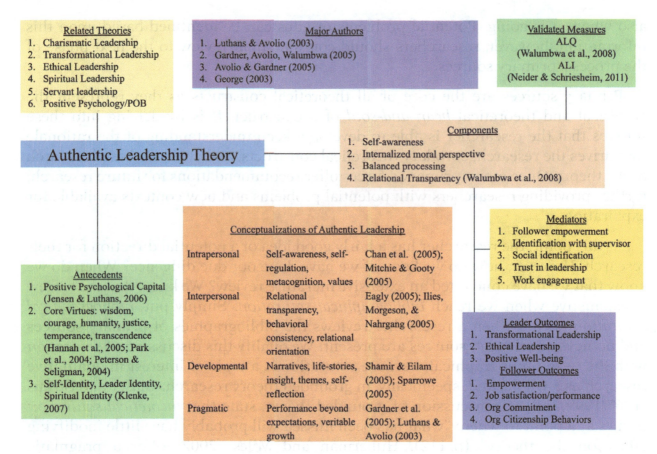

Figure 2.3 Literature Map of Authentic Leadership

Source: Joshua Henson.
Data Source: Gardner, W.L., Cogliser, C.C., Davis, K.M., & Dickens, M.P. (2011). Authentic leadership: A review of the literature and research agenda. *The Leadership Quarterly, 22*(6), 1120–1145.

map that helps to visualize the theoretical development, components, antecedents, and outcomes of a theory. Be sure to highlight problems in any of these areas and the corresponding source(s) from which you have derived this information.

Based on the literature review, we have a good idea of some potential areas of research. It is important to note at this point, there is a difference between *conducting* a literature review and *writing* a literature review. There is a good possibility that you have not typed a word at this point. We research for understanding, and then we write for clarity. Equipped with perspective, we now turn our attention to the biblical pericope. Given that you are reading this book, it is fairly evident that the research methodology will be exegetical in nature. Because of this, the next question to be asked is: How do I choose a biblical text to study?

Selecting the Right Pericope

In selecting the right pericope for research, there are a series of questions that should be considered. But first, we need to address your first question: What is a *pericope*? Biblical studies, like other fields, is littered with jargon. This is one of those cases. *Pericope* is another word for biblical passage or biblical text. In this book, these terms are used interchangeably. It is worth noting, however, there is a difference between a *pericope* and a *verse*. For example, John 3:16 is a verse while John 3:1–21 is a pericope. It is almost always considered poor form to exegete a single verse without researching the context that surrounds it. As will be discussed in later chapters, effective exegesis will flow from the text to its context and then back to the text. Thus, in the case of John 3:16, one cannot fully understand its meaning without understanding it within the entire conversation between Jesus and Nicodemus. When selecting a pericope for study, be sure to select *an entire passage*: this will include the full thoughts of the author. Generally, the easiest way to identify the boundaries of a passage is to look for the bold headings that develop the sections in most Bible translations. These; however, are modern additions and do not constitute part of the biblical canon. The most effective way to distinguish these boundaries is to read through a text until it seems that the author has finished the thought. In this case, you will recognize a shift in the content of the text or notice the use of a transition word or phrase. As we have learned previously, it is necessary to support our selection with research. In the case of exegetical research, researchers depend upon commentaries, peer-reviewed journal articles, and scholarly books to make these choices. Those with a background in Greek will note that the Greek language does not identify punctuation or paragraphs. It is only through experience with the original language that biblical scholars are able to get a feel for a specific author's writing style. For everyone else, look to quality sources for these answers.

As we begin the process of selecting a pericope, a new process of funneling begins. This time, our focus is on selecting a pericope that will most effectively produce data to answer the problem that we have identified from the literature. There are four questions that will guide this phase of the research process as we consider how to narrow the Scripture in search of a text that will align well with our research problem (Figure 2.4).

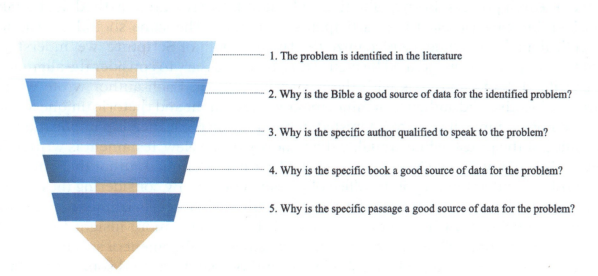

Figure 2.4 Narrowing the Scriptures

Source: Joshua Henson

Why Is the Bible a Good Source of Data for Identified Problem?

If we were conducting standard qualitative research, there would be many data sources at our disposal; however, we are conducting exegetical research. Therefore, the problem should be addressed from a biblical perspective. While the Bible is applicable to a plethora of contemporary contexts, this does not necessarily mean that it is the best source of data for every situation. For example, if you are interested in conducting a study researching how the forced termination of senior administrators in Christian universities affects the relationships between the university's board of trustees, then exegetical analysis would not be the best research design. With that said, exegetical analysis would be applicable if you were interested in exploring what the Scriptures teach us concerning how Christians should respond in the midst of leadership change. Please notice that, though the problems are similar, the change in context warrants different research designs.

Of primary concern is ensuring that the research problem is aligned with biblical research. Remember, that the goal of the research is to identify and answer problems in the literature. First, we must ask if we *should* research the problem from a biblical perspective. Second, we ask *if* it has already been researched from a biblical perspective. Researchers do not research a problem because they *want* to research it, they research a problem because it needs to be researched. Thus, the problem is not only present, but it is also significant. Given this, it is important to explicitly demonstrate through the literature that exegetical analysis expands the existing body of knowledge.

Why Is the Specific Author Qualified to Speak to the Problem?

At first glance, it would seem that a question about the qualifications of any biblical author is unnecessary. From a spiritual perspective, we offer the rebuke: "Of course, they're qualified. It's the Bible." However, this conversation should be had as it is part of the research process. Both qualitative and quantitative research methodologies take considerable care to select the participants of a study. The same should be true for exegetical analysis. While we recognize the Divine origin of Scripture, we understand that the Scriptures were penned by men. Thus, it is necessary to consider the alignment of specific authors and texts with the research problem. Each author wrote with a specific objective and audience in mind; making the content and rhetoric unique to that author. For example, if you are interested in researching the leadership implications of the office of the priest, while arguably the majority of the New Testament is written by Jews, it is actually the one New Testament book with no identified author that offers the most robust understanding of the office of priest: Hebrews. By considering the content of the book, the researcher can infer that the author of Hebrews is intentionally and overtly espousing Jewish themes and most likely will offer more insight than other authors on this topic. Thus, it is necessary to consider the alignment of specific authors and texts with the stated problem. While one author may be a good source of data, it may be that another author is more closely aligned to the research objective.

Why Is the Specific Book a Good Source of Data for the Problem?

Closely connected to the preceding section, we should reflect upon our rationale for choosing a specific book of the Bible for study. Once more, while there is a possibility that the majority of books in the Bible offer some degree of insight on a given topic, we are concerned about alignment. As we continue to narrow our research topic to a specific passage, we cannot overlook the book in which our passage is contained.

At this point in the research, there is a good chance that you have already chosen a pericope. However, this logical process ensures quality research. During the literature review, it is possible to identify a problem or gap in the literature while reviewing tertiary sources; however, it is not until you have reached *bibliographical saturation* that you can claim due diligence. Similarly, without carefully considering the book in which a pericope is found, you cannot rule out the possibility of taking the text out of context.

Parallel to the discussion of the book of the Bible, is considering its genre. Osborne (2006) states: "Genre functions as a valuable link between the text and the reader" (p. 182). Identifying the genre aids in understanding the structure, rhetorical patterns, and content of a book. Identifying the genre of a book provides a hint into the authorial intent of the book. Historical books are narratives: they tell a story. Conversely, most epistles contain few narratives, because they are letters, containing salutations, greetings, and contextual instructions. Given this, the analysis of a historical book may look significantly different than that of an epistle. Further, these differences should be considered in light of the stated research problem. For example, if one wants to research the dynamics of the leader–follower relationship, it may be difficult to glean data from many epistles. Yet, by selecting the relationship between Moses and Joshua or Jesus and Peter, there is a possibility of extrapolating more data.

Why Is the Specific Passage a Good Source of Data for the Selected Problem?

Last, we ask the most obvious yet essential of the four questions: will a given text answer my research problem? For those new to exegetical analysis, it is common to choose a wrong passage. This happens for one of two reasons: (a) we misunderstand the meaning of a text, or (b) we still have a limited knowledge of the theory that we are trying to research. Hopefully, a quality research process will address the second; however, the first is a significant obstacle for some.

There are a few reasons why researchers misunderstand the meaning of a text. First, they assume that similar language equates to similar meaning. For example, the terms *servant* and *steward*, carry with them, first-century connotations that may or may not apply to contemporary conceptualizations. Second, they generalize the characteristics of biblical characters without taking into account the totality of their story or the social and cultural context in which they lived. For example, we can research King David and not balance our research with both his successes and failures. Third, as discussed earlier, they fail to consider an entire thought, limiting the research to a few verses out of context. Fourth, they come to the exegetical process with theological, cultural, or doctrinal biases that they have not adequately reflected upon. Vyhmeister and Robertson (2014), while recognizing the ever-present interaction with our presuppositions, write: "An important task in research thinking is to ask the question: 'Which of my presuppositions affect the way I think and write?'" (p. 101). Given this, we should approach the selection of a biblical text with scholarly precision and humility. It is from the place of honest, reflective thought that the researcher is prepared to assess the relational alignment of a biblical text and a theoretical problem.

How can we ensure that we have selected the right text? While it may be possible for dozens of passages to provide data, we want to optimize our research by selecting a passage that provides the best fit for the stated research problem. It may be that no other research has been conducted on a text, or that the text has never been applied to a specific context. Caution should be taken here as there is the chance that it has not been studied for a reason. Below are some considerations to guide you:

- Read the text repeatedly until you have a good grasp of its structure, content, and rhetorical patterns.
- Identify and research key words and phrases that you do not fully comprehend.
- Consult commentaries and quality journals to gain insight regarding the themes and historical, social, and cultural nuances of the text.
- Read the passages before and after the text to ensure that you did not limit the content of the text; leaving out key information.
- Reflect upon how the content of the text possibly offers data to answer your research problem.

Writing the Introduction

This section may seem like an exercise in the obvious. However, when we discuss *starting off on the right foot*, it is essential that we focus on the *starting off* part of it. The first few pages of a research article or dissertation are essential. Given this, Creswell and Creswell (2018) dedicate an entire chapter to the introduction and another chapter to the purpose statement. The purpose of the introduction is to establish an argument that ends with an explicit purpose statement. After many years of reviewing exegetical and qualitative research papers, it is clear that researchers struggle with the introduction. Yet, the introduction tells a reader everything they need to know about whether they should invest their time in reading the rest of a research paper.

At this point, the researcher has spent hours researching the literature and has identified a research problem. Prior to constructing the research question(s), it is important to communicate the purpose of the research in the introductory pages of the research paper. The majority of readers will make judgments about the research based on the first few pages. Until now, the focus has been on synthesizing the literature of a theoretical construct and a biblical pericope. Now we move to writing our argument. Creswell and Creswell (2018) identify five parts of an effective two-page introduction:

1. State the research problem.
2. Review studies that have addressed the problem.
3. Indicate deficiencies in the studies.
4. Advance the significance of the study for particular audiences.
5. State a problem statement (p. 105).

Begin by writing an opening sentence that contains a "narrative hook" (p. 108). This sentence will both create interest for the topic while communicating the problem to a broad audience. It is essential that you state the research problem, or problems, succinctly and clearly while establishing your argument with numerous high-quality sources. By the end of the first paragraph, the readers should be able to understand the research problem or problems to be studied.

Next, review recent studies that have addressed the problem. The key term here is *recent*. Recent may be different based on the topic. Further, some constructs are more researched than others. It is important to make ensure that you have found the most recent studies: those in the last 10 years. However, if you are researching a topic with little-to-no recent research, this may be one of the problems you address in your study. Creswell and Creswell (2018) recommend grouping the sources at the end of a paragraph or summary when writing this section as it de-emphasizes single studies and draws the reader's focus to the larger problem being discussed.

After reviewing the recent literature, the introduction moves to indicate deficiencies in the studies. These deficiencies are not necessarily a critique of the stated studies. Generally, the deficiencies we identify come from the *suggestions for future research* sections of the research. The body of knowledge, through offering limitations and suggestions, provides a road map for future research. Notice, that there are certain phrases that will be repeated in research articles

- There is *little research* on the topic.
- There are *few studies* that address the topic.
- There *is a need for* continued study of the topic.
- The problem has not been researched *in this specific context*.
- The problem has not been researched from a *biblical perspective*.

The following section deals with stating the significance of the study. It may be true that a topic has not been researched adequately. There may be a reason for this. An argument not only needs to establish the *need* for research but also the *significance* of it. This section should contain at least three points that state what the study will add to the existing research on a topic.

Last, the introduction section should end with a purpose statement. It is this statement that will guide the rest of the research and will help to construct the research question(s). The purpose statement should explicitly use words like purpose or objective and should identify the research design of the study: *"The purpose of this exegetical study is/was/will be to."* The next segment of the purpose statement involves the use of action words that are in line with the qualitative inquiry: *"The purpose of this exegetical study is/was/will be to explore."* Use action words that keep the purpose statement open-ended and communicate an emergent design (Creswell & Creswell, 2018). Next, the purpose statement is to identify the phenomenon or construct to be studied: *"The purpose of this exegetical study is/was/will be to explore [the identified phenomenon]."*

From this point forward, we will use our example from earlier in the chapter: *"The purpose of this exegetical study is/was/will be to explore how followers interact in the midst of leadership crises [phenomenon]."* Typically, this is the point in the construction of the purpose statement that you would identify the participants; however, this is an exegetical purpose statement, therefore, we will identify the biblical pericope: *"The purpose of this exegetical study is/was/will be to explore how followers interact with one another in the midst of leadership crisis [phenomenon] through a Socio-Rhetorical Analysis [the methodology] of the crucifixion and post-crucifixion narratives in the Gospels [the sample]."*

For most exegetical research papers, this is a good purpose statement. However, as you will notice, there is a lot of ambiguity in the phrases: *leadership crisis* and *post-crucifixion narratives of the Gospels*. Using the information gleaned from the selected pericope(s), explicitly state why the selected pericope(s) offer beneficial data related to the research problem. The purpose statement should be further developed as follows:

> *The purpose of this exegetical study is/was/will be to explore how followers interact with one another in the midst of leadership crisis through a Socio-Rhetorical Analysis of the post-crucifixion narratives in the Gospels. The study will seek to understand how the disciples interacted with each other during and after the crucifixion of Jesus as described in the Gospels. The study will conduct an exegetical analysis of Matthew 26:36–28:20, Mark 14:43–16:20, Luke 22:47–53, and John 18:1–21:25; ranging from the betrayal of Jesus to the Ascension of Jesus. These passages potentially provide data on leadership crisis, because the crucifixion narratives contain multiple events that impacted each disciple individually and the disciples as a group.*

The introduction ends with a clear, concise purpose statement. As you will notice, the reader will have no questions as to what the above study will seek to research. By building an argument that ends with a purpose statement, the researcher has laid a foundation for constructing the research question(s).

Constructing the Proper Research Question(s)

As demonstrated in Figure 2.5, marrying a theoretical problem and an aligned biblical pericope requires a two-phase funneling process. Phase One involves narrowing the literature to an identified problem. Phase Two involves narrowing the Scriptures through asking hermeneutical questions that help to identify a text. Now, we discuss how to construct research question(s).

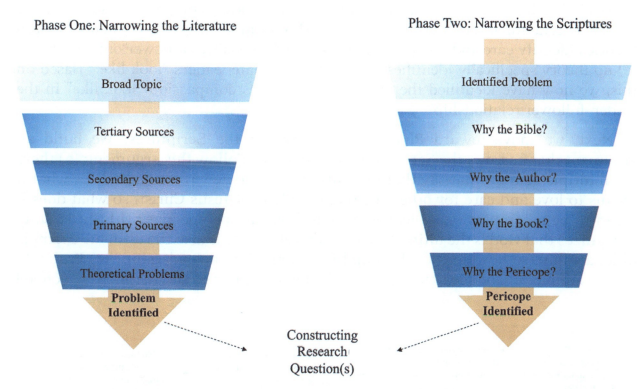

Figure 2.5 Constructing Research Questions
Source: Joshua Henson

In the final stages of narrowing the Scriptures to the selected pericope, the researcher hypothesizes potential relationships between the theoretical construct (based on the literature review) and the text. Qualitative research generally asks one or two central questions (Creswell, 2009). These questions are open-ended and relates each question to the specific qualitative strategy employed (Creswell). Research questions will most often begin with *what* or *how*, and, occasionally, *why*. They will never be answered by a simple yes or no. There are four elements of a strong exegetical research question. At minimum, at least one question should include each of these elements:

- Beginning: Why, What, or How
- The stated problem from the literature review (Phase One)
- The selected biblical pericope (Phase Two)
- Reference to the methodology

To illustrate this, the next few paragraphs will outline a hypothetical argument as seen in Figure 2.6. For an extensive example, including citations, see Appendix A. First, we begin with a broad topic: I am interested in learning more about compassionate leadership, and, more specifically, what the Bible says about leading with compassion. Second, we explore theoretical constructs that relate to compassionate leadership: servant leadership, spiritual leadership, leader-member exchange, and so on. Third, we review the literature to find potential problems, gaps, or suggestions for future research. We find: (a) feminine styles of leadership (love, compassion, support) are quickly overtaking masculine forms of leadership as more effective; (b) many modern theories identify care and compassion as essential to positive follower outcomes; and (c) no theory specifically identifies what compassionate leaders "look like." Based on this, we now have identified the problem: What does compassion "look like" in the leader–follower relationship?

Next, we move toward Phase Two: narrowing the Scriptures. We build an argument that narrows the Scriptures toward a text. Follow this argument: (a) there are multiple sources that say that the Christian worldview recontextualizes what it means to love and care for others through the lens of Jesus Christ, so what does it mean to be a compassionate leader from a Christian perspective? (b) Christianity recognizes that God is the ultimate leader; therefore, He is also the ultimate example of leadership, so how does God exemplify compassionate leadership? (c) Psalm 23 is an example of God's leadership, and (d) the metaphor of the shepherd is echoed

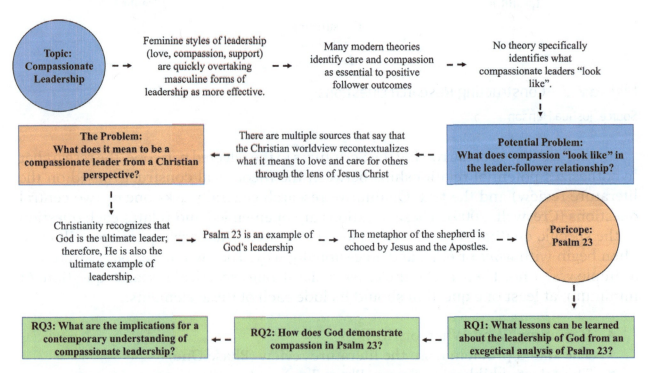

Figure 2.6 From Topic to Thesis

Source: Joshua Henson

by Jesus and the Apostles in the New Testament. Therefore, Psalm 23 may be a good source of data to understand compassionate leadership from a Judeo-Christian perspective.

Last, we combine the two constructs to develop a research question. We begin by identifying the purpose statement. This statement should be a clear, concise description of the study.

The purpose of this exegetical study is to explore compassionate leadership from a Christian worldview by conducting a Socio-Rhetorical Analysis of Psalm 23. The study will seek to understand how God demonstrated compassion toward the Psalmist as described by the Psalmist.

Based upon this research statement, we can now develop our research questions:

RQ_1: What lessons can be learned about the leadership of God from a socio-rhetorical analysis of Psalm 23?
RQ_2: How does God demonstrate compassion in Psalm 23?
RQ_3: What are the implications for a contemporary understanding of compassionate leadership from the analysis of Psalm 23? (Figure 2.6)

Conclusion

We have walked through the literature review process from selecting a topic to constructing the research questions. There are a lot of considerations as you begin this process. It is time-consuming and detail-oriented; however, this reflective process provides the rigor necessary for scholarly research.

Begin with a broad topic and narrow it until you have identified potential problems. The narrowing, or funneling, of a topic requires that the researcher establish a logical argument, or supported opinion. It is from this argument that we are able to pinpoint potential problems in the literature.

The key to building quality arguments is beginning with quality sources. Tertiary sources, while they provide a summary of a construct, should never be relied upon to build an argument. Secondary sources deepen our understanding of a construct while providing the empirical research upon which a construct is developed. Primary sources provide the theoretical heart and soul of a theoretical construct. It is best to build arguments through the use of primary sources.

Selecting the right pericope is not a matter of right or wrong as much finding the best fit. In order to yield the best data to answer the research questions, it is essential to identify passages that align with the stated purpose of the research. Researchers should reflect upon the content of a passage and consider potential relationships between a construct and a text.

A great research paper begins with a great introduction. It is in the introduction that we identify the problem, review recent studies, and identify the significance of the study. It is from here that we develop a purpose statement that will guide the construction of the research questions and provide focus for the study.

Good exegetical research questions are structured to encourage inquiry. Create open-ended questions that begin what, how, or why. Be sure to identify the theoretical relationship between the selected theoretical construct and the biblical text.

Chapter Two Reflective Exercises

1. You have a general topic of interest that you are considering. Discuss the process through which you will arrive at a problem or problems in need of research.
2. Choose a hypothetical theoretical construct. By using the information in the chapter, identify a biblical pericope that could possibly be a good source to answer a research question about the selected theory. Then construct a purpose statement for the research. Be sure to support your answers with engagement from this chapter, support from the literature on the selected topic, and support from the selected biblical pericope.
3. Practice constructing research questions using the hypothetical scenarios below:
    a. The purpose of this study is to explore gender relations from a socio-rhetorical analysis of Judges 4.
    b. The purpose of this exegetical study is to examine the cause and effect of negative feedback from a biblical perspective by examining the relationships of Jesus and Peter, Paul and John-Mark, and Elisha and Gehazi.
    c. The purpose of this exegetical study is to explore how Jesus addressed the social and cultural boundaries of His day through an exegetical analysis of John 4.

Part 3
Answering the "Hows"

Chapter 3

The Various Approaches to "How"

In the process of hermeneutics, there are several approaches as to how or in the use of method in the research of Scripture and biblical interpretation. Some of these approaches are rather holistic with principles to be applied in all different areas of Scripture. Other approaches simply look at a narrow aspect of interpretation like the author or the generation of the text itself. Though it is beyond the scope of this chapter many of these methods of interpretation can be traced back through history. A few of them can be traced back at least in part to some early schools in the early centuries of the church like the School of Antioch or the School of Alexandria. This is an intriguing study. In addition, these ways of interpretation can be traced through the history of the church and even back to eras before the church in Jewish hermeneutics. There are even issues of dispute between Jesus and the Pharisees that had to do with hermeneutics and Old Testament interpretation. Hermeneutics or biblical interpretation has a long history that is filled with insights, surprises, and controversies. Nevertheless, in this examination of interpretation, the focus will be upon a few of the different approaches to interpretation that are relevant and important for biblical interpretation in the present context. The deep dive into the historical origins and the nuances of these controversies will be reserved for another study. Presently, the examination of a few of these different approaches will give the student a foundation for further study in Socio-rhetorical analysis (SRA) and an ability to use some of these insights in the process of doing the five textures of SRA.

Grammatical-Historical Interpretation

Grammatical–historical interpretation is the use of exegetical analysis to examine the words, the sentences, the paragraphs, and books of the text of Scripture to understand the meaning of the text. This interpretation includes the issues of historical background and contexts as well. This interpretive method looks for the meanings

of the text in their context using an understanding of language and grammar as well as the historical and even literary setting. There are many books written based upon the premise of grammatical–historical interpretation. Since the middle of the 19th century grammatical–historical interpretation has been a basic premise of serious interpreters (Mickelson, 1972). This method is a movement from the text and its context to the understanding of the text through understanding the sense of the words in the context that it was written. This grammatical approach looks for the meaning as intended by the author, which is firmly rooted in historical truth. There are many other methods that focus on authorial intent and this concept has a long history in several methods. However, this is a pivotal point in this method. In other words, the message made sense in the context of history that it was authored. This is the message that can then be applied to contemporary contexts, but it cannot be changed. Grammar is the architectural blueprint of communication showing how the parts of an utterance relate together and this is the key to word meaning and semantic analysis (Osborne, 2006). The understanding of how the words fit together forms the foundation for understanding the meaning of the sentence and even the meaning of the words in an endeavor to understand the message of the pericope of Scripture being examined. Grammatical–historical interpretation involves the careful, honest, intelligent use of grammatical and historical knowledge for the interpretation of these documents written in foreign languages within several different historical contexts and this includes the issues of the meaning of words as well as using figurative language while understanding special issues of types and genre (Corly, Lemke, & Lovejoy, 2002). This kind of examination includes the issues of how language is used in figurative ways as well as being sensitive to the literary genre of the text.

Since there is a focus on language and its words as well as its grammar, there is a need to study and use these languages in understanding the texts. For the understanding of Scripture, this would include the study of Hebrew and Greek. However, this does not preclude the researcher from using this method. There are many study helps that can facilitate this process with some excellent computer-based programs that can be used effectively with some foundational knowledge of Greek and Hebrew. This can be done on an introductory level, then language study would be the next step.

This method is designed to help the researcher overcome the gaps of understanding between the author and original hearers and themselves. These gaps in understanding are historical and grammatical but they also include areas of culture, genre, and possibly even religion. These gaps can be overcome by the study of other's research in these areas. There are several good resources for developing an understanding of the cultures, history, genres, and religions of the era and places of these writings. These resources can become effective tools for interpretation with the focus on finding the meaning intended by the author for the intended audience. However, this focus does not exclude the authorship of the Holy Spirit. Nevertheless, it should be considered that in Scripture God used human words to communicate divine truth to specific people in that moment of history. These are divine and human words at the same time. How is that possible? It is possible in the same way that Jesus is fully divine and fully human without confusion.

This type of research focuses on the need for textual criticism as well. Textual criticism is the attempt to ascertain the original wording of the text since there are no original manuscripts and the existing ones must be compared for accuracy (Virkler & Ayayo, 2007). This process brings the text to a place with the proper wording for the message of the text. There is no major variant in the study of these texts. However, the proper wording helps the interpretation for accuracy in finding the correct words especially when examining grammar. The goal of this precision is to accurately understand the message to be able to form good biblical theology as a foundation for appropriate understanding and living.

How does this process work? The first step is to find a good translation of the Bible. The best process for research would be to find a translation that is a good working translation and then to use several others for reference that are good to be able to compare these translations for words and concepts (Fee & Stuart, 2014). Once this is done, there is a turn to the content of the text for analysis. There are four kinds of issues of content: the actual wording of the author or textual criticism, the meaning of these words, then the grammar or the relationship of the words to each other and the historical–cultural background and then there is a careful integration of these concepts (Fee, 2002). The first part of the actual wording can be found through use of good translations and research on any texts with issues of variants. Then, as to the meaning of the words, this can be done through the use of a good lexicon. Do not use generic dictionaries. For instance, many of the concordances, including online concordances, have dictionaries attached to them and it makes it easy since they are keyed to certain numbers, so you do not have to read Greek and Hebrew. However, there is a problem here in that these dictionaries use gloss definitions. A gloss definition is taking several definitions and making them shorter but merging them all together. When there are multiple definitions to a word, those definitions must be separated and then the proper one chosen by the context of the discussion or the sentence. An example in English is the word "table." It is a flat surface to put things on, it can be a certain way to measure water, it can be a math explanation, it can be at the front of a book listing contents, it can even be used as a verb to table a motion. In each situation, the correct definition must be chosen. As English speakers, this is done automatically in the mind of the hearer. However, when the language is changed to Greek or Hebrew, this is not automatic. The good news is that there are some good lexicons with these separate definitions that are still keyed to the numbers in the concordances. Use these lexicons.

Then the process moves to grammar. Greek or Hebrew grammar is helpful here, but research can be done in these areas to facilitate this process. Then these good English translations will generally follow the grammar of the original languages though there can be some nuances that are not seen in English. Again, this is where good research is necessary. In this examination of these word relationships, the researcher needs to view the context of the pericope being studied. The context around the section being studied needs to read with a view for a general overview of the text and its context. You need to become thoroughly acquainted with the pericope being studied by reading it several times in several translations (Fee, 2002). This helps to see the message in its setting and gives the general idea of the direction of the message and even some of the grammar being used. Then you analyze the sentence structures and syntactical relationships along with the grammar in these sentences (Fee, 2002). This process can point out any special words that need further research.

Finally, the historical–cultural background needs to be researched. This includes the meaning of persons, places, and/or events in the passage; the cultural–social milieu of the author and audience of the text, their customs, their thought world and the intertextuality used by the author and audience (Fee, 2002). These several ideas or concepts can be researched through books for this purpose and even commentaries. However, it is important to use commentaries properly here. At this point, the researcher is looking for these issues of context more than for the conclusions of the commentator. This is an important component of this method of interpretation. The meaning of a text cannot be interpreted with any degree of certainty without historical–cultural and contextual analysis including the general context, the knowledge of customs, the spiritual disposition of the audience, and the immediate context (Virkler & Ayayo, 2007). This research has many different aspects and it needs careful development. Then at this point, the researcher must wrestle with the question of context having to do with various genres (Fee, 2002). The understanding of the proper genre will greatly help the researcher to understand the message of the text. This study of genre has become a greatly nuanced area of research that spans several different methods of interpretation. This study of genre helps to set the literary context.

The grammatical–historical method of interpretation has a long history used by many in the development of biblical theology. Grammatical–historical interpretation suggests the meaning of a text is the author's intended meaning and this can be found most accurately through observing history and rules of grammar as they apply to the text (Virkler & Ayayo, 2007). Though this method can be highly technical and the arena for biblical scholars, it can also be adapted for use by other researchers. It can be a foundation for other methods in looking for the intended message of the author to the intended audience remembering that in this method a text has a meaning related to its grammar and historical context. This way of interpretation gives momentum to finding the message to be able to apply it to the present context since there is a clear message to be found.

Textual Criticism

As briefly mentioned earlier, textual criticism is the attempt to ascertain the original wording of the text (Virkler & Ayayo, 2007). This is not nearly as important to our current methodology as we utilize modern English translations and accept the accuracy of said translations. With that said, however, there is a need to provide an overview of the methodology as it applies specifically to the grammatical–historical approach. The rise of textual criticism occurred during the time of the Reformation as scholars recognized that the most common reading of Scripture may not be the most accurate (Bray, 1996). Further, textual critics argue that accurate interpretation requires a solid knowledge of the original documents. Textual criticism, especially of the New Testament, is considered relatively stable as there are over 5,000 documents known to exist (Osborne, 2006). The discovery the *Dead Sea Scrolls* in the mid-20th century ignited a fresh interest in textual criticism and yielded many of the modern translations in use today. Though small differences were discovered in the *Dead Sea Scrolls*, scholars were able to confirm the remarkable accuracy of the Bible. The field of textual criticism tends to be more conservative given that it focuses on the accuracy of the text in comparison to the original document (Bray, 1996; Osborne, 2006). Because of this, textual scholars are not nearly as interested in what a text means as they are with ensuring and preserving the accuracy of its translation over time.

As social scientific researchers, some may wonder why there is a need to overview a critical method that does not concern itself with the actual meaning of a text. Since, the majority of those reading this book will research the Scriptures using English translations, it is important to remember that the accuracy of these translations was established through the work of textual critical scholars. Further, it is often helpful to research not only a chosen pericope but to also consider the nature of the English translation. For exegetical research, it is beneficial to choose a translation that is as close the original manuscripts as possible. By doing so, researchers ensure that the author's original intent is preserved.

Inductive Biblical Analysis

Inductive Biblical Analysis is a way of studying Scripture or doing exegetical analysis that is done on both a popular and a scholarly level. These methods are widely used and taught in different contexts from Bible Study groups, to churches to informal workshops and seminaries. It can be taught at different levels for use by different groups of people for the study of Scripture. It is a scientific or a systematic way of studying Scripture. This systematic way of biblical analysis yields a great amount of data that can be examined, interpreted, and applied to contemporary contexts. This examination of IBA will follow the teachings of Dr. Garwood Anderson. This process has many pieces to it and a certain philosophy behind it that is implied in the name. This Inductive Biblical Study or Inductive Biblical Analysis is fiercely text centered and based upon inductive thinking in its interaction with the text.

Induction is a way of thinking that is focused on the internal evidence of an issue. Inductive describes a mode of reasoning. Inductive moves from particulars to general concepts, from evidence to conclusion, from data to theory. It is a way of logic and conclusion and it can be used in many different contexts or applications. However, here it is going to be applied and used in the examination of Scripture to exegete or to draw out what is actually there in the text. This helps to understand the text well and thoroughly. A good interpretation of a text will survive a close reading of the text. This is a search for that which is in the text. It is not a superficial examination, but it is a deep or close reading of the text. In the broad sense, induction in exegetical analysis is a commitment to form the evidence of the text to possible conclusions or inferences regarding the meaning of the text, it is evidential over against a deductive approach that is presuppositional (Bauer & Traina, 2011). This inductive process looks at the data in the Scriptures rather than working from an external concept or idea as a construct for the interpretation of Scripture. The process of inductive is a commitment to the evidence in and around the text allowing this evidence to determine the meaning of the text with a desire to hear whatever the text has to say (Bauer & Traina, 2011). It looks at the evidence to test the theory. Induction starts with observation and deduction starts with theory. Sherlock Holmes used inductive reasoning even though he told Watson consistently that it was deductive reasoning.

This method of inductive study looks at issues in the text, not issues that are behind the text or in front the text. Behind the text issues are an examination of the areas of authorship and dating of the particular book. It is not concerned with proving who wrote Romans. This does not imply that this is unimportant it is just not the focus of this examination of Scripture. In addition, the focus is not in front of the text issues. In front of the text issues answer questions like what this means to me today. This question will be answered as the issue of appropriation is addressed but the initial examination is about looking at the text issues before looking for anything else. In the initial stages of this study even comparing the verses that are examined with other biblical texts will be suspended for a moment, though we will include echoes from older texts if they are part of the discussion on the text. In this passion for the message of the text, the search is for authorial intent, but it is ardently looking for the message as it was understood by its original audience. It is likely that the original audience of many of the books did not have access to the other books. The New Testament audience had access to the Greek Old Testament but not too many other letters or gospels. The Old Testament audience had access to the Torah but not all of the other books.

It must be remembered that these texts were written to peoples of oral cultures. The literacy rate in the biblical cultures seems to have ranged from about 5% to 20% depending on the culture and group, so these documents were necessary surrogates for oral communication and these documents were composed with their aural and oral potential in mind (Witherington, 2009). These documents were written with very intentional use of words for people who would need to remember and to interact with the material that was read to them. This intentionality in communication gives rise to some of the clear communication techniques seen in Scripture that may not appear obvious to us as literate readers of the text. Therefore, observations need to be made carefully to see the data and evidence for the message as found in these books. In this process, anachronisms need to be carefully avoided in reading the data in a way that it would be understood by the original hearers knowing that they are separated from us culturally by time, language, societal differences, and even method of communication.

This evidence or data from the text comes from observations that are a detailed part of the process. These observations begin broadly by evidence gathered from the book that is examined as a whole or as a complete book. This macro-observation comes from reading the book in a single read through and making observations about its structure, its divisions, and its emphases. The goal is to get a very clear picture of what is being said by looking at the whole and then once the overall story or writing is seen then to examine the parts and to do micro-observations and then ask the question of how these parts fit together. In this way of doing biblical study learning happens through the process of discovery. This has profound pedagogical significance in that the student participates in the discovery process creating deep impact on both the person and the memory. This Scripture discovery process is transformational for the person and significant for the mind in leaving an imprint for memory. In other words, the process changes the students and helps them remember what they learned. In these observations, we are looking for what is there in the text not what we assume is there or what we have put there to make sense to us. The goal is not to make everything fit together well and some tensions might be found. However, these tensions need not be resolved too quickly.

There are three building blocks of Inductive Biblical Analysis. They are observation, interpretation, and appropriation. These must be done carefully observing certain systems for using these concepts and they must be done in this order. In zeal for pragmatism, the Western mind is trained to aim for application. As a result, the temptation in biblical interpretation is to move from reading the text to application. However, there are other necessary processes to be able to understand the text of Scripture clearly. The idol of pragmatism has helped the Western world create great cities and great technologies, but the worship of this idol comes with some problems that go unseen at first. In the rush to apply or make things work, some of the nuances of reality are lost or ignored as unimportant. Nevertheless, in hindsight it is found that these nuances and warnings are important.

In the study of Scripture, this means that this process must be slowed to a pace that begins with observation and gathering data. This observation then becomes the primary stage and the place from which to build the other two blocks of interpretation and appropriation. Nevertheless, there is a problem with observation in that one often finds that which is looked for in the data. This is part of the problem of presuppositions and this needs to be addressed in this process. When people walk through a city, different people see different aspects of the physical reality around them. Some see the people, others see buildings and landmarks, while others see the trees along the side of the streets. All these observations are part of reality but different aspects of it. This difference in observation is influenced by what we expect to see in that place and what is important to us and has priority in our worldview.

Another important aspect of induction that needs to be noticed is that the hypotheses that we draw from inductive study are always tentative and open to adjustment in light of more evidence or a more satisfactory explanation. In addition, reasoning is ultimately a combination of inductive and deductive. Nevertheless, with Inductive Biblical Analysis, the examination needs to begin with the process of observation and inductive study in data from the text. As can be seen here, there are some weaknesses in method in our presuppositions and in the tentative results. It is important to become aware of these presuppositions and then intentionally expose them to biblical evidence with a willingness to change; this is the essential character of induction (Bauer & Traina, 2011). In this way, these presuppositions can be addressed at least in a tentative way. The good news here is that this method of biblical analysis can be used in conjunction with other methods and provide some strengths and insights that other methods do not offer.

In this method of study, the text is an end in itself. Ultimately, it is God who is the end here in that we want to discover God and what He is saying in and through the text. However, the point is that we are not asking questions of better manuscripts or if Paul was the true author. The text is the final product as we view it for observations. The text is a window through which can be seen God and His purposes and His ways. In the text everything is connected, a piece of the text cannot just be held off by itself. The parts norm the whole of the book and the whole norms the parts. It is like the issue of the hermeneutical circle. What comes first in the text—the parts or the whole? They become norms for each other. A piece of the text cannot be held out or cut out of its context to fit a desired meaning.

This way of inductive study of Scripture encourages a close reading of the text as opposed to a casual reading or a reading to make it fit with other unrelated texts. This way of reading the text has a robust view of Biblical authority. It matters what is said and how it is said, the message matters therefore it must be read closely and understood clearly. In this way, the text is prioritized over every other agenda, over apologetics, over application over all other issues and questions. The Bible does not just answer my questions it questions my questions—it is much more profound than answering questions. This close reading of the text is a submissive position of being open to the Lord and what He says.

In Inductive Biblical Analysis, there is the concept of the implied author. This does not mean that Luke did not write the book of Luke. It means that Luke wrote two books, Luke and Acts and his purposes and methods are different in the two books though they have an overarching theme. When discussing the implied author, it is examining what the author is doing or implying or communicating in that book. Vanhoozer (1998) declares that an implied author is a rhetorical construct used to convey a sense of authorial presence as an effect of the text however; he goes on to warn that the readers must also believe in real authors otherwise they will fail to perceive the agency at work in the text. The implied author is created as a sense of the text, but we cannot remove this implied author from the real author who existed at the time of the writing of the text. This implied author concept helps in understanding the text, but the real author ties it to real time and history and the authority of the text. Then it must be remembered that the Holy Spirit is the author who must be considered here as well. This concept of the implied author helps us to think realistically about this dual authorship without doing damage to the human author and his presence in the text. The human author was carried along by the Holy Spirit as declared in 2 Peter 1:21 This dual authorship is seen in the implied author.

The Process

In observation, seeing what is really there is a hedge against eisegesis or superficiality. Observation begins by looking at the broad scope of the book then it moves to the narrow scope of the words, sentences, and pericopae. In this observation process, the researcher is looking for data. It is not the issue of what it means at this point. The meaning question is suspended until after gathering the data of observation.

The big picture is that we begin by searching for data—what is really there. The second step is interpretation—what can be made of and found from what is there. Then the third step is appropriation, which is evaluation and application. To appropriate means that we deeply understand the original issue and then we bring it to the present context.

Observation (Broad)—Foundation

Since there are several different levels and systems of IBA this examination will interact with the teachings of Dr. Garwood Anderson on these issues. The first part of the observation process or step one is to survey the book of the Bible that is to be studied. This survey has several steps that develop the broad perspective of the text to be examined. This process begins with an uninterrupted read through of the book. This should be done in one sitting to hear the message as a whole. In this reading, the researcher needs to pay attention to several important items that come through this type of reading. In this survey, the researcher sees the general features of the book and notices significant details (Bauer & Traina, 2011). In this reading pay attention to these items and write down some comments on them. The items of interest include the characters, the major themes, the atmosphere, and the plot. What kind of atmosphere is found in the text: is it foreboding or optimistic and does it change at any place in the text? Themes in a book are generally the issues or concepts that recur. The main recurring participants are the characters in the book, but it could be important to notice a participant that shows up for a short time and has a significant part to play in the text.

The second step in this survey of the book is to go through and separate the book into pericopae or sections that are shorter than chapters but longer than a verse or two. In this step, the researcher is looking for cohesive story or teaching times. What are the verses that need to be considered together? Then give them a short description like healing story, conflict story or discussion, and so on. In this process, it is important not to use the pericope separations of an already printed Bible's larger segments for maximum effectiveness in data gathering. Once these are done, the structural unit needs to have some explanation as to the reason it fits tighter or that the material is related. As the text is examined in these ways, there are two other issues that need to be noticed in the reading of the text. The first is a cruciality. There can be several in a text. These are changing points in the story or in the direction of the teaching. An example is found in Mark 3:6 when the Pharisees and Herodians collaborated against Jesus trying to find a way to destroy Him. The story of Mark turns foreboding after this time as this plot against Jesus is running in the background of the rest of the events in the story. The second issue is in looking for the climax. There is usually only one climax. In Mark this is the crucifixion. The climax is the high point in the narrative or the argument of a book.

Observation (Narrow)—Process

In this area of observation, there are four levels of examination and then there are different specific areas that need to be studied for discovery of data. The first level is the book level in looking for implicit connections between segments. The second level of observation is the segment level in looking for implicit connections between paragraphs or episodes. The third is the

paragraph level looking for connections between clauses and these are usually grammatical connections. The final level is the clause level in looking for connections and insights in the way's words are used (Anderson, 2003). Many of these observations will be in how language is used in the text.

Then there are four kinds of observations that will help in understanding these connections. The first kind of observation is looking at basic content in the text of who, what, where, and when. Notice that the why question is not in this list, it will come later. The second kind of observation is verbal/conceptual looking at the connections between words and certain concepts in the pericope. The third is the logical structural issues looking at some of the larger issues of the connections in the text. Then the fourth level is the grammatical in examining the words themselves. There will not necessarily be data in all four kinds of observations.

Following is a list in using this process of these four kinds of observations:

1. **Basic content**—who is there, what is happening, where is this happening, and when in considering time as a factor
2. **Verbal conceptual**
    a. Repetitions of words or concepts; this is an issue at every level of book, pericope, paragraph, or sentence
    b. Contrasts that are verbal as in sentences or conceptual that are found in the pericope or book level
3. **Logical relationships**
    a. Cause and effect which is also called causation or effect and cause, which is also called substantiation (many times these sentences will use the words for or because)
    b. Cruciality—this is a pivot point in the story where a significant change occurs
    c. Particularization—this is a movement from general to particular and it is often an introductory summary with particulars to follow as in the creation account in Genesis
    d. Generalization—this is a movement from particular to general and it is often an encapsulating summary of preceding material
    e. Climax—this is a high point in the narrative (or argument)
    f. Echoes—this is when the text uses a previously known event or text from other parts of Scripture, like using Old Testament concepts or references to Old Testament events especially when they are not mentioned as such in the text itself
4. **Grammatical relationships**—these are found by language use, but the researcher must push past simple word use to find the relationship in that instance in that connection or sentence
    a. Instrumental—look for this when these words are used, "through" "by means of" "by"
    b. Purpose or Result—look for this when these words are used, "in order that" "so that" "that"

c. Implication—look for this when these words are used, "therefore" "thus"
d. Explanatory—look for this when this word is used, "for"
e. Conditional—look for this when these words are used, "If" "since"
f. Concessive—look for this when these words are used, "although" "even though"
g. Adversative—look for this when this word is used, "but" (Anderson, 2003)

Many of these categories are explained more completely in the Bauer and Traina (2011) text on Inductive Biblical Study. However, it is more important to notice or make an observation than to label something. The categories are meant to enable the student to notice, not to limit observations to the available categories. These categories are to facilitate observation and to help categorize them when they are written down.

In addition, these types of observations are unevenly distributed in the biblical text. Not all, or even most will be found in each document. Do not worry if the significance of the observation is not immediately evident and remember that ultimately "observation" is just very slow, careful, and self-conscious reading of the text. Once the observations have been noted, examined and written down then the researcher can move to the interpretation phase (Anderson, 2003).

Interpretation

The way ahead in moving from observation to interpretation is in asking good interpretive questions. These questions are based on the data that was collected in the observation stage. In answering these questions, the solution is not found in commentaries or other bible helps books or resources, but the answers are found in the observations of the text. The one exception to this reality is in answering background questions but this will be considered in the discussion of that type of question. There are different types of questions that can be asked and answered in this interpretation phase of the study. These questions are specific and are not just questions about curiosity that cannot be answered by the text. We cannot find answers to questions like what the apostles had for breakfast before they were sent out two by two. In addition, simply asking the question of meaning for a verse is not specific enough. However, there are several types of questions that can be asked. Remember these

are interpretive questions not application questions. Therefore, the questions are looking for meaning in the context of the 1st century audience not a 21st century audience. That comes later.

Good interpretive questions are a bridge from observation to interpretation and they are specific enough in that when they are answered something has been learned by that process. These are genuine questions not just questions for the sake of asking questions. There are five different kinds of questions in this process (Anderson, 2003).

Following is a list in using these five different types of questions:

1. **Questions of definitions**—this is about the meaning of words or expressions wherein the lexical (dictionary) meaning of the original language is the starting point. The range of possibility is chosen by context and the specific meaning is the goal. Do not use gloss definitions. In addition, meaning includes both denotation as the idea content as well as connotation as the emotion content of the word or phrase
2. **Questions of inference**—these search out the issues from the observations with questions like: Why? Of what significance? For what reason? For what purpose?
3. **Questions of implication**—these search for the issues that the text presupposes like background knowledge assumed for the reader or the worldview assumed by the text and what follows naturally from the text. A good question in this section could be: What truths or principles are implied by the text?
4. **Questions of unresolved difficulties**—these questions search for issues or concepts that do not make sense or what does not seem to fit or just does not seem right. These are issues that the researcher needs to know more about in this situation. Yet it is important here to acknowledge dissonance when it is found without resolving it prematurely.
5. **Background questions**—a background question is an interpretive question in which sociohistorical information is sought to reconstruct the repertoire of the reader. These are issues that the original audience would have known but the 21st century is not aware of these issues. It is here that secondary sources must be used but it must be done carefully not looking for commentary as much as information about the background of this situation in the biblical world. Then the further question here is once discovery has been made, what is the significance for this reality in connection to the text (Anderson, 2003).

Systematically pursue the answers to these interpretive questions from the text and the data gathered or observations from the text. Since the questions are asked of the text, answers are to come first from the text (Anderson, 2003). The exception is needing lexical aids for the meanings of words, but the researcher must determine the meaning in the context of the text. The other exception is in pursuing background questions but again the researcher must determine the implications of the new information from the background issues. In these answers look for relationships, patterns, and correlations. Press for detailed answers that fully answer and develop the issues of the text and the question. This will take more than a sentence or two if the questions are asked effectively.

Up to this point, the researcher has written documentation of the broad observations concerning the book dealing with structures and large connections. In addition, the researcher has documentation of the narrow observations of the sections that are to be examined. Then the documentation also includes a third section with good interpretive questions and fully developed answers to those questions. Nevertheless, this process is not yet complete until appropriation is developed for this text.

Appropriation

Appropriation is the act of setting apart or assigning to a particular use, it is taking a message that has been given to another and taking it to one's self. This final step of appropriation has two aspects. The first aspect is evaluation in the context of the canon. This is where comparison is made to other texts that may be similar or distinct or explanatory. This process is saved until the end so that the message of the original text will not be influenced or even misdirected by this comparison. This preserves the integrity of the message of the text before this message engages with the messages of other texts. It also preserves the message in that these documents were written to be read to a group so the message is preserved and as it would be to the original audience who heard it read to them.

The second issue of appropriation is a contextual synthesis. This is where the original message is brought to bear upon the reader's current context. It is here that application takes place. However, it must be done carefully without flattening the process of simply bringing everything into the present context without first looking for universal principles and being aware of cultural context that may not be brought into the present. Why does this need to be done so carefully? This carefulness is due to two realities that must be considered and addressed. The first is that any section of Scripture is only a partial witness to the whole message of Scripture. The second is the issue of particularity. The message of every text is conditioned by and specific to a particular social, religious, and historical context.

This application process must be contextual. This is moving the message from one context to another context. Therefore, the message or event must be decontextualized and then recontextualized into the present. To facilitate this process, there are some questions that can act as guidelines. Here are the three basic questions:

1. What is the function of the biblical instruction in its original context?
2. How is our context the same and how is it different?
3. How can that instruction function analogously in our context? (Anderson, 2003).

This process is about first moving from understanding the message in its original context, then finding the aspects that transcend time and space then importing it to the present. The transcendent message is not to take the cultural particulars of the original message and transport that into the future. Instead it is to take the message that is in the context of one culture and put it into the context of another as a divine message. Contextual appropriation is similar to language translation in that the message is the issue and it must be translated in a way that is faithful to the original message and yet understandable in the receiver culture.

The final area of documentation is to take the interpretive answers and then appropriate them to the current context in the areas that they apply. They will apply in many areas such as theology, marriage, relationships, leadership, or many other areas of concern in the 21st century. This is where the researcher is able to bring the art of pragmatism to the process in answering 21st century issues and discovering the transcendent Word for the present generation. This final process needs to be written as well. Then this can be added to and interact with other research in these areas. This is the final part of the process that brings the Word of the Lord to bear upon the contemporary believer, church, and society.

The Value of IBA

The value of Inductive Biblical Analysis can be seen in several areas as it stands alone in the process of hermeneutics or as it is used in conjunction with other analysis methods. First it has value as a system of exegetical analysis in its passion and single focus on the text. This focus brings many effective tools into the process of analysis from the world of linguistics, philosophy, and theology. It also deals with issues of context that is a central issue in good hermeneutics generally. Added to this is the systematic process it uses in all three areas of observation, interpretation, and appropriation. This way of analysis also clearly separates the processes adding strength to the focus on interpretation before application.

Inductive Biblical Analysis can also be used in conjunction with other systems. First it can be used with basic hermeneutical principles of interpretation cooperating with basic exegetical analysis based in grammatical–historical interpretation. Grammatical–historical interpretation is about analyzing the text looking for the message with its focus on certain principles of exegesis in the verses and words of the text. Inductive Biblical Analysis can add its unique strength to this process, and they can be used together for a more robust understanding of the message. IBA can reinforce the concepts of grammatical–historical pursuits of the message.

Inductive Biblical Analysis can go farther in helping in other systems as well like SRA. SRA uses the concept of inner texture that is a focus on words and even repetitions in some areas of analysis. These two systems are similar here but not the same. SRA focuses on the repetitions but then goes on to focus on other issues like ascetics. IBA can add the strength of looking into these words and their connections even further in looking for issues of

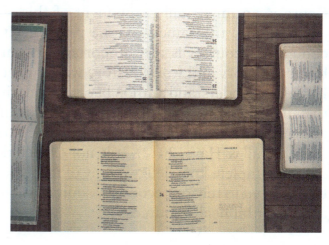

contrast or cause and effect or even grammatical connections while at the same time expanding the search into larger issues of crucialities. Then the interpretive section of IBA can bring some strength into the process as well. SRA looks to interpretation and application but the process of interpretive questions as seen in IBA can enhance the interpretive phase of analysis. Finally, the concepts of appropriation can add further insight and clarity to the application process in SRA.

Inductive Biblical Analysis is a robust yet very practical method of biblical study that systematically guides the researcher from observation and data gathering, through interpretation to application by the appropriation of the message from a previous context to a present context. This process adds depth and strength to the hermeneutical process, and it becomes an effective tool for the exegete who studies Scripture with the purpose of deep understanding and practical application to the present realities of believers, the church, and the world.

The Interpretive Journey

Similar, in some ways to IBA, is Duvall and Hays' (2012) Interpretive Journey (IJ). While IBA is primarily focused on the content of the text, the IJ is focused on the social–historical context that surrounds the text. This is not intended to suggest a better/worse approach—rather, the two methods have different emphases.

The IJ starts out quite similar to IBA. It requires a meticulous reading of the text that highlights textual markers in sentences, paragraphs, and the overall discourse including: repetition of words, contrasts and comparisons, lists, causes and effects, figures of speech, the placement and importance of conjunctions, verb tenses, pronoun antecedents, interactions between characters, the uses of questions and answers, the rationale for including dialogues between characters, any purpose and result statements, conditional clauses, the actions and roles of God compared to the actions and roles of people, emotional terms, shifts and pivots in the focus of the content, connections to other passages, and unique words used (Duvall & Hays, 2012).

IJ also seeks to bring in literary and historical–cultural elements to interpretation. Genre is an important component of this since one should not read Song of Songs (a love song) the same way one reads Leviticus (ancient ritual practice). Historical context, of course, is also important. When the passage was written in relation to biblical history and world history will impact our understanding of the passage. Thus, IJ seeks to understand author, background, time of writing, nature of author's ministry, the audience and their relationship to the author, the occasion for writing, the author and audience's relationship to God, and cultural elements that are embedded into the text (Duvall & Hays, 2012). It is not expected that any student of Scripture is going to have a complete knowledge of any of these historical–cultural insights and thus should be expected to rely on secondary sources such as commentaries, atlases, introductions, and other biblical resources.

All of this allows the researcher to begin to grasp the text in the ancient context. This is a critical step as the interpreter seeks to avoid eisegesis and/or anachronism. Eisegesis is the placing of meaning into the text that the original author never intended. Anachronism is attributing a contemporary value, ethic, custom, or item as part of the world of the past without evidence of its presence. Grasping the text in the ancient context seeks to avoid both these flaws.

Once that understanding is accomplished, the next IJ step is to measure the width of the river that separates the ancient from the contemporary. Three primary elements separate the ancient and the contemporary: culture, time, and language (Duvall & Hays, 2012). For instance, the pledge of Joseph to marry Mary (Matt 1:18) is as strong as a marriage vow and thus required a divorce statement to exit (Matt. 1:19). This is quite different than the marriage engagements that contemporary Western cultures experience. This widens the river at this point in the text. The further back in time that a passage is situated, the wider the river becomes as what was once well-known becomes forgotten over time. Language and all its constructs also pose a widening of the river. While many components of ancient Hebrew, Aramaic, and Greek are known to contemporary scholars, still, there is uncertainty in some parts of its usage. All of this places a river between the ancient and contemporary that varies in its width. When we come across a passage like Ephesians 4:25, the river is not very wide: we understand well the ideas of falsehood and speaking the truth. However, when we wade into Leviticus 5:2–6 and its discussion on cleanliness and uncleanliness, we find the river to be quite wide.

All of this requires a bridge. Duvall and Hays (2012) suggest that the interpreter, once they have a firm grasp of the ancient meaning, can identify the theological principle that is transhistorical. In other words, a bridge that crosses the river and allows the ancient to speak into the contemporary, irrespective of where that contemporary point in time might be. Again, it is important here to avoid eisegesis and anachronism. There are four elements that ensure that the principle is firmly anchored to the meaning of the text: it is drawn directly from the text; it is timeless; it is transcultural; and it is relevant to both the biblical and contemporary audiences. When the principle is drawn out of extra-biblical meaning, tied to a specific event, bound to a culture or is irrelevant to either the biblical or contemporary audience, it is less likely to bridge the river separating both times.

The next step recommended by Duvall and Hays (2012) is to consult the biblical map. In other words, how does the principle align with the rest of Scripture. It is possible to identify the right principle for one part of Scripture but to be unaware that the principle changes over the course of Scripture. So, for instance, the need for blood sacrifices for forgiveness is a principle taught throughout Leviticus. However, as we come to the New Testament, (Hebrews 10:4 and 1 John 1:9) we see that the multiple sacrifices have been subsumed into the single sacrifice of Jesus. He is the sacrifice. However, without an understanding of the multiple sacrifices of Leviticus, we lose the multifaceted impact of Christ's sacrifice. Starting with either without consulting the rest of the biblical map will lead one to an incomplete picture of what Scripture has revealed. Thus, one will want to identify explicit parallels with other parts of Scripture as well as echoes that represent similar ideas or themes that may be repeated. It is also appropriate to understand how the principle has been understood throughout Christian history. While it is possible for contemporary thinking to speak truth into past understandings, it is also possible for past understandings to correct contemporary thinking. All of this will necessarily require a wordsmithing of the original principle to nuance this statement.

Finally, we are ready to interpret the application of the principle to a contemporary context. It is important here that the meaning of the original author and context does not change, nor does the transhistorical principle. Rather, what changes is the application of the material to the contemporary context. For instance, 1 Corinthians 6:19 declare our flesh and blood bodies as temples of the Holy Spirit. In the context of the passage, Paul is rebuking the Corinthians for their sexual immorality that had become rampant in the Corinthian church, not unlike the culture surrounding that church. The principle that our bodies are the temple of God is transhistorical and of course could be more deeply understood by studying the material throughout Scripture on the tabernacle and temple in the Old Testament. When we go to apply it to our contemporary situation, it would touch upon any body-based conversation from eating to tattoos to addictions to, still in our day, sexual immorality.

Genre Analysis

Another method of studying Scripture is through the study of a pericope's genre or literary style. There is some discussion about the practicality of discussing genre across a text, such as Scripture, that has been developed over several hundred, if not thousands, of years (Osborne, 2006). Additionally, it is not uncommon for Scripture to embed and amalgamate multiple genres within a single pericope. While these difficulties to genre analysis are recognized and not always resolvable, at the same time, for most of Scripture, there is enough uniqueness between genres and sufficient characteristics of each to identify genre(s) for most passages.

Even if that hurdle has been passed, one must decide on the number of unique genres that compose most of Scripture. The numbers vary by analysis. For the sake of this summary of genre analysis, it will be presumed that there are at least 10: (a) narrative, (b) ritual law, (c) historical chronicles/annals, (d) poetry, (e) wisdom, (f) prophecy, (g) gospel, (h) parable, (i) epistles, and (j) apocalyptic.

Narrative Genre

Without a doubt, narrative comprises the most common form of genre for Scripture. Of course, other forms of genre are integrated into these stories, but narrative forms the backbone for the following books: Genesis; portions of Exodus; Numbers; Joshua; Judges; Ruth; 1 & 2 Samuel; Ezra; Nehemiah; Esther; portions of Daniel; Jonah; and Acts. This genre includes what we typically think of as story with all the distinctive elements of plot and time (Duvall & Hays, 2012).

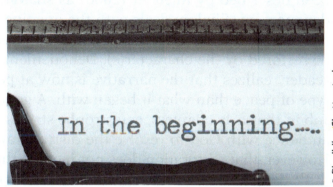

We tend to be drawn to the narratives of Scripture because they capture the attention of all ages, have action that propels them along, and can most easily be paralleled with our own lived experience (Duvall & Hays, 2012). However, because the story can become so vivid, the principle that the author is trying to convey in the text can become elusive. For instance, the story of David and Goliath (1 Sam. 17) is familiar to many and we often think of comparing those two characters coming to the interpretation that with God the small can defeat the large. However, a closer reading of the context shows that the contrast is less about David and Goliath and between David and Saul, a comparison that will play out throughout the rest of 1 Samuel (Carter, Duvall, & Hays, 2018). Additionally, this genre may be difficult to interpret because the whole story must be considered, which can span several chapters. While we rightly peg Genesis 3 as a primary place where we see the effects of sin, really, this story spans all the way to chapter 11, including sins effects: on our relationship to God; on our relationship to others; on our physical health; on the righteous and the unrighteous; and on nations. While each of these could rightly be broken down and interpreted separately, to interpret what has happened in chapter 3, this larger narrative needs to be taken into consideration. Ultimately, narrative is included in Scripture not simply for the retelling of stories nor even for its historical value—although both of those are true—but it has been included by the author to support a particular theological truth (Carter et al., 2018). Without understanding that theological principle, we are likely to miss the point of the story in our interpretation.

As narrative might imply, there is a narrator who is the author as s/he wants to be presented through the story (the implied author). The narrator has the ability to present the thinking of characters, suggest what is right and wrong, immediately move from one location to the next, move from one time to the next, decide which words get placed on the lips of which characters, and order the events (Osborne, 2006). All of these should be considered especially when there are multiple examples of the same narrative presented in Scripture.

Additionally, one must consider the plot of the story. The four elements of plot have been described by Allender (2006) as shalom, shalom shattered, shalom sought, and denouement. Shalom deals with the opening setting of the story and the character(s) at peace. Shalom shattered represents a disruption of that peace that is then sought to be restored by the character(s). Denouement is the conclusion of the story where the reader realizes that the narrative is now at peace, although it may be a very different type of peace than what it began with. A good example of this is Job. All is good with Job in the early chapters, catastrophe strikes and his shalom is shattered, he seeks an audience with God to resolve the distress, and in the end has a form of restoration. However, that restoration does not include the resurrection of his first seven sons and three daughters, a grief that he would need to bear for the rest of his life.

Finally, one must consider the words that are spoken by the characters and the implied commentary that the author is developing by choosing those words (Osborne, 2006). The author of the Gospel of John makes this explicit in the conclusion of his gospel: he has witnessed all that happened but only a portion of what happened is included (John 21:24–25). Again, this harkens back to the theological intent of the original author. Thus, to interpret this genre well, we must consider not only what is said, but why were these words chosen to be said by the author.

Ritual Law Genre

If contemporary readers are most comfortable with narrative, the opposite side of that spectrum lies in ritual law genre. Part of this is, undoubtedly, the foreign concept of a sacrificial system and cleanliness codes. Many, although certainly not all, contemporary readers have little connection with any type of animal sacrifice for sacred ritual. Additionally, the increased understanding of pathologies creates cultural codes of cleanliness that are far removed from sacred codes. As such, the portions of Scripture devoted to these topics—primarily portions of Exodus, Leviticus, and Deuteronomy—are difficult to interpret.

Additionally, the historical approach to interpretation for ritual law has been to identify the specific code as either civil, ceremonial, or moral law. This was done in the hopes of teasing out moral law that would still be applicable to those who are no longer under the civil or ceremonial aspects of the law. However, as Duvall and Hays (2012) point out, this is far more difficult to do than might be expected at first glance. The primary difficulty is its underlying presupposition: that the intention of the law was to provide a code that, if followed, could produce righteousness. However, the law was not given until after God had already rescued the people out of their enslavement and sealed their place as His people with the crossing of the Red Sea. In other words, the law was given as a response to what God had already done, not as a means to become something that in fact, they already were (Exod. 20:2).

This suggests that our interpretation of the ritual law has more to do with how theological truths are acted out in the individuals and nation of God's people in such a way that they could worship Him with their whole body and spirit. This theological approach to ritual law interpretation has four primary components: covenant, cleanliness, sacrifice, and remembrance. The interpreter of this genre must always consider how the material being analyzed fits into the larger covenant narrative of ancient Israel that began with Abraham in Genesis 12 to be a blessing to the world (Duvall & Hays, 2012). This required a degree of holiness, since God is holy, that is consistently expressed throughout the law as a contrast between that which is clean/sacred/holy and that which is unclean/profane/unholy (Osborne, 2006). When one became unclean, profane, or unholy, God was gracious to provide a means of renewal through the sacrificial system (Osborne). Thus, while one would not expect to live without sin, one could live blamelessly through the law (Phil. 3:6). And, since humans tend to be a forgetful bunch, the law provided by God was structured around seasonal feasts that would remind His people of what He had and would accomplish for them so that they would be impelled to continue to be sanctified through adherence to the law. For Christians, this ritual narrative was fulfilled in Jesus who provided a new covenant that secured holiness through His sacrifice that would be remembered through the sacraments of the church. Thus, focus on these four elements of the law is likely to provide a stronger interpretation that is both relevant to the original author/listeners, its impact upon Christianity, and its application in contemporary settings.

Historical Chronicles/Annals Genre

Four books of the Christian Scripture are dedicated to specific historical chronicles (1 & 2 Kings and 1 & 2 Chron.) and then scattered throughout Old and New Testaments are genealogies. While the historical chronicles are easier for contemporary readers to grasp due to their reliance on some narrative, the genealogies are a bit more difficult. This is especially so for cultures where the remembrance of ancestors may only go back a half dozen generations. However, both chronicles and genealogies follow a similar format. Both tend to introduce the character of focus, identify something

significant about the character, and give the span of their life or rule. This is why it is probably better to think of chronicles less as royal narrative and more like narrative genealogy. Additionally, we can rightly presume that God did not place this genre in Scripture to bore us—in other words, it has purpose within the larger scope of God's revelation.

Several interpretive steps assist with analyzing these elements of Scripture (Adams, 1999). First, while Kings is probably written during the exile to explain the demise of the unified and split kingdom(s), Chronicles is probably written after the exile to explain the rationale for the exile to encourage future faithfulness to the law (Adams). Irrespective of whether chronicle or genealogical material, one should always identify its starting point and its terminus. This will provide further insight into the narrative that underlies most chronicle and genealogy genre. The interpreter should highlight important figures. The importance may not always lie in their biblical fame but rather in the stories that underlie their mention. For instance, Matthew's genealogy of Jesus contains four women: Tamar, Rahab, Ruth, and the wife of Uriah (Bathsheba). Understanding the unlikeliness of these characters being part of the genealogy of the Messiah assists in properly interpreting their role within the genealogy. In this case, it is important for the interpreter to understand what else Scripture has said about each character. Often, there are branches of the tree that are followed and those that are not. These typically represent those whom God is choosing as His instruments to accomplish His will. Finally, the interpreter should highlight unusual components of a genealogy. Returning to Matthew 1, while reading this genealogy would prepare the reader for an important Jewish (son of Abraham) King (son of David), what is unexpected is the presence of an incestuous relationship, a prostitute, a Moabite, and an adulterer. These are not only names that, from Matthew's perspective, need not appear in a genealogy (most genealogies contain only the male progeny), these are names that no one would expect to be associated with the Messiah. Yet, perhaps Matthew, knowing the scorn from his fellow countrymen of being a tax collector for the Romans, prepares us theologically for a Messiah King who will fulfill the blessing of Abraham for, truly, all people.

Poetry Genre

Whole libraries of books have been written on Hebrew poetry and so we will not rehash what is readily available in any of them. While the books of Psalms and Lamentations are the most obvious resources for this genre, Hebrew poetry is by far the most prevalent genre to intersect with the other genres and so can be found throughout Scripture. It should be noted, however, that one of its most fascinating elements is that it is the only genre that is specifically focused on responding back to God. While every other genre in some form is God speaking to us, Hebrew poetry is God giving us the words to speak back to Him.

Four elements are critical to the proper interpretation of Hebrew poetry: type, form, structure, and use of figurative language (Duvall & Hays, 2012; Osborne, 2006). Nearly every author that writes about Hebrew poetry has their own list of types of poetry. An overview would include regal, lament, praise/thanksgiving, and imprecatory, within which there can be additional subcategories. Additionally, the interpreter must realize that the form of Hebrew poetry may differ from their cultural experience of poetry. For instance, Western culture is often concerned with some form of rhyme or rhythm within their poetry. Hebrew poetry, on the other hand, is less concerned about these elements and instead focuses on thematic patterns within the text (Osborne). This, necessarily, affects its structure. Those more familiar with a linear development in poetry or expecting a form of plot to be included will often find themselves unable to find these elements in some Hebrew poetry. Rather, a chiastic structure is often employed where there are matching themes on opposite ends of the poem with the ideological emphasis of the poem being revealed in its middle. This cultural poetic structure was so ingrained in ancient and 1st century Jewish thinking, that it can impact writings from other genres as well. Finally, as might be expected in poetry, the interpreter must not only identify the use of figurative language but also conclude its meaning. Sometimes this is quite simple: if God is my rock, then there are characteristics of a rock (although not all) that can explain God's character. Other times, like God being a shepherd, require a much deeper knowledge of how the image would have been understood in its original context for us to grasp the significance of the image.

Wisdom Genre

Another genre that finds itself intersecting with many other styles of Scripture is wisdom literature. Four books are primarily dedicated to this form: Job, Proverbs, Ecclesiastes, and Song of Solomon. Much like poetry, on which its form is based, there are a number of types

of wisdom literature including proverb, saying, riddle, admonition, allegory, prayer, dialogue, confession, lists, and beatitudes (Osborne, 2006).

Recognizing its intersection and influence on a number of different genres, the four books of wisdom in Scripture have unique but complementary purposes that allow one to grasp equilibrium in our understanding of wisdom. Duvall and Hays (2012) provide a helpful analysis of each. Proverbs provides the reader an understanding of how life usually works. These are not rules (not every child that is brought up well will age well—Prov. 22:6) as much as principles of life. This is underscored in Job where a righteous man suffers not because of what he has done wrong but because of his righteousness. Where Proverbs is more likely to supply the 'why' of life, Job is left unable to answer any of God's questions. This seems irrational and, indeed, Ecclesiastes agrees: rational, logical approaches to life based on a set of principles—even wise principles—will ultimately fail in providing meaning for life. Yet, all is not hopeless. Even in the midst of an irrational, illogical life, in Song of Solomon we find romantic love for others that itself is not solely rational or logical yet an invaluable blessing.

Thus, to interpret well, the wisdom saying(s) must be placed within the context of their biblical setting and their type of saying must be identified (Osborne, 2006). Wisdom literature is especially prone to hyperbole and so it is important to analyze whether the point being made is being overstated as a literary form of bold–italics–all uppercase writing or whether it truly means that the overstatement is generalizable to humanity. The interpreter must also be careful about anachronism in wisdom genre interpretation. There are typically customs and phrases embedded into the text that must be understood in their original context before they can be applied to contemporary settings.

Prophecy Genre

Nothing seems to quite pique our interest like a bit of prophecy. We seem to like the challenge of figuring out how a particular prophecy might be hiddenly revealed in our own day. However, it is important to remember that Old Testament prophecy was primarily related to three broad themes: broken covenant, impending judgment, and God's faithfulness throughout (Duvall & Hays, 2012). All three of

these themes require us to not look forward when interpreting, but probably to look backward to the establishment of the covenant that has been broken, what happens when it is broken, and whether God will remain faithful. This idea of the prophets primarily drawing upon the past to describe the present and near future is called forthtelling, as opposed to prophets primarily looking into the distant future, which could be called foretelling. A vast majority of the prophetic material contained in Isaiah, Jeremiah, Ezekiel, Hosea, Joel, Amos, Obadiah, Micah, Nahum, Habakkuk, Zephaniah, Haggai, Zechariah, and Malachi is primarily written as forthtelling. These books all heavily rely upon the law genre, particularly Deuteronomy and principally drawing from chapters 28–30. To be sure, there is evidence of foretelling that occur throughout prophetic genre but in many cases, it is unlikely the prophets fully understood the gravity of the foretelling that they were providing (e.g., Isa. 7:10–25)—they were often simply forthtelling.

To interpret prophecy genre well, it is necessary for the interpreter to identify the setting, time, and audience. For some prophets, we can identify this pretty easily. For others, we have few if any of these cues. However, when this context is provided, it will assist with us interpreting the passage without ancient anachronism (i.e., bringing in later historical events into earlier times unless the foretelling nature of the text requires us to do so). Additionally, it is necessary to understand the biblical history of those mentioned in the prophetic oracles. Edom is the son of Esau who had, to put it mildly, a strained relationship with his brother Jacob, who was later renamed Israel. When reading about Edom in the prophetic genre, it is important to know the history and genealogy of these nations from a biblical perspective. All of this will serve as a governor that keeps us from jumping to futuristic speculation (Osborne, 2006). Due partially on its heavy reliance on poetic genre, but also as an inherent aspect of the prophetic genre in its own right, there can be important symbolic language that is provided in the material. Interpreters of this genre must do the diligent and tedious work of identifying what is literal and what is symbolic (Osborne). All of this will assist in making sure that the interpreter first identifies a passage's original meaning before jumping to the Messianic implications, which might range from non-Messianic, analogous, or direct foretelling (Osborne). Since theological perspectives can taint the interpretation of any passage, but historically especially prophecy, it is important to draw from a spectrum of Christian perspectives and try to hold those different perspectives in tension (Osborne). None of this is to suggest that there are no contemporary applications for prophetic material. However, more often than not, we will find that those applications mirror the threefold themes of the genre: how we break relationship with God; the consequences of that unfaithfulness; and God's faithfulness throughout.

Gospel Genre

Some might argue, and quite convincingly, that the four gospels belong under narrative. Certainly, Matthew, Mark, Luke, and John contain all the elements of the narrative genre and they very much read as such. If some would subsume gospel genre under narrative, they would not be wrong to do so. The strongest argument for this would be Luke—a

gospel writer who also penned the Acts narrative. Certainly, the gospels are somewhat biographical with theological themes woven throughout. Despite the variety that occurs in the gospels, only four events are repeated in all the gospels: Jesus feeding the 5,000; Jesus walking on water; the death of Jesus; and the resurrection of Jesus. While the feeding and water walking are used differently by each author to support their theme, all four identify the death and resurrection events as proof that Jesus is who the author says He is (Carter et al., 2018).

Given this aspect of the gospel genre, it is important to ask three questions (Duvall & Hays, 2012). First, what does the account that is being analyzed tell the interpreter about Jesus? Without trying to overgeneralize, this will typically be an emphasis on Jesus' divinity and/or His humanity. Since Jesus, to the writers of the gospels, represents divine God revealing Himself and the fullness of humanity in the person of Jesus, it is critical for the interpreter to understand what the gospel writer is saying about God and about the intentions of humanity as both are displayed in Jesus. A second question is how the pericope being analyzed fits into the surrounding stories that are being strung together for a purpose. For instance, we may miss the irony that John is displaying when a Pharisee cannot understand the teachings of Jesus (John 3) but a Samaritan woman can (John 4). Finally, the interpreter must ask how the pericope under analysis fits into the larger theme of the death and resurrection of Jesus. For example, throughout Matthew's narratives, he keeps highlighting different types of kings. How shocking it is then when we find that the king he is going to hold up as the greatest of kings is a crucified king (Mt. 27:27–37). It is this consistent emphasis on a proclamation of Jesus as the crucified and risen One that separates gospel genre from the broader narrative genre.

Parable Genre

Primarily intersecting with the gospel genre, but also in other portions of Scripture, the parable genre is a comparison literature that provides insight into kingdom realities using easily recognizable images (Osborne, 2006). Blomberg (1990) suggests that rather than trying to find a single lesson from a parable that its comparison nature presents multiple lessons to learn.

Generally, most parables have three characters who each represent a unique lesson about heavenly, earthly, or a combination of both realities (Blomberg). Most parables have a significant reversal of expectations that need to be understood in their ancient context to interpret the full weight of the parable (Osborne). These turns of expectations point to both kingdom eschatology and kingdom ethics (Osborne).

As with nearly all biblical analysis, context—both historical and cultural—is usually critical to interpretation (Osborne, 2006). To whom is the parable addressed or in what venue? How does that change the emphasis of the different lessons? Since the parable is, by its very nature, a story, many of the elements listed under narrative apply to this genre as well (Osborne). Typically, the parables are part of the proof that the author of the pericope is using to support the theme of the book. As such, parables should be interpreted within this context rather than jumping immediately to doctrinal application (Osborne). What all of this will avoid is the unhealthy allegorical interpretations of parables that have been offered throughout church history where often interpreters would make every element of the parable have an ecclesial meaning of significance. Instead, we should see parables as masterful narratives that embed deep meaning in easy to handle, although not always easy to understand, ways.

Epistle Genre

While travel and communication were at a height in the first century, still, it was a timely endeavor to lead from a distance. Epistles, or letters, resolved this tension by standing in the place of the author (Duvall & Hays, 2012; Osborne, 2006). In this sense, they carried quite a bit of authority with them. However, they were also always written to a specific context or situation and as such were not first and foremost theological in nature, although they contained a high degree of practical theology. Thus, each of the epistles of the New Testament (Rom., 1 & 2 Cor., Gal., Eph., Phil., Col., 1 & 2 Thess., 1 & 2 Tim., Titus, Philem., Heb., James, 1 & 2 Pet., 1, 2, & 3 John, and Jude) were written by leaders of the church to be used as authoritative direction.

Due to their epistolary nature, most letters follow a relatively linear, logical progression. Grasping this progression throughout the epistle will assist the interpreter in identifying the meaning of the pericope (Osborne, 2006). Obviously, this will need to be coupled with not only an understanding of rhetorical devices that might be used in an epistle in the first century, but also the events that might be happening in the lives of the author and recipients that could affect proper interpretation. Thus, while epistolary interpretation is sometimes the easiest to come to a conclusion on because of its logical format, it is deceptively easy. Interpreters must dig deeply into the original meaning for the author and audience. Interpreters should also beware of their own biases, especially theological, that may cause the text to communicate something that it was never intended to say. Finally, it is important for interpreters to determine whether the commands within an epistle are normative or prescriptive. Normative commands are commands that would apply to all Christians of all ages. Prescriptive commands would have a specific application to the original context, although there might be principles embedded in these commands that could be applied in a contemporary environment.

Apocalyptic Genre

Finally, we come to the apocalyptic genre. All Scripture interpretation should be approached with care—exponentially so with apocalyptic genre. If we said that prophecy genre primarily looks backward as a function of its forthtelling, then apocalyptic genre looks forward as a form of foretelling. However, unlike prophetic material, which is typically written in an easier to understand format, apocalyptic literature is filled with symbolic images that can be quite difficult to interpret. Revelation is the primary book with this genre (although it also contains epistle and prophetic genres). This genre is also spread throughout other books such as Daniel and Ezekiel.

Due to the nature of apocalyptic genre, it is critical to understand the meaning of its symbols in their original context. That context often included significant knowledge of Jewish Scripture and so drawing image meanings, when appropriate, from existing biblical images is a solid start. While there is typically some type of development within apocalyptic literature, one should proceed with caution about developing chronological maps or timelines (Duvall & Hays, 2012). While we can be sure that Revelation will unfold one day as described in the book, much like Jesus' first coming, it may not play out exactly the way we would have expected it to from an overly literal reading of apocalyptic genre. Perhaps in this genre more than any other, it is important to take a bird's-eye view of the entirety of the writing rather than getting

overwhelmed in the small details. It is not that these details are insignificant, only that interpreting them would be like a person a generation before Jesus trying to map out the ministry of Jesus including His death and resurrection. We should not allow our 20/20 hindsight of the Old Testament in light of Jesus to make us arrogant about our ability to identify the details of apocalyptic literature. Thus, we should approach our theological applications and predictive tendencies with humility (Osborne, 2006). The healthy interpreter of apocalyptic genre will be heavy on transhistorical principles and short on fulfillment predictions.

Conclusion

This chapter obviously represents only a brief overview of several different exegetical methodologies. It is neither intended to be exhaustive nor to be inclusive of all the variations that are available to the researcher. It does, however, set the groundwork for the focus of this book—SRA. As will be seen in the chapters that follow, many of the elements of these various methodologies are available to the researcher through SRA. It is in the intersection of these approaches that SRA tends to hold out a strong promise of allowing the analysis to review many of the dimensions of interpretation inherent in scriptural interpretation.

Chapter Three Reflective Exercises

1. Consider a value or ethic from your culture's past that is no longer held by your culture. How could the IJ be used to identify its meaning in the past, the principle that is transhistorical, and consider ways that principle could be used in the contemporary context?
2. To understand the value of genre analysis, find a love letter and an end-user license agreement either online or that you have personally. If you read the love letter like a license agreement, how would it change the meaning of the letter? If you read the license agreement like a love letter, what negative outcomes could occur? How might the different genres of Scripture be misread?
3. In using grammatical–historical interpretation, describe how textual criticism is an important foundation for this process. Then describe the next three stages of interpretation having to do with the words, the grammar, and the context of the text. Finally explain the process of using a lexicon for the understanding of the words of the text.
4. Inductive Biblical Analysis is a method for a close examination of the text. Explain how the researcher examines the data of the text using verbal concepts, logical relationships, and grammatical relationships. Then describe how the researcher is to move from gathering data to the interpretive process and finally to the appropriation of the text for the contemporary setting.

Chapter 4

Timing Matters—Dealing with Authorship and Dating

One of the key terms in exegetical analysis is *location*. As interpreters, we are interested in the location of the original author and the original audience. *Location* is a term that is widely understood in a variety of arenas and understanding some examples of determining location can help us better comprehend its importance in the hermeneutical process. There are lessons that can be learned from considering these.

From a mathematical perspective, location is measured by calculating mean, median, and mode. Mean, or average, considers all of the data in a data set. Median determines the midpoint, or center, of a data set. Mode identifies the value that occurs most often in a data set. From a geographic perspective, location can be expressed using a three-dimensional Cartesian vector: latitude, longitude, and elevation. Thus, location is determined by calculating the point of intersection of each of these vectors. Each of these measures provides valuable insight into how we can determine the social and cultural location of the people in a given text.

First, like the *mean*, we take into account all of the social and cultural information available about a given text. Second, like the *median*, we identify the central social and cultural realities that surround a text. Third, like the *mode*, we consider the concepts, events, and social norms that would have been common to the people living in the world around the text. Given the distance that exists between the interpreter and the world of the text, researchers also must determine the social and cultural location by pinpointing the intersection of key vectors of textual data: (a) the original

author, (b) the original audience, (c) the date, and (d) the purpose. By identifying these core elements of a passage, researchers are better equipped to interpret the author's original meaning, and then, best apply it to its applicable contemporary context.

Determining the Author

The first vector we will consider is authorship. It is important to begin by recognizing that there are many hot button issues in biblical interpretation and one of these is the matter of authorship. Given one's understanding of the nature of Scripture, faith tradition, or theological leanings, the issue of authorship can serve as a pivotal part of the interpretive process. In some cases, authorship is fairly obvious; however, in other cases, such as the Epistle to the Hebrews, identifying the author can be challenging. When seeking to determine the author, researchers must do their due diligence while also recognizing there will always be potential for disagreement. Given that we acknowledge the potential for various faith traditions to utilize this text, it is necessary to begin with a call for mutual respect and honest dialogue. We echo the hopes of Klein et al. (2017) that, though we may not agree with one another's conclusions, we can view them in light of faith tradition and the diligence and care given to Scripture. Thus, the impetus falls upon each researcher to make an informed decision regarding controversial issues such as authorship and then support said decision with diligent, scholarly precision.

How Do We Determine the Author?

While determining authorship may seem arduous, it is far from a lost cause. Given that no one has personal knowledge of the original author of any given text, researchers rely upon identifying the *implied author*. We infer certain information upon the author based upon data we glean from the text itself and a variety of other sources. Given this, the "implied author of a work is never completely identical to the flesh-and-blood author" (Bauer & Traina, 2011, p. 43). Since we are unable to interview the original author and get his response to our interpretation, we cautiously construct an understanding of the implied author with the interpretive purpose of getting a better sense of the meaning of the text.

The most obvious way to determine the implied author of a text, though not without its own controversy, is to look to the text itself. Found often in Epistles, being letters to a specific church, the salutation often sheds light on authorship. As stated in earlier chapters, we take a strong stance on our belief that the Scriptures are the inspired, inerrant, and infallible Word of God. Simply, the Bible does not lie. Therefore, if the Bible is in fact truthful, then we as interpreters can identify the author of a text by first looking to see if the author is identified. For instance, in the New Testament, only nine books do not explicitly state the author. With the exception of the Epistle to the Hebrews, each of those nine has an author connected by way of its title. On the surface, it would seem simple to identify the implied author of most of the New Testament; however, in cases like the Pastoral Epistles, this simplified approach is often rejected (deSilva, 2004). While the Pastoral Epistles are traditionally connected with the Apostle Paul, modern scholars tend to reject this; however, this is not universally accepted. Henson (2015) argued that we must reject a theory that would propose that any portion of the Scripture would intentionally deceive its audience. Thus, we tend to lean toward a position that, if the text identifies its author, then we should accept it as such unless presented with irrefutable evidence. Therefore, the traditional view of authorship in the New Testament is that every book in the New Testament, with the exception of the Epistle to the Hebrews, has an author who can be identified either through the text itself or through its title.

Arguments challenging the traditional view of authorship are often made based on the style of Greek, syntax, or even the content of a text. These arguments are fair and must be given consideration. With that said, implied authorship comes with some caveats that must be addressed. There are two writing practices common in Scripture that are beneficial for consideration.

- **Amanuensis** is the literary practice in which a literary assistant takes dictation or copies manuscripts. This is the case in some of the Pauline corpus where Paul, either due to his health or imprisonment, utilized an amanuensis to transcribe his words (Fee, 2011; Witherington, 2006). Most likely, the amanuensis was a close confidant or protégé of the Apostle. The practice of dictation is common even in modern times. For instance, an executive may ask an assistant to dictate a letter. Though the assistant writes the letter, no one would argue that the words and intent are not fully those of the executive. Thus, the practice of *amanuensis* is best understood as the author's words but another's quill.
- **Editing** was also a common practice in ancient times just as it is today. Absent of a printing press, copies of ancient manuscripts were transcribed by hand. Further, given the bardic nature of the Early Church, many of the early manuscripts of what we now call the New Testament Canon were copied by hand and distributed to the people long after they were originally written. Returning once more to the Pastorals, it is fully possible that the epistles were compiled into a codex after Paul's death (Quinn, 1990); thus, creating a church manual of sorts for early Christian leadership. There are

many questions and theories surrounding the Gospel of Mark. Significant debate exists as to the original content of chapter 16 with the longer ending considered as canon. It is clear; however, no matter the original content of Mark, that editorial changes were made to the Gospel and these changes were accepted as part of the canon. Given this, it is perfectly reasonable to assume that minor editorial changes may have been made as the documents were prepared for mass consumption and that these changes do not significantly change the message of these manuscripts nor their place and value in the canon of Scripture.

Authorship in the Old Testament

Interpreting the Old Testament brings with it the task of its own set of issues concerning authorship. Unlike the New Testament, Old Testament authorship is not as always clearly identified and, given the dating of many of these texts and the chaotic times in which they were written, researchers must carefully examine the evidence from both biblical and non-biblical sources. Traditional perspectives of Old Testament authorship rely heavily upon the earliest attributions of authorship from Hebrew traditions, Jewish commentaries, and early Christian writers. A familiar case-study of the complexities of determining Old Testament authorship is the traditional view that Moses was the author of the Pentateuch. Most conservatives refer to Moses as the "essential author" of the first five books of the Bible (Longman & Dillard, 2006, p. 42). It is widely accepted that there are non-Mosaic portions of the Pentateuch: the most obvious being the record of Moses' death (Deut. 34). Our earlier discussion of *editors* addresses this issue. It is reasonable to assume, that sometime after the death of Moses, a Jewish historian would have recorded such an important event as a concluding chapter in the life of Moses. We see this in the New Testament as well as Luke, the writer of Luke-Acts, goes into great detail to provide a historical narrative of the ministry of Jesus and the early Church.

Likewise, while the Old Testament, for Christians, is a deeply spiritual document that prophetically points to Jesus Christ, for the Jewish people, it is the history of their nation and their religion, but, more importantly, it is the story of the Jewish people. Researchers must be careful not to remove the text of the Old Testament from its deeply historical context (Longman & Dillard, 2006). It is clear that, whether or not Moses wrote every word of the Pentateuch, he is the implied author. Israel's history is important to the way we view authorship in the Old Testament. When one considers the destruction of Jerusalem, the exilic period, and the many seasons of revival and apostacy that preceded them, it is understandable that much of the Old Testament has been preserved and compiled by Jewish scholars. Like the monks of the Dark Ages, Jewish rabbis protected Jewish history, religion, and traditions in the midst of perilous times. The fact that the Old Testament exists is a miracle in itself.

While most Old Testament books were clearly compiled and edited over time, and while some do not offer clear evidence of authorship, interpreters can generally understand the implied author through other means. Researchers can look to Judaic tradition, early Christian documents, historical records, and archeology to shed light on the specific origins of any given text. But, for Christians, the New Testament offers a specific perspective that is essential to understand: if the New Testament narrative infers an author, then that author becomes authoritative. For instance, no matter the debate regarding the nature of the titles within the book of Psalms, Peter clearly identifies David as the author of Psalm 16 and 110 (Acts 2:25–28, 34–35). Further, there are multiple occasions in the Gospels that the narrative references words that "Moses wrote" (Mar. 12:19; Luke 20:28; John 1:45, 5:46, ESV). Thus, from a New Testament perspective, Moses is the *implied author* of the Law found in the Pentateuch and David is the *implied author* of many of the psalms.

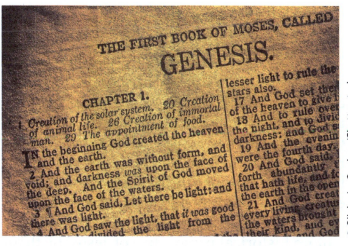

God as the Original Source

While scholars wrangle over minor details, in actuality, the Scriptures are remarkably consistent. This consistency comes because, while there are many authors, the Bible has one source: God. It is through this paradigm that we should view all interpretive endeavors: "All Scripture is breathed out by God and profitable for teaching, for reproof, for correction, and for training in righteousness, that the man of God may be complete, equipped for every good work" (2 Tim. 3:16–17; ESV). The fact that God is the ultimate source of all Scripture should undergird the necessity of exegesis, and the reality that we are seeking His Truth should challenge us to rigorous scientific research. In summary, the Bible is God's Word spiritually transferred through the pen of anointed men. No matter the debate regarding authorship, pursuing, and preserving God's original intent must be the primary goal of exegetical analysis.

Determining the Audience

The second vector used to determine the social and cultural location of a text is the intended audience of the text. Just as there is an *implied author*, there is also an *implied audience* or *reader* (Robbins, 1996). Bauer and Traina (2011) identify the implied author and reader as corollary concepts: "the reader whom the text envisages and projects, the sense of the reader one infers from the text itself. The implied reader is the creation of the implied author" (p. 46). Therefore, the complexities of determining authorship now roll directly into our discussion of the audience. For instance, if the Apostle Paul, in fact, is the implied author of the Pastoral Epistles then there are specific limitations placed on the location and timing of the text; thus, narrowing our search for the implied audience.

As with authorship, in most cases, the intended audience is implicitly or explicitly communicated by the author. In the New Testament, we see a very similar pattern to that of authorship. The Gospels are more covert with their intended audience. Only Luke-Acts is addressed to someone: Theophilus. However, this is considered by most to be an honorary title and yields little light on the intended audience. Most likely this is because the Gospels were written for a more general audience. However, each Gospel has individual characteristics that may illuminate the author's intended audience. For instance, Matthew emphasizes Jesus' Jewish lineage while Luke offers a more historical perspective of Jesus' birth and points to Jesus as the "son of Adam, the son of God" (Luke 3:37, ESV). Given this, it is more likely that Matthew was written to a more Jewish audience while Luke was written for a Gentile audience. The Pauline corpus offers a straightforward answer to the question of audience as each epistle specifically identifies the church or person to whom it was written. The writer of Hebrews infers an intended audience both by the title of the letter as well as its language and content: "God spoke to our fathers by the prophets" (Heb. 1:1, ESV). Likewise, given that both letters refer to those of the dispersion, both James and 1 Peter seem to be directed toward Jewish Christians. Second Peter, 1 and 2 John, and Jude are the only epistles that do not specifically identify to whom they were written. Like the Pauline corpus, the Book of Revelation identifies the churches to whom it was written (Rev. 1:4).

The implied audience of the Old Testament is fairly easy to discern. For the most part, it is the nation of Israel as a whole, and the Old Testament's final composition as we understand it today was intended for the postexilic Jewish people. There are a few exceptions that must be considered. In these cases, it is best to consider the intended audience as both direct and indirect audiences. For example, often when a national leader gives a public speech, he or she is speaking directly to a specific audience; however, often the rhetoric of the speech is meant for a larger audience. The same is true with biblical texts. This is visible in the rhetorical nature of some of the Old Testament books. One has the sense that the Book of Proverbs is written by Solomon to his sons; however, Proverbs is a compilation of multiple authors whose audience was fairly generic. The book of Nahum follows a convention that is unique to the Minor Prophets. Whereas the book of Nahum is attributed to Nahum and addressed to Nineveh, there is an indirect audience as well. While Nahum pronounces a judgement upon Nineveh, the intended audience was the Jewish people who were being oppressed and distressed by the armies of the Ninevites. Therefore, while the book Nahum pronounced judgement upon Nineveh, it also served to give hope to Israel that God would deliver them from their oppressors. This also sheds light on the nuanced nature of the implied audience; the language and content of a text can yield great insight into the intentions of the author.

Determining the Date

As is hopefully evident, our discussion of authorship informs our understanding of the audience. By locating the implied author and the implied audience, the interpreter is closer to identifying the social and cultural location of a text. At first glance, it seems that we should have enough data at this point; however, we do not. A third *vector* sheds light upon the social and cultural location of a text: the approximate date. In the New Testament, the majority of the books were written within a 30-year period. The Church and its theology evolved quickly during that time. Given this, placing an epistle just 10 years earlier or later than its actual date could have profound interpretive ramifications. In other cases, dating is a matter of maintaining biblical accuracy. For instance, the prophet Amos dated his prophecy "two years before the earthquake" in the days of King Uzziah (Amos 1:1, ESV). There has been considerable debate over the accuracy of Amos' prophecy because of the lack of evidence of an earthquake. However, in the mid-20th century, biblical archeologist Yigael Yadin found evidence of an earthquake in strata V and V1 in Hazor; dating the damage to the time of Jeroboam II (Austin, Franz, & Frost, 2000; Thomas, 1967). This archeological discovery proved Amos' prophecy to be accurate.

So then, how do we determine the date of any given text? There are a few strategies to consider. First, it is important to remember that identifying the author and the audience has narrowed the possible timeframe of the text. Second, look for textual evidence, such as the earthquake in Amos, that identifies people, places, or events that better construct the timeline. Third, and this is the most important, consult quality, scholarly research and commentaries. Rather quickly, researchers will discover that the issue of authorship, audience, and date for some texts come with a broad spectrum of opinions.

It is important to give proper care to the issue of authorship, audience, and dating; however, our goal is to accurately interpret a text and we need to determine the author's purpose. Rather than becoming bogged down in the research on the background of a text, interpreters must reach a conclusion and then move forward in the research. We have examined the research on authorship, audience, and dating, and now it is time to make a decision. Here we offer the most important advice: trust your scholarly opinion. You have consulted the literature. You have explored the text. Make a decision and support it with a logical argument. While there is potential for criticism, the goal of the researcher is to make an informed decision and then logically state that decision with scholarly support.

Determining the Purpose

The last *vector* we will consider is the author's purpose. The author's purpose is often referred to as the *occasion for writing* as well. Every book has a purpose, and each author seeks to make an argument to support that purpose. The purpose is closely connected with the audience and the date. Earlier, we stated that the *implied audience* is a creation of the *implied author*. To further extend this, the *implied purpose* is a construct of the *implied author* and the *implied audience*. This is especially true and evident in New Testament epistles. Given the nature of the epistles as actual letters written from a *real* person(s) to *real* people, the logical flow of thought leads to the recognition of *real* situations or occasions for which the epistle was written. Consequently, the social and cultural location of a people of a text should not only be considered geographically and historically, but also sociologically.

Consider the following example. In his first letter to the Corinthians, it is clear that the Apostle Paul is addressing a church with significant conflict. He addresses a variety of issues including sexual immorality, marriage, proper worship, idolatry, and even lawsuits amongst believers. While there are social and cultural commonalities between the Corinthian church and the broader Corinthian society, Paul's letter focuses specifically on issues that were happening within, and unique to, the Corinthian church. Thus, the Corinthian church operated as a subculture within the larger Corinthian culture. No doubt many of the issues of which Paul wrote were common in the social context of Corinth; however, their spiritual, theological, and sociological nuances made them specifically unique to the church. Here we see the necessity of careful consideration of authorial intent within the highly specific context in which the text was written.

This, however, raises an issue of *generalizability*. If a text was written for such a specific purpose, how can the interpreter extrapolate relevant data? First, each text that we examine is included in the biblical canon, and, therefore, applicable to the entire Church. Second, given that exegetical analysis falls under the umbrella of qualitative research, there are some qualitative principles that can help us here.

Exegetical analysis, being a form of qualitative inquiry and part of the hermeneutical process, has two parts as we have learned earlier: the *exegesis* (original intent) of a text and then the *contextualization* (significance for today) of a text (Osborne, 2006). The primary focus of exegetical research, as with qualitative research, "lies in the particular description and themes developed *in context* of a specific site" (Creswell, 2009, p. 193). The danger of attempting to contextualize biblical texts to modern society without fully exploring the author's original purpose is *proof-texting* or *eisegesis*: the logical fallacy of selecting isolated biblical texts to prove one's presuppositions or conclusions rather than developing one's conclusions based upon fundamental hermeneutics of biblical texts. By ignoring the context of an author's purpose, the interpreter fails to distinguish between the author's intended meaning and what it means to *us* (Osborne, 2006). Thus, the interpreter, in essence, allows their contemporary social and cultural location to supersede the social and cultural location of a text, and, thereby, creates the fallacy of *hasty generalization* (Damer, 2009). By focusing on the author's purpose, the interpreter is able to understand the "dynamics underlying the relationship, that is, the 'why' of what is happening" (Huberman & Miles, 2002, pp. 21, 24). So then, once we understand the *why* behind the *what* of a text, we can engage the literature that ties together proposed relationships between the text and contemporary society; providing generalizability to the text (Huberman & Miles).

Last, it may be appropriate to shift our paradigm for a moment and consider biblical analysis as a case study. The case study approach goes hand-in-hand with our discussion of particularity given that case studies explore the "dynamics present within single settings" (Huberman & Miles, 2002, p. 8). Yin (2003) poses that it is possible to generalize qualitative research to some broader theory as long as the researcher expands the research to additional cases or studies. Treating biblical texts as case studies is not a new concept. Lakey (2010), in exploring the "relationship between the Bible, gender, and hermeneutics in the Christian tradition," sought to better examine the interplay between practical situations in contemporary society, Scripture, exegesis, hermeneutics, and theology in how the evangelical faith tradition addresses disputes related to gender and authority. Methodologically, Lakey follows a typical qualitative approach while integrating exegetical, hermeneutical, and theological perspectives: (a) exploring the literature related to the problem; (b) engaging the specific text (1 Cor. 11:2–16) through rigorous exegesis and hermeneutics; (c) exploring the literature relating to the theory and theological issues surrounding the topic; and (d) offering a logical, robust proposal for contemporary application. So then, it is possible that by carefully and conscientiously exploring the author's specific purpose, the interpreter is able to effectively determine the social and cultural location of a text and utilize hermeneutical principles in concert with theory to apply biblical principles to contemporary contexts.

Conclusion

As many read through this, there is no doubt that some wonder why so much time is appropriated to exploring the issues of authorship, audience, dating, and purpose. It is a convoluted topic that may challenge the *practical* nature of this *practical guide* to biblical research. With that understood, for most, it will be convenient to simply review the various commentaries and scholarly publications on the topic and move forward. While it may seem *practical* to gloss over this topic, it is far from prudent. While it may not be necessary to spend hours of research on the topic, it must be considered prior to moving forward on the interpretive journey. Thus, we end this chapter with the words of Bruce (1981):

> That Christianity has its roots in history is emphasized in the Church's earliest creeds, which fix the supreme revelation of God at a particular point in time, when "Jesus Christ, His only Son our Lord . . . suffered under Pontius Pilate."

This historical "once-for-all-ness" of Christianity, which distinguishes it from those religious and philosophical systems which are not specially related to any particular time, makes the reliability of the writings which purport to record this revelation a question of first-rate importance (p. 2).

Chapter Four Reflective Exercises

1. In this chapter, we said that there is a difference between the *flesh-and-blood* author and the *implied author*. What is meant by this? In what ways are they different? Are there ways that they are similar? How do we handle this in the interpretative process?
2. In the interpretative process, we recognize the presence of the *implied audience*. This means that the interpreter is inferring an identity upon the audience that may or not be accurate. How do we guard against mischaracterizing the social and cultural realities of the audience? Further, how do we address our own social and cultural biases and ensure that we do not transfer these biases to the implied audience?
3. Why does accurately dating a biblical text matter? What are the theological implications for dating a text? What are the interpretive implications for dating a text?
4. Select a biblical text of your choice. Read through the text multiple times. Use the contextual clues within the text and surrounding passages to identify the purpose of the author. Be sure to engage the material in this chapter, the plethora of scholarly sources available to you, and the contextual clues in the passage to support your claim.

Chapter 5

Why Socio-Rhetorical Analysis?

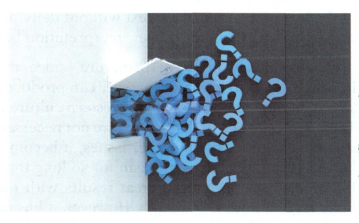

Why is socio-rhetorical analysis (SRA) to be used in exegetical analysis? Why does it matter? Why this method and not another one? These are more than questions of style and preference since the answers impact how one analyzes, interprets, and understands Scripture.

This approach invites detailed attention to the text itself and it moves interactively into the world of the people who wrote the texts and the present world in viewing the text as a thickly textured tapestry (Robbins, 1996). Thereby, this way of exegesis analyzes the details of the text with its nuances and implications as seen by the original audiences. It takes the best from Inductive Biblical Analysis (IBA) and Interpretive Journey (IJ) from chapter 3 and combines them together with other important missing elements. Scripture like an excellent painting has details that need to be noticed to understand the message of the piece. However, a casual observer can see the general form and discuss its message in a superficial but understanding way. This is the issue of the perspicuity of Scripture wherein it can be understood by those who read even if it is only a casual perusal. Nevertheless, the secrets of the kingdom, the mystery of the kingdom, and the nuances of the kingdom of God belong to those who seek. As in examining a good painting, there is a process to understand its message and intent. This message can be glossed over or even misunderstood by a casual observer or even manipulated to the purposes of the observer. The safeguard against this kind of gloss understanding is good research to be able to hear the message of the author, both human and divine, as it was given to the original audience. This authorial intent has been challenged by many modern and postmodern authors; however, it remains the foundation for effective interpretation whether of a painting, literature, or Scripture. To leave this foundation is to leave the moorings of reality whether that is divine or human and whether it is a painting or Scripture. Since the Reformation commentators have made the author's intended meaning their exegetical goal and recovering the author's intent remains the goal of much modern exegesis since without the author there is no possibility of meaning in the texts (Vanhoozer, 1998). Since this authorial intent is foundational, a way is needed not just to read the text and transfer it into our own time or our own image, a way of analysis is needed that can move interactively between the world of the author and the message and into the present world in the context of the realities of that time and this one without gloss or confusion. In looking at the biblical texts, there are two tasks in finding out what was originally meant and to understand that same meaning in the present contexts (Fee & Stuart, 2014). This task must begin with a clear understanding of the text in its original context without deifying the original contextual issues but in understanding them for proper interpretation before the jump to application.

The tendency in Western culture, since there is a focus on pragmatism and information, is to look for whatever can produce practical results. Then, since there is so much information, people in Western culture tend toward gloss rather than details. These issues in and of themselves are not necessarily negative. Nevertheless, when they become exalted above all other issues, it becomes a problem. The Western world has bowed at the idol of pragmatism for so long that it is barely noticed that this occurs. Pragmatism has produced great results with the ability to build large cities and to build large amounts of wealth. However, it has not solved all the issues and problems of modern society like large numbers of people still going hungry. Pragmatism is good it just tends to miss the finer nuances of life and even solutions. So, it is in studying the text of Scripture in the modern world. The tendency is to look immediately for how this message applies in the present context and to look for the macro-message. These in combination create an interpretation that is hurried, general and culturally contingent. This message is then relevant to modern society without asking how it was relevant to their context or society to whom the message was sent. This is an important issue. If you want to build a house, you cannot just take a picture of it and go reproduce the look of it somewhere else. You need to understand the workings of how the house is built and some of the science of what makes it work and stand like it does so that it does not fall in the first storm. In Scripture, there is a word for those who build houses that easily fall.

In the interpretation of Scripture, this issue needs to be addressed and solved. This combination of pragmatism and information overload leads biblical interpreters to rush to the overall message and how it can be applied in the moment. Both have value but not as the initial stage of interpretation but instead as the final stage. This zeal for pragmatism can be maintained but in its proper place. For the message to be useful, it must be brought into the present world. In addition, the overall macro-message must be seen as well. Nevertheless, this macro-message must be seen first in its historic context and the nuances need to be noticed to build a proper macro-picture. This analysis moves the interpreter toward a close reading of the text with a clear understanding of the issues of the world of the text and even the world of those who are the actors in the text. These actors would include not just the author and the audience but also some of the other people mentioned in the text as well as issues that are referenced. The problem is that when the message was given, there were some common understandings and even ways of using words that modern interpreters hear but do not understand. Therefore, a way is needed to effectively bridge this gap in understanding to really hear the message before forming the big picture and how to use this message in the present context.

How does socio-rhetorical analysis help with this situation? There are several ways that this method helps solve this dilemma. As already mentioned, it moves the interpreter to a close reading of the text and of the situation of the text. Then it asks questions of the text that are underlying issues of the text in areas of language, culture, society, context, ideology, and even theology. When these questions are answered, it causes the text to move to more clarity with an understanding of the details or the nuances in its message. Then once the message is seen, it can be appropriated to the present context with more force since in it is a divine message not just our message about the divine message. There are three reasons this method is important and useful here in that it is scientific, it is systematic, and it is holistic. These three aspects of this method make it practical in that it has a good foundation for effectiveness, it is user friendly in that there is a way that it can be used that can be followed by different interpreters with consistency and it covers many of the areas that need to be viewed that may not be initially obvious to the interpreter. These different areas cover the needed aspects for the interpreter to begin to hear the message from the original author as it was intended for the original audience. In this is heard the human and the divine author as the Holy Spirit who inspired the text helps the interpreter hear the full message. The work of the Holy Spirit helps here but He is not opposed to diligent work in finding the message. The Holy Spirit is the one who inspired Paul to write to Timothy and instruct him as a church leader to make every effort to present himself to God, to be an approved worker for God. How is he to do this? By rightly handling the word of truth (2 Timothy 2:15, ESV). Becoming a diligent researcher is part of the way to fulfill this imperative from Paul and the Holy Spirit to make every effort by handling the word of God well and correctly. This is a message to Timothy in his context and setting. What are the full implications of this message as it is appropriated for today? Well this is for you to search out and discover. It is the glory of God to conceal a matter; to search out a matter is the glory of kings (Proverbs 25:2, ESV). Searching out the matter is for those leaders of wisdom and for those to whom the secrets of the kingdom have been given. This is for you. It was Timothy's turn in the 1st century now it is your turn.

It Is Scientific

Science is a systematic search for truth using the scientific method. This method involves empirical observation and data gathering with conclusions made from this process. Science takes many forms such as the traditional sciences of biology and geology or the social sciences like sociology and leadership. In one sense even theology is a science or the study of God, which is literally the definition of the Greek word.

Medieval theologians thought that theology was the Queen of the sciences and that philosophy was her handmaid (DeWeese & Moreland, 2005). It was believed that theology held all of the other sciences together in unity as the study of God would bring not only unity but clarity to the other disciplines. Science and theology are both concerned with search for truth and they share common ways of approaching this search for understanding and a common conviction that there is truth to be sought (Polkinghorne, 2007). The broad term for the science of interpretation is hermeneutics (Fee, 2002). Not only are science and theology connected in a search for truth, they use similar methods especially when it comes to hermeneutics.

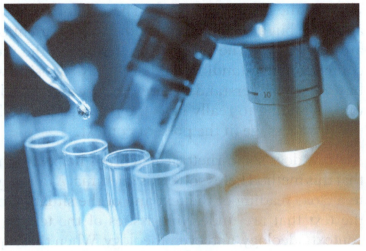

SRA is scientific on several levels. On one level, it is in this search for truth that it finds common ground with other sciences. However, it does not stop here at this general commonality. It is scientific because it uses proven methods of empirical research and data gathering for the process and the conclusions of this analysis. In general, SRA uses the scientific method of observation. As in other scientific research, first data is gathered. Then the data is analyzed and grouped together in ways that make sense. Then finally a hypothesis is formed. However, it is subject to further research that can impact the final theory. In this final stage, the desire is to use this discovery for some application for scientific advancement. In SRA, first data is gathered. It is grouped together for sensemaking and finally a hypothesis is formed. Then finally a theory and then to application. The process moves from data gathering to interpretation to appropriation. This process though remains open to new observations as well from more data gathering. Since there are five different areas of SRA, it facilitates this process of hypothesis and theory development. It helps us to answer the question of meaning in the text and then to move from meaning to application then to practice.

Inner texture focuses on the words and word patterns as well as senses that are evoked in the words. Many of these are issues of rhetoric and even of linguistics. Linguistics is the study of language and the study of the science of linguistics is not entirely new but linguistics studies languages in general and issues they have in common (Cotterell & Turner, 1989). This is a study that focuses on words and how they are used to form meaning. Biblical scholars are aware that they need new tools to accomplish the task of interpretation and linguistics is a tool that studies issues of the social context of language and discourse analysis (Cotterell & Turner, 1989). These aspects are part of SRA in the area of inner texture and in social and cultural texture.

The purpose of inner textual analysis is to gain an intimate knowledge of words, word patterns, voices structures, devices, and modes in the text as the context for meanings (Robbins, 1996). This involves the science of linguistics. However, it does not stop here in that this analysis also involves social sciences and even the discipline of rhetoric.

SRA engages with social-scientific approaches in interpreting the text in the study of social class, social systems, personal and community status, and people on the different ends of the spectrum concerning power (Robbins, 1996). These aspects are seen in areas wherein people act and interact in groups and this includes issues like anthropology and even the way people act and interact in religious groups. Most modern critics recognize that there is a distinctive rhetoric in religion and this religious rhetoric can be found in the Bible (Kennedy, 1984). This religious rhetoric can be found in social and cultural texture in the area of specific social topics in the discussion of different religious worldviews. These worldviews then have implications for the context and even the message of the text of Scripture. These concepts of interpretation are based upon Brian Wilson's typology of sects developing seven kinds of religious responses to the world (Robbins, 1996). This scientific approach gives insight into the context of the text where the interpreter can see some of the important social interactions at play in the interchanges between people in the text. Sociology is the science searching for understanding in how people interact with each other and their environment. SRA uses some of these discoveries to understand and interpret the text and the nuances of the text of Scripture.

This method also uses rhetoric or the analysis of rhetoric in observation and interpretation. Rhetoric is the quality in discourse by which a speaker or writer seeks to accomplish his or her purposes and the writers of the books of the New Testament had a message to convey and sought to persuade others and as such they are rhetorical (Kennedy, 1984). This is also true of the prophets and writers of the Old Testament. The term "rhetorical" in SRA refers to the way language in a text is used as a means of communication among people and this method integrates the way people use language with the ways they live in the world (Robbins, 1996). Rhetoric can be seen here in this method in both sections of inner texture and intertexture since both have to do with use of words and even to some extent with the meaning in context and the relationship between words in different contexts. Argumentative texture in inner texture has to do with the use of words in arguments using certain forms of logic and even classical rhetoric. Rhetoric had a long history before the New Testament authors were born and most ancient peoples used rhetoric and were avid consumers and critics of its practitioners (Witherington, 2009). The text of Scripture was born into societies that were oral cultures. This orality put a premium on rhetoric and proper communication and this kind of communication found its way from the oral speeches to the written texts and the texts of Scripture. The question is whether this included both macro- and micro-rhetoric but that is a question for another day. In the West, the Greeks were fascinated by oral speech even after the advent of writing, which showed in the elaboration of the vast, meticulously worked out art of rhetoric, the most comprehensive academic subject in all Western culture for 2,000 years and this was mostly the paradigm of all discourse including that of writing (Ong, 2002). In examining rhetoric, the researcher is searching for the meaning in the message in the text. It is this search using methods for gathering and interpreting data for discovering truth that is at the foundation of SRA making it scientific.

In it all SRA uses proven methods from different disciplines to discover meaning in the text through a process of observation, interpretation then application in a similar fashion to the scientific method. There is a cousinly relationship between the ways that theology and science each pursue truth though there is a difference in subject matter, yet the idea is that both are forms of the human search for truthful understanding (Polkinghorne, 2007). This search for truth in the theological writings of Scripture shares not only convictions but the use of methods that are developed in this search for truth. In addition, some of the methods used come from different sciences from linguistics to sociology. This exegetical analysis is a form of qualitative analysis that is used in the social sciences for research. These different methods and concepts come together in a system of analysis with the goal of effectively interpreting Scripture with all of its textures and nuances.

It Is Systematic

This method is systematic and this systems concept flows from the previous concept of it being scientific. SRA is a method that is in search for truth using inquiry and observation. SRA brings together disciplines from literary criticism, social-scientific criticism, rhetorical criticism, postmodern criticism, and theological criticism into an integrated approach (Robbins, 1996). These disciplines could also be called literary analysis or interpretation. To effectively bring these disciplines together, there is a system of study or analysis that can be followed in the search for truth. It is like a road map in systematically searching in areas where truth could be found. Good exegesis is the careful integration of all of the data from the careful examination of content and context into a presentation that is as close an approximation of the author's original intent as careful examination can bring us (Fee & Stuart, 2014). To facilitate this thorough examination, hermeneutics needs to follow a process or a system. Systematic simply means that there is a method or pattern that can be followed. There are some different methods that follow a system but SRA has this systemic thinking built into it. SRA has five sections that are each broken down into further systems. Then each subsystem has a clear path for the development of data and interpretation with appropriate questions in each category.

This system has a clear starting point in the examination of inner texture. Robbins (1996) declares that inner textual analysis focuses on words as tools for communication and this stage of analysis is prior to the "real interpretation" of the text but it is to gain an intimate knowledge of the words and related patterns. This is a close examination of the text on the level of words and their relationships moving from repetitions to patterns to argument and narration as well as their aesthetic nature. This inner texture then forms a foundation upon which to look for insights in the other sections of the method. Here in inner texture, this part of the analysis lends itself to developing tables and figures of this data from words and their relationships enabling the interpreter to look at the data systematically and comparing it to other data. In this way, the different patterns of words can be seen and examined for emphasis and comparison with other patterns and to see possibilities for other textures. This getting inside the text gives the interpreter the ability to see not only patterns but places or issues of emphasis that need further work in definition, implication, or contextual understanding.

Then it is important to note that each major area of texture examination has subcategories with a way of processing through each category. Every category may not necessarily be relevant to the particular pericope, but it can be examined for relevance. For instance, social and cultural texture has three subcategories, but it does not stop there. In each of these subcategories, there are options to be decided. In specific social topics, there are seven possibilities that can be examined, and the researcher can decide which of these options or worldviews can be found in the pericope. Then moving on to common topics there are several topics that can show up in different ways in the text. There are many of these but some of the more common ones can be searched out for implications for the text. Then finally there are the final cultural categories in deciding which of the five ways of thinking and living are seen in this text. Each of these can be examined and then the researcher decides which to include by those that are relevant to this section of the text in that not all of these concepts are seen in every pericope.

Since there are categories and subcategories with options for understanding in each area, this system can be used in whole or part. In other words, the researcher can use one texture like inner texture or social and cultural texture to examine a text of Scripture. Conversely, the interpreter could examine all of the textures in a given pericope and discuss all of them in interpretation or choose the ones that are the most relevant and important for the interpretive process. Since they are independent areas yet related it is possible that some from different textures will need to be connected in the interpretive process. For example, the researcher may find some inner texture word patterns that are related to sacred texture or intertexture. Since these textures are connected in a system of exegesis, they can be easily related together and even interact with each other. Finally, when this system is followed, it is a safeguard to develop observation or gathering data from the text before moving on to interpretation and application. This zeal for pragmatism that was referred to in the previous section pushes many researchers to rush to application before the observation and interpretation are completed. SRA gives a systematic, scientific tool for research and good exegesis that searches out the textures of a text in the observation and interpretive stages of the text.

It Is Holistic

This way of examining the text of Scripture is holistic and this concept flows from the other two issues of SRA in that it is scientific and systematic. In this search for truth based upon scientific research concepts, the method has systems that can be followed that are expansive. They are expansive in that they cover a great deal of material with many different concepts and even ways of looking at the text. This examination of the text using SRA is nuanced and detailed while being broad enough to discover the broad issue of the message. This method is diverse. It is diverse in how the text is examined as in looking at words and patterns as well as looking for the issues of worldviews and ideologies. It is diverse in examining different issues of the text ranging from cultural issues of the time of the text to the issues of the past connections of this text with other texts or looking for the divine connections as well as the social ones. In essence, it examines a wide range of issues using different methods and strategies for finding answers to important questions or issues as found in the text.

It is holistic meaning that it allows or helps the researcher to examine a wide range of issues that could be important for interpretation in the text. It is similar to archeology in this way in that the researcher goes looking for what is there in the dirt. This archeologist cannot find what is not there. However, she or he must use many different tools to find what is actually there in the dirt. This research for artifacts of past societies is driven by a search for the truth. In this search, there are different tools that have been developed for how to examine the area. Then there are certain tools for digging large amounts of land and then there are tools to dig up the small delicate materials of this dig. Ultimately, many tools must be used to find the truth of this earlier civilization. The lack of using the right tools or of asking the right questions could lead to error or even to missing the civilization altogether. So, it is with SRA in that these are tools of examination in doing exegesis in the overall task of hermeneutics to discover the tapestry of truth in the text of Scripture.

Since Scripture is finely nuanced and an expression of real life as well as divine intention and prerogative it is indeed a tapestry. Interpreting a biblical text is an act of entering a world where body and mind, interacting with one another create highly complex patterns and configurations of meaning wherein argument, social act, and belief intertwine like threads and yarn in a richly textured tapestry (Robbins, 1996). This type of text or tapestry needs to be examined carefully and knowledgeably from different perspectives and with great care. SRA gives the researcher specific tools for this type of examination in the text of Scripture. Many interpretive methods do not seriously incorporate literary, rhetorical and semiotic modes of analysis and in their resulting discourse they exclude meanings that are highly pertinent to addressing current issues (Robbins, 1996). This view is holistic in that it examines the issues of words and linguistics while addressing areas of society and culture on both the detailed level as well as the worldview level. In addition, SRA addresses the issues of a text's connection to other texts or events of the past or present to the text and the direct issues of theology and its implications for living. Then SRA examines rhetoric and its purposes of persuasion in the text and it examines the implications of different ideologies and implications of cultural norms. It is holistic in that it includes spirituality as part of the process of interpretation. This is a process, but it is spiritual process as well in that it engages the researcher on the level of connection with God for illumination and encounter resulting in change and personal transformation.

Scripture itself teaches that God's wisdom is multifaceted. In Ephesians 2, Paul is talking about preaching the mystery of Christ. Then in verse 10, in this preaching of Christ, the mystery that has been hidden is now revealed as the manifold or many-faceted wisdom of God. This is the concept of a diamond that has facets and since there are so many facets you cannot see all of them at once. You must examine it from different angles to see the complete diamond. This is what the wisdom of God is like as revealed in the Scripture. This message or wisdom from God needs to be seen in many ways. It is not that the Scripture has multiple meanings, but the many facets of God's wisdom are seen here. These concepts or revelations of God's wisdom held together as a whole are the truth about God. To discover this truth, a method is needed that allows for the examination of these many facets of God and his word. This holistic method of SRA helps the researcher to examine these different facets in the text for interpretation that is true to the intent of the author of the text. The Holy Spirit seeks to reveal to us this multifaceted wisdom of God. To do less is to not take this search for truth seriously. It is not a civilization that could be missed but it is an aspect of the wisdom and truth of God that could be missed.

This method even asks about the social or ideological location of the researcher in a quest to determine if the difference between interpreter and writer impacts the interpretation. This would have to be considered in the research to develop a message that aligns with authorial intent. This method then takes a micro-view through words, a macro-view through sociology, a view to style through rhetoric with attention to theological teachings through divine texture, and a historical view from different aspects of history from events to texts. This holistic view even examines the social and cultural location of the writer, the audience, and the researcher. This is a full-orbed method that is based in research from many disciplines bringing a holistic examination to the text of Scripture for a fully textured interpretation.

Conclusion

Since Scripture is a finely nuanced and developed text with both human and divine authors, it produces a message that at the same time is straightforward yet nuanced and complex. This multifaceted nature of the text is also driven by the fact that it speaks of a multifaceted God with multifaceted wisdom in the context of societies and cultures that span over 1,600 years with at least two languages. This complexity and diversity in Scripture brings a rich message that is textured and nuanced and filled with truth to be discovered by the researcher. This method of SRA is designed to meet the challenge here in finding this rich textured message from the Scriptures.

The scientific aspect of SRA brings important and effective tools to the process of observation and interpretation of the text. These tools are used in a method that is scientific looking for truth in the text and these different areas of research are put together in a system. This system gives guidance to the researcher in the process of this search for truth that is finely nuanced. In addition, this method is holistic in looking in many different possible areas for clues in finding these profound concepts of Scripture.

The question comes to forefront of this discussion then as to why this is so complex. There are at least two reasons for this as seen in this study. The first is that it is the glory of God to conceal a matter (Proverbs 25:2). It is God's way of working with humans. The Kingdom of God does not belong to the passive but to those who passionately pursue God and His word and His truth. Jesus said to the disciples in Mark 4 that the secrets of the Kingdom had been given to them. There are secrets or mysteries that need to be revealed. It is also the honor of kings to search out a matter (Proverbs 25:2, ESV). Whether in science or Scripture there are obvious truths that can be seen that can help us. You do not have to be a scientist to know that rain and sunshine are important for plants and crops to grow. However, if you are a scientist, you understand how this works and you will be able to find more truth in how to be effective in growing crops or plants. You do not have to be a biblical researcher to know that salvation is a free gift of grace that is provided based upon the work of Christ in dying for sins on the cross and rising from the dead. However, a biblical researcher can find the answers to the issues of living in Christ on the earth in a way that brings honor to God and to find ways to be effective in making disciples of others. It is important to know that believers are to make disciples but then it becomes very important to know how to become the believer that can effectively make disciples. This is where research helps us. This is why the researcher needs a way of exegesis and analysis that is scientific, systematic, and holistic.

Chapter Five Reflective Exercises

1. How does SRA overcome the tendency toward pragmatism in Western culture? What method could the researcher use to overcome this tendency? Explain why it would work. Give an example of how SRA could overcome this tendency with a certain Scripture text and the application of SRA.
2. How is SRA scientific in its approach to biblical interpretation? Give an example of one of the methods used in SRA that is scientific in its approach. Then explain how SRA is related to the general concept of Science in biblical interpretation.
3. How is SRA systematic and show how this method is systematic. Outline a method for addressing a text in a systematic way. Where do you begin? What texture would you examine first? How would it show a process that leads to a conclusion?
4. Explain how SRA is holistic in that it examines the broad issues of the text as well the finer nuanced issues of the text. Why is this important? How can this holistic view be seen or accomplished in the study of a text?

Chapter 6

Working Through Socio-Rhetorical Analysis—Inner Texture

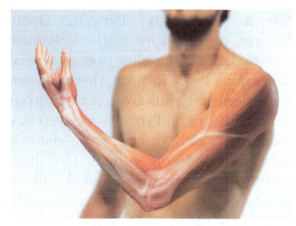

If Scripture is a person then Inner Texture is its anatomy. Much like anatomy, the inner texture is concerned with the parts of a pericope, its structure, and how those parts work together within that structure to represent a completed whole. Literate adults rarely take into consideration the complexity of the language that they use. However, try to learn a new language—especially as an adult—and that complexity will be writ large in the struggle that ensues.

Every language has structures governing its communication dictating not only the representation of words but also the way genres are properly expressed. Those structures are conveyed in a variety of techniques within each language. The simplest parts, of course, are the letters of its alphabet that represent the most basic elements from which words are bonded together like molecules. In the English language, these words are typically categorized into eight types: nouns, pronouns, adjectives, verbs, adverbs, prepositions, conjunctions, and interjections. This does not include numbers, articles, and identifiers. These words are placed into a purposeful whole that creates a single concept called sentences. Those sentences are also structured together into divisions of common ideas called paragraphs. Those paragraphs are strung together to make a passage that has a common theme. Of course, there are all sorts of rules and exceptions that dictate each of these structures, not to mention how genre affects all of this. For instance, a perfectly acceptable sentence in poetic genre may not be considered a typically complete sentence while the perfectly acceptable sentence in legal genre in other genres would normally be considered a run-on sentence.

When we come to the interpretation of Scripture for application to the social sciences, all of these complexities come to bear in drawing the meaning out of the text. Of course, there is an added complexity of translation. Few social scientific researchers will have fluency in ancient Hebrew, Aramaic, and/or Greek. However, English translations of Scripture are highly accurate although, at times, with nuances that should be considered when exegeting a pericope. All of this means that using translations in deeply established languages that triangulate results from multiple versions can allow the researcher to exegete Scripture in their own heart language or another fluent language that they possess.

Inner textual analysis passes a pericope through six filters to determine the meaning in its parts, structure, and message. These filters consist of Textual Units, Repetitive Patterns, Progressive Patterns, Opening-Middle-Closing Patterns, Argumentative Patterns, and Sensory-Aesthetic Patterns (Robbins, 1996a, 1996b). It is important to note that the researcher does not necessarily need to follow this exact order when analyzing a text. However, there is a sense in which the filters are getting finer as they move along and thus are ordered purposefully. It should also be noted that researchers will not always find strong—or even any—results in every filter. This is to be expected. The authors did not have socio-rhetorical analysis (SRA) structure sitting in front of them to write to our benefit. They had their own purposes in writing, following the structures of their day. What the filters allow us to do is to determine the types of structures that are being used in each pericope, which will then make the author's meaning in the passage clearer.

Textual Units

In the ancient languages of Scripture, there were no paragraphs and little if any punctuation, let alone chapters or verses. But neither did ancient writers simply present a stream of consciousness. This means that the divisions that assist us in understanding changes in themes were embedded by ancient writers into the text. The researcher can identify these markers by carefully identifying narrational units. Common markers can include time indicators, a shift of focus within the text, or a shift from narrative to commentary. Conjunctions (e.g., and, but) and conjunctive adverbs (e.g., therefore, however) also play a role in separating units of text.

Sometimes these units will reflect well the paragraphs, chapters, and verses (or even the section headings that are not part of the original text that are included in most Scripture versions) that English speakers have imposed on the text. Other times, these markers are not as clearly recognized within our contemporary structures and need to be identified by the researcher. In other words, the researcher should not presume that section headings, paragraphs, chapters, and/or verses fully identify the textual units of the original author.

An example of a highly structured textual unit would be Matthew 5. We see that the chapter begins with a time marker (typically, *now* or *when*) that sets it apart from the previous material in chapter 4. At v. 3, Jesus' speech begins with his statement of blessings on those who follow Him. At v. 13, the narrative shifts to a description of the impact that the blessed will have on the world around them in the images of salt and light. While most versions combine these into a single unit under an added heading, the researcher would want to separate these out into two units since they address different images. Before Jesus starts revealing deeper truths about the Law, starting in v. 17, He explains this new revelation in relationship to His fulfillment of the Law. From there through the rest of the chapter, units begin with the phrases similar to "You have heard that it was said . . ." (vv. 21, 27, 31, 33, 38, 43, ESV). We also see the adverbial conjunctive *therefore* in v. 23. Another potential unit exists at v. 25 where a shift to judicial matters is covered. Thus, in chapter 5 we have at least 13 textual units identified. In most English versions, these correspond to the paragraph and verse markers but possibly not all the inserted headers. However, researchers should not presume that the headers, paragraphs, chapters, or verses are the definitive unit markers.

Textual units are important to the researcher because they assist in breaking down the pericope into themes that are within based on the writing of the author. This assists the researcher in understanding and interpreting the structure of the passage in a way that reflects the original author's intention. While contemporary interpretations have done some of this work for us, we should not presume that the unit marking is complete. Identifying these units will also assist in recognizing possible patterns in the other filters that are used for inner texture.

Repetitive Patterns

Repetition in contemporary writing, with its vast access to written information, is eschewed. However, in the much more oral cultures of ancient times, repetition was an important mnemonic device (Loubser, 2005). Often, theological significance was communicated through these repetitions such as through the genealogies of Matthew and Luke (Loubser). Thus, it is important to establish these repetitions so that they can be considered for their potential influence on the understanding of the pericope.

Often times, these repetitive patterns are identified through tables in which each row represents a unit/verse and each column represents the repetitions that occur throughout the pericope. Pronouns are usually associated with the noun that they represent. For example, in John 11, the *she* of v. 20 would

© David Carillet/Shutterstock.com

be in the *Martha* column whereas the *she* of v. 29 would be in the *Mary* column. The columns represent less of distinct words and instead distinct ideas. Thus, it is very possible in a column to see the words *go*, *went*, and *traveled* since, although distinct words, they represent the same concept. Additionally, it is possible for a column to be made up of a repeating phrase rather than simply a repeating word.

We can take a look at an example from Genesis 5. Typically, genealogies are dismissed as repetitive and superfluous parts of Scripture. However, the original authors probably did not intend them to be and instead were conveying a significant message in a genre much more familiar to them than it is to us. As we look at this passage several repetitions occur, primarily in phrases: Names/naming, image/likeness, fathering timing, additional years, total years, and he died. When we map these out according to verses, we get Table 6.1.

When the repetitions of this passage are structured in this way, four distinct areas of deviation from the repetition occur. The first difference in vv. 1–2 is to be expected. As the text indicates God created Adam and Eve rather than fathering them and so the pattern that develops with Adam does not exist in the first 2 verses.

The second deviation occurs between vv. 1 and 3. While Adam and Eve are created in the image/likeness of God, Adam's son is birthed in his image. With God and His creation of Adam and Eve, no death is mentioned. Adam's image, as v. 5 makes clear, includes death. So, throughout the rest of the genealogy—as if to hit us over the head with the obvious—the author lets us know that each father died. If there is anything superfluous in genealogies, it is this statement—"and he died"—that occurs throughout and only in this biblical genealogy.

Which leads us to the third deviation from the repetition. In v. 23, where we would expect the statement "and he died", it does not occur. Instead, we have already been informed that Enoch walked faithfully with God for 300 years (v. 22). The explanation of the omission from v. 23 is provided in v. 24: "Enoch walked faithfully with God" and then "was no more, because God took him away" (ESV). The silence concerning his death is deafening in this genealogy.

The final deviation occurs in vv. 28–29. Rather than mentioning Lamech and Noah together, as has been the norm throughout the genealogy, the author changes the wording here. Lamech has a son who is different in that his name is not mentioned with his father's and is interpreted within the text. This tends to suggest a removal of Lamech's influence on his son since Lamech loses the creative act of naming his son (Bledstein, 1977). Noah seems to have a unique place within this genealogy, just as Adam, Eve and Enoch did.

What does all this repetition provide us in terms of interpretation? Something significant happened with the sin of Adam and Eve. While humanity retains its divine value because all are created in the image of God (Gen. 9:5–6; James 3:9), humanity has also inherited the image of Adam with which comes the curse of death. This brokenness extends to all of the sons and daughters of Adam and Eve;

Table 6.1 Repetition in Genesis 5

Verse	Names	Image	Fathered	Add'l Years	Tot Years	and he died
1	Adam's/God/human beings	Likeness of God				
2	He (God)/male/female/human beings					
3	Adam/Seth	Own likeness/own image	130 years			
4	Seth/Adam/sons/daughters			800 years		
5	Adam				930 years	and he died
6	Seth/Enosh		105 years			
7	Enosh/Seth/sons/daughters			807 years		
8	Seth				912 years	and he died
9	Enosh/Kenan		90 years			
10	Kenan/Enosh/sons/daughters			815 years		
11	Enosh				905 years	and he died
12	Kenan/Mahalalel		70 years			
13	Mahalalel/Kenan/sons/daughters			840 years		
14	Kenan				910 years	and he died
15	Mahalalel/Jared		65 years			

(Continued)

Part 3: Answering the "Hows"

(*Continued*)

Verse	Names	Image	Fathered	Add'l Years	Tot Years	and he died
16	Jared/ Mahalalel/ sons/daughters			830 years		
17	Mahalalel				895 years	and he died
18	Jared/Enoch		162 years			
19	Enoch/Jared/ sons/daughters			800 years		
20	Jared				962 years	and he died
21	Enoch/ Methuselah		65 years			
22	Methuselah/ Enoch/God/ sons/daughters			300 years		
23	Enoch				365 years	
24	Enoch/God					
25	Methuselah/ Lamech		187 years			
26	Lamech/ Methuselah/ sons/daughters			782 years		
27	Methuselah				989 years	and he died
28	Lamech		182 years			
29	Noah					
30	Noah/Lamech/ sons/daughters			595 years		
31	Lamech				777 years	and he died
32	Noah/Shem/ Ham/Japheth		500 years			

except Enoch. If we are to escape the curse of Adam, we must walk with God. Perhaps, this passage holds out, Noah will be another example of what that looks like.

For the Christian social science researcher, this type of analysis provides insights into the value of human life and escape from the brokenness of this world from a Judeo-Christian perspective. Obviously, only a single pattern of inner texture is used here and there is likely more within this passage than just what this pattern reveals but it is still a compelling example of how this pattern might be used in other social science environments.

Progressive Patterns

Closely associated with Repetitive Patterns are Progressive Patterns. These patterns couple with the repetition of the pericope to indicate advancement or structure within the passage. Typically, the exegete will want to look for four forms of Progressive Patterns: chiasm, encapsulation, development, and connection (Robbins, 1996a). Chiasm is an ancient writing structure that places the resolution of the passage in the middle of the passage, as opposed to typical Greco-Roman structure that starts with a dilemma and, through linear, logical deliberation, results in a conclusion. Encapsulation provides insights to a particular thought through bookended repetitions, providing explanation between the bookends. Development occurs when a particular theme shifts to a new meaning as the pericope progresses. Connection occurs when distinct ideas, themes, or images are purposely connected together by the author. To exemplify each of these, we can look at John 1:1–18. The Repetitive Patterns of this passage are provided in Table 6.2.

Chiasm occurs when multiple parallel themes converge on a resolution to the theme. Chiasm is a common poetic element (although not exclusive to this genre). This is why so often we read the first verses of many Psalms, connecting to the emotion expressed in them. So, we read to the end of the Psalm to find the resolution to that emotion and find that the end of the Psalm seems to repeat the beginning, which leaves us unsatisfied. This is a non-chiastic reading of the Psalm. When an author uses chiastic structure, the resolution is always in the middle of the parallel themes. Typically, this is easier to spot when Repetitive Patterns have been identified like they are in Table 6.2. If a line is drawn between v. 1 ("in the beginning") to v. 7 ("believe") and back again to v. 15 ("before"), a progression can be seen that could be a chiasm. It is likely, then, that Figure 6.1 represents a chiasm that occurs in John 1. What this suggests is that an important message that John is portraying is the importance of belief in Jesus (v. 7). This plays itself out throughout the Gospel where belief expressed in testimony/witness will present as an important theme. This does not undermine the critical statements of the deity of Jesus that are also provided in this passage—there are multiple elements of writing that John is intertwining into this passage. But, certainly, John seems to be focusing on the importance of testimony.

Another progressive element in this pericope is the encapsulation in vv. 14–17 (cf., Table 6.2). Encapsulation tends to provide some form of explanation or identification of the bookended topic. In the case of John 1:14–17, we see "one and only" repeated.

Table 6.2 Progression in John 1

Unit A										
1	in the beginning	Word (3)	God (2)							
2	in the beginning		God							
3				made (3)						
4					life (2)	Light				
5						light/darkness (2)	did not comprehend				
Unit B										
6			God					testify/witness			
7						light		Witness	believe		
8						light (2)					
Unit C										
9						light (2)					
10				made			did not recognize			World	
11							did not receive			world (3)	
12			God				received		believe		
13			God								
Unit D										
14		Word								one and only	grace/truth
15	was before						testified				
16							received				grace (2)
17							came [realized]			one and only	grace/truth
18			God				made known [explained]				

Chapter 6: Working Through Socio-Rhetorical Analysis—Inner Texture

```
□ In the beginning (v. 1-2)
  • Word (v. 1)
    □ God (v. 1-2)
      □ made (v. 3)
        □ Light (v. 4-5)
          □ Witness (v. 7)
            □ Believe (v. 7)
          □ Witness (v. 8)
        □ Light (v. 7-9)
      □ Made (v. 10)
    • God (v. 12-13)
  • Word (v. 14)
□ Was Before (v. 15)
```

Figure 6.1 Chiasm in John 1:1-18
Source: Russel Huizing

Within these bookends are the repetition of grace and truth. This suggests that John is setting up for his writing an identification of the one and only Son of God—the one who throughout his writing is an expression of grace and truth.

A third type of progression is development. In Table 6.2, we can see that in v. 5, we have the statement of not comprehending, in v. 10 not recognizing, and in v. 11 not receiving. John seems to be offsetting this with the receipt of Jesus in v. 12 (offsets v. 11), the coming of Jesus resulting in realization in v. 17 (offsetting v. 10), and making known, or explained, in v. 18 (offsetting v. 5). This then develops the idea that those who are uncomprehending, unrecognizing, and not receiving, through Jesus, can receive Him, realize Him, and know Him. In other words, those that were opposed to Jesus can change to be aligned with Jesus.

A final type of progression is connection. In v. 5, we see that John is introducing an important motif for his writing: light and dark. "The light shines in the darkness, and the darkness has not overcome it" (v. 5, ESV). This idea is expanded in v. 9 where the light comes not into the darkness but into the world. When these verses are connected to each other it is not outside the realm of possibility that John is connecting the darkness of v. 5 with the world of v. 9 and the light of v. 5 with the one who comes into the world of v. 9. These connections are important to the understanding of John's continuing motif of light/dark and the world/the one coming into the world throughout John's writings.

Once again, while only one inner texture pattern is used here, important insights are provided for the Christian social scientist. In the midst of our studies, we will be challenged to adopt the light or the dark. The way of light will result in illumination that will result in a message equally balanced with grace and truth that is anchored in the testimony and witness of the Word, Jesus Christ. From this passage, we should expect that the world in its darkness will have difficulty comprehending this message and exert pressure to adopt the dark that the rest of the world lives within. John challenges Christian social scientists to stand firm in the truth that the interpretation of Scripture—and its ultimate expression in Jesus—leads us to.

Opening-Middle-Closing Patterns

Communication is done for a purpose. Rarely does a person write anything down for no reason. In this sense, there is an explicit and/or implicit narrative to nearly everything that is written. Scripture is no different. While, as we have seen in the previous section, the structures of writing may not be as linear as we are used to in Western thinking, still, there is a purpose to the writing—an end that one is writing toward. As such, most writing has some form of narrative or plot to it. This plot can be thought of as Opening-Middle-Closing (OMC) Patterns.

OMC considers the plot of each textual unit and how it contributes to the overall pericope. Most plots have four scenes as described by Allender (2005). The first scene could be described, as Allender did, as shalom. This is the beginning of the plot (although it may appear later as a flashback). It represents the innocence before things go wrong. It is the opening credits of a movie where the sun is shining, and people are walking about happy. The second scene is shalom shattered. This is the crisis that arises that causes shalom to be broken or lost. It is the introduction of the villain and his or her villainy. Shalom sought is the third scene. In this scene, protagonists seek to restore shalom with no success. This can be through both moral and immoral means—however, the central character(s) are trying to get back to the shalom that is known to be missing from their current state. The final scene is denouement. While in Disney movies this typically results in a restoration of shalom, in the best of stories it is a loosening of the tension that the shalom shattered has caused. It is more nuanced than reversing everything. In the narrative of Jesus, the crucifixion is not reversed—rather Jesus is resurrected and yet still with his hand, foot, and side wounds.

OMC patterns identify these plot features (typically, middle refers to both the shattering of shalom and shalom sought) for the sake of understanding what shalom looks like, what the shattering and seeking of shalom looks like, and what denouement looks like. OMC analysis studies these plot progressions. In a highly structured narrative, it is possible for every textual unit to have OMC elements. Sometimes, OMC is spread throughout the entirety of the pericope. Still other times, it requires the stringing together of multiple pericopae to begin to see the emergence of OMC.

The story of Joseph in Genesis provides a rather protracted but detailed example of OMC. In Genesis 37:1–11, we see Shalom experienced, at least by Joseph. His brothers have already drifted into Shalom Shattered because of their lack of love from their father and their jealousy toward Joseph. Their Shalom Shattered results in Joseph's Shalom Shattered as described in Genesis 37:12–36. Perhaps Shalom can be restored through one of the brothers? Genesis 38 makes clear that this will certainly not happen, at least not through Judah. Shalom will also not be restored through either Joseph's dreams or his favored status, as he moves from favored son, to favored slave, to favored prisoner, to nobody (Gen. 39–40). While God can use both dreams and favored status, it is clearly God who orchestrates the Denouement that restores Joseph to his family (Gen. 50:19–21). Although a larger set of pericopae, this story provides in broad strokes the type of OMC that we are analyzing in the smaller pericopae that social scientists are more likely working with.

Argumentative Patterns

What authors have decided to include in their writings is purposeful because they are trying to provide reason to a particular outcome or belief. This is explicitly stated in John 21:25 and presumed throughout the rest of Scripture. This, of course, goes against some documentary, fragmentary, and supplemental hypotheses (Bray, 1996). While it is recognized that some Scripture developed over time with multiple contributors, still, the final composition was not simply cobbled together haphazardly. The Argumentative Pattern in inner texture then is designed to unveil the reasoning of the author in the pericope. In some ways, Argumentative Patterns within a pericope are the springboard for Ideological Texture since it is the reasoning of the inner texture that is used by the author to support underlying beliefs that are being promoted.

Several elements—although not necessarily all—can assist in composing an Argumentative Pattern. These include a thesis, rationale, contrary, restatement, analogy, example/testimony of antiquity, and conclusion (Robbins, 1996a). The exegete would identify each of these elements within the text and show the progression of argument. Typically, although not always, the author is working toward the conclusion supported by example/testimony of antiquity. To exemplify each of these, we will examine Mark 12:13–17.

In this passage, the Pharisees and Herodians approach Jesus with a question: "Is it right to pay the imperial tax to Caesar or not?" (v. 14, ESV). The thesis that they approach Jesus with differs depending on one's perspective. The answer from Rome, of course, is "Yes, one should pay taxes." The rationale here is that it is a civic duty and even a religious obligation in order to sustain the Pax Romana. The answer from the Jewish nation, however, is "No, one should not pay the tax." The rationale here is that Rome represents everything that is against Jehovah and therefore should not be supported—supporting them supports their evil. As the passage states, the religious leaders were purposely asking Jesus this to set Him up to be hated by the Jewish people or to be considered a traitor by Rome (cf. v. 13, 15). Jesus presents a contrary thesis based on analogy. He requests a denarius and asks whose image is on it. They rightly reply Caesar's. Jesus restates the thesis by indicating that what is Caesar's—his gold and silver—should be given back to him, however, what is God's should be given to Him. Unsaid here is both an explanation from antiquity and a conclusion. If Caesar's image is on the coins, and thus they belong to him, what has God's image on it that belongs to God? The obvious answer from Genesis 1–2, the explanation from antiquity, is humanity. Therefore, the conclusion is that we should worry less about our material possessions and more about giving ourselves completely to God who has created us in His image.

Sensory-Aesthetic Patterns

If I were in a classroom teaching this and I were to ask you at this point, "Do you see what I am saying about inner texture?" you would understand that I am asking a question about comprehension. You would not think that I am asking whether you can literally see with your eyes the words that I am speaking. Language is filled with such sensory-aesthetic idioms and this analysis is intended to tease them out of the text.

There are three primary zones of sensory-aesthetic patterns: emotion-fused thought, self-expressive speech, and purposeful action (Robbins, 1996a). Emotion-fused thought is expressed through explicit representations of either emotion/feeling or thought/knowing. However, in addition, anything having to do with either the eyes or the heart is also possibly tied to this zone as well. Smell is typically most associated with memory and so could also fit into this zone. Self-expressive speech zone is connected with anything having to do with communication including speaking and hearing. The physical representation of this is anything having to do with the mouth (including lips, teeth, tongue, throat, and voice) or ears. Purposeful action, as might be expected, includes any specific physical behavior. Physical representation of this would include nearly any appendage including hands, arms, legs, and feet. While one should certainly not expect that every physical expression in a passage has an idiom attached, still, it should be considered whether emotions/thoughts, expressions, and/or actions are being communicated.

Typically, researchers can use a similar approach as used in the Repetitive Patterns. By analyzing each zone on a verse-by-verse structure, one can ascertain the various interactions both within a particular zone as well as across multiple zones. Table 6.3 presents the results of a sensory-aesthetic analysis of 1 Corinthians 12:15–31.

Chapter 6: Working Through Socio-Rhetorical Analysis—Inner Texture

Table 6.3 Sensory-Aesthetic Patterns in 1 Cor. 12:15–31

Verse	Emotion/Knowledge	Expression	Action
15		Say	Foot/Hand
16	Eye (2)	Ear/Say	
17	Eye/Smell	Hearing/Ear	
18			Placed
19			
20			
21	Eye/Head		Hand/Foot
22	Weaker		
23	Honor(able)/Unpresentable		
24	Presentable/Honor		
25	Concern		
26	Suffer (2)/Honor/Rejoice		
27			
28			Placed
29			
30			
31	Eagerly		

a stretch?

Clearly, this analysis presents a picture of Paul arguing against emotion/knowledge and for the inclusion of expression and action. This is even a stronger argument if we can move dishonorable/unpresentable to the expression/action columns (although this particular analysis does not support that step). Certainly, the pursuit of knowledge/wisdom was causing dissension within the church of Corinth (1 Cor. 1:18–31; 2:6–16). Paul, through his use of the body metaphor, seems to be placing expression and action on equal standing with knowledge. This carries through later in the book as he speaks of the actions of love (1 Cor. 13) and the importance of tongues and prophecy (1 Cor. 14:5). Paul seems to be advocating a balance between knowledge, expression, and action throughout the book.

For social scientists, this is an important insight. Too often in an information age, we believe that having the right knowledge/education is sufficient for effectiveness. However, according to this passage, not only must that knowledge be aligned with truth, but it must also be able to express itself properly and result in actions that themselves are a manifestation of both the knowledge and expression. In other words, all three are necessarily linked with each other.

An Example from John 21

To illustrate how all of these methods are used in social science research, John 21 will be analyzed and applied to the field of leadership. Irrespective of results, each pattern will be followed to show both relevant and irrelevant results. Then, some conclusions regarding the application of the passage to leadership will be offered. The ESV will be the version used for this analysis.

Textual Units

Time-bound units can be identified in vv. 1 (After this), 4 (Just as day was breaking), 7 (therefore), 9 (when), 15 (when), and 19b (And after). Additionally, there is a commentary shift that occurs in v. 24 (This is the disciple). Thus, the seven narrational units of this pericope would be: v. 1–3; v. 4–6; v. 7–8; v. 9–14; v. 15–19a; v. 19b–23; v. 24–25.

Repetitive Patterns

Table 6.4 provides a visual analysis of the repetitive patterns. While pronouns are not included for the sake of space, they could also be added to the table to identify further emphasis on the material.

Progressive Patterns

The Repetitive Patterns of the pericope (Table 6.4) provide a basis for Progressive Patterns. While there is no clear indication of chiasm in this passage, encapsulation and development are explicit while the connection is alluded. Encapsulation occurs with the parallel statements of "Follow me" in v. 19b and 22. The material between this encapsulation emphasizes a personal responsibility of faithfulness. Development can be seen in the shift from an emphasis on fish (vv. 3–13) to an emphasis on shepherding (vv. 15–17). This development is further extended when Jesus commands following Him: perhaps a subtle reference to Jesus as the Great Shepherd (John 10). The connection element is less explicit but seems apparent upon close examination. Throughout the pericope Peter is identified as either Simon Peter or Peter. However, when Jesus references him, He only uses the term Simon son of John, a name that Jesus has not used to reference Peter since Peter first started following Jesus (John 1:42).

Table 6.4 Progression in John 21

Unit A								
1	Jesus							
2		Disciples Thomas, Nathanael, Sons of Zebedee, Two others	Simon Peter					
3			Simon Peter	Fishing				
Unit B								
4	Jesus (2)	Disciples		Fish				
5		Children		Fish				
6								
Unit C								
7	Jesus/ Lord (2)		Peter/Simon Peter		Loved disciple			
8		Disciples		Fish				
Unit D								
9	Jesus			Fish				
10				Fish				
11			Simon Peter	Fish				
12	Jesus/ Lord	Disciples						
13	Jesus			Fish				
14	Jesus	Disciples						

(Continued)

(Continued)

Unit E						
15	Jesus/Lord	Simon Peter, Simon son of John		Love (2)	feed	Lambs	
16	Jesus/Lord	Simon son of John		Love (2)	tend	Sheep	
17	Jesus/Lord	Simon son of John		Love (3)	feed	Sheep	
18		Peter					
19a							
Unit F						
19b			Loved disciple				Follow me
20	Jesus/Lord	Peter					
21	Jesus/Lord	Peter					
22	Jesus		This disciple				
23	Jesus						Follow me
Unit G						
24			This disciple				
25	Jesus						

OMC Patterns

Table 6.5 provides a review of the OMC for each unit in the pericope. It is clear that each unit has OMC elements that contribute to the larger narrative of the chapter. This analysis assists the researcher to identify how the story develops through its many smaller iterations.

Table 6.5 OMC in John 21

Unit A (v. 1–3)	
Opening	Appearance of Jesus
Middle	Going fishing
Closing	Caught nothing
Unit B (v. 4–6)	
Opening	Jesus on the shore
Middle	Throw your nets
Closing	Large number of fish
Unit C (v. 7–8)	
Opening	It is the Lord
Middle	Jumped in water
Closing	Net full of fish
Unit D (v. 9–14)	
Opening	Fish and bread
Middle	Come have breakfast
Closing	Jesus' third appearance
Unit E (v. 15–19a)	
Opening	Finished eating
Middle	Questions
Closing	Foretelling
Unit F (v. 19b–23)	
Opening	Follow me
Middle	What about him?
Closing	Follow me
Unit G (v. 24–25)	
Opening	Disciple who testifies
Middle	Testimony is true
Closing	Not enough books

Argumentative Patterns

The thesis of the pericope seems to focus on what happens when Jesus fulfills His promise to fill the nets of His followers with fish. In some sense, the testimonies throughout the Gospel of John show that Jesus has already accomplished the promise to make the disciples fishers of men (Luke 5:2–11). Jesus presents a restatement of His expectations that after catching the fish, He wants His disciples to become shepherds. This is most clearly exemplified with the life of Peter who, despite his wavering from Jesus, is still challenged to go beyond being a fisher of men and become a shepherd of the Great Shepherd. Thus, this passage includes thesis, rationale, restatement, analogy/example, and conclusion.

Sensory/Aesthetic Patterns

The patterns, as indicated in Table 6.6, show an emotional emphasis on vv. 15–17. Throughout the pericope there is a significant emphasis on what Jesus is communicating rather than the disciples. The action orientation seems to focus on the past (catching fish), the present (shepherding), and the future (in the foretelling of Peter's demise).

Table 6.6 Sensory/Aesthetic in John 21

Unit A			
1			Appeared
2			
3		Told them They Said	Going to fish Go With/Went/ Got in boat/Caught Nothing
Unit B			
4	Did not realize		Stood on shore
5		Called out/ Answered	
6			Throw nets/They did Unable to haul
Unit C			
7		Heard him say	Wrapped garment Jumped in water
8			Followed in boat Towing net

(Continued)

(Continued)

Unit D			
9	Saw fire		Landed
10		Jesus said	Bring fish
11			Climbed in boat
			Dragged net
12	They knew	Jesus said/ None dared ask	Come have breakfast
13			Jesus came
			Took bread
			Gave to them
			Did same with fish
14			Appeared
Unit E			
15	Do you love me/ You know I love you	Jesus said he said	Finished eating Feed lambs
16	Do you love me/ You know I love you	Jesus said he answered	Take care of sheep
17	Do you love me (2)/ Peter was hurt/You know I love you	He said Jesus asked him he said	Feed my sheep
18		I tell you	Dressed yourself Went where wanted Stretch out hands Someone else dress Lead you
19a		Jesus said	
Unit F			
19b		He said	Follow me
20	Peter Saw/Jesus loved	Had said	Turned Leaned back
21	Peter saw	He asked	
22		Jesus answered	
23		Jesus did not say/ only said	Rumor spread
Unit G			
24	We know testimony true	Wrote them down	Testifies
25	I suppose		

Application to the Field of Leadership

While the analysis of this pericope could be applied to a variety of social science fields, the leadership field will serve as an adequate example. The encapsulation of v. 19b and 22 emphasize the importance for Christian leaders to be faithful to their individual calling. The significant communal context of 1st century culture makes this individualistic statement all that much more significant. The development of the passage could emphasize the need for Christian leaders to go beyond quantitative measures and instead focus on relational care of followers. The connection between Peter's former name and current name offers an analysis of the identity of the leader and how that identity changes, especially through a relationship to Jesus. This is further strengthened through the argumentative patterns that introduce a new way of looking at leader/follower relationships. In a world that is beholden to quantitative outcomes, Christian leaders are refocused on character and relational outcomes through this pericope. While the other inner texture areas of analysis do not seem to hold as much value to the leadership conversation, it is very possible that through further digging into the passage coupled with additional scholarly support, that there are many other riches to be unearthed in this text.

Conclusion

After reviewing a number of passages, it is important to return to our original metaphor. Our goal through SRA is to determine the meaning of the original passage to the original author and audience. One step in accomplishing that is to identify the unique details that exist within the passage. Certainly, we want to also understand how these passages relate to the larger narrative of the books that they are included within, not to mention the larger salvation narrative of Scripture. Whereas these broader themes should (and will through other textures) be examined, it is important to understand these internal aspects of the text. While it is important to know how a person walks, there are skeletal systems, muscular systems, cardio-vascular systems, nervous systems, and many other anatomical systems at work in order for what seems relatively simple to most of humanity to occur. In the same way, while the larger themes of the passage will certainly be addressed, an important step in understanding that larger theme is to bring a microscope to the text and understand its internal components. Inner textual analysis accomplishes this in a methodological approach that can be replicated by multiple researchers to come to a verifiable outcome.

Chapter Six Reflective Exercises

1. Develop a list of idioms that are used in your culture that are associated with parts of the body (e.g., "I see what you are saying"). These would be contemporary examples of sensory aesthetics. Are certain body parts in your culture associated with emotional thinking, communication, and/or action? Are there other associations that you could make with these idioms?

Chapter 6: Working Through Socio-Rhetorical Analysis—Inner Texture

2. Conduct an inner textual analysis of Matthew 28 using the following steps:
   a. Identify the textual units that create natural breaks throughout the pericope. These might be time markers, change in focus of primary characters, or responses. List these off in a table similar to Table 6.4.
   b. In the same table, track repetitive patterns. Be sure to include repeating references to people, words/ideas, or places. Remember, that a repetitive pattern does not have to be an exact match of words. For instance, the angel's reference to "disciples" in v. 7 is likely connected to Jesus' reference to "brothers" in v. 10.
   c. As you review your table, do you see any patterns that emerge? Do you see any elements that might be chiasm, encapsulation, development, or connection?
   d. Go back to each textual unit and map out the plot of each unit indicating its opening, middle, and closing. As you review these, do you see any unexpected parallels or differences?
   e. Review the rhetoric of the passage. How do the conversations that occur connect with each other and are there any noticeable patterns that emerge?
   f. Create a new table with your textual units and plot out the sensory aesthetics of the passage. Remember, text that references eyes or any explicit emotion or thought goes under emotion fused thinking. Any references to mouth/ears or explicit mentions of speaking/hearing go under expressive speech. Any references to hands or legs or specific actions go under action.
   g. As you review each of these patterns, what new insights do you have about this passage?

3. Write out a 1-page story from a third-person perspective about a significant event in your life that you would be willing to share. Exchange your story with someone else who has done the same exercise. Go through the steps in the previous question on their story. What new insights did you come to about this person? Share those with the person to see how accurate your interpretation of their story was.

Chapter 7

Working Through Socio-Rhetorical Analysis—Intertexture

Continuing the use of metaphors, if *inner texture* analyzes the anatomy of a text, then *intertexture* explores the relationship of a text being interpreted with the "world outside" (Robbins, 1996a, p. 40). The difference between the two textures is best understood by defining their prefixes: *inner* refers to the internal workings of a text and *inter* refers to the reciprocal relationship and exchange of ideas between a text and outside sources. Central to the relationship between a text and outside sources is the communication of meaning. It may be easier to conceptualize the work of intertexture analysis by considering the components of communication: context, sender/source, message, medium, receiver/interpreter, feedback, and interference (see Figure 7.1).

From a hermeneutical perspective, we understand that God (the sender) is the original source of all biblical content and His Word is the medium through which His truth (the message) is conveyed to humanity (the receiver). As with all forms of effective communication, the goal of biblical interpretation is to properly interpret God's intended meaning while accounting for interference in the interpretative process. According to Osborne (2006), biblical interpretation involves a *spiral* from "text to context, from its original meaning to its contextualization": allowing "the God-inspired meaning of the Word to speak today with as fresh and dynamic a relevance as it had in its original context" (pp. 22–23). Biblical researchers seek to apply biblical truth to their contemporary context. There is, as with any communication, the problem of interference. In the case of biblical interpretation, interference comes in the form of the problem of "distance": time, culture, language, and geography (p. 25; Klein, Blomberg, & Hubbard, 2017).

In order to understand a text in its original context, special attention must be given to how the author configures the world outside of a text to convey an intended meaning (Robbins, 1996a). Intertexture analysis "enables an interpreter to begin to address the myriads of ways a text participates in networks of communication throughout the

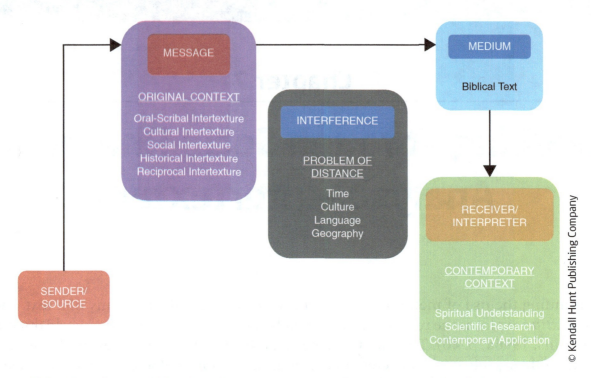

Figure 7.1 The Original Meaning Communicated to Contemporary Society

Source: Joshua Henson

world" (Robbins, 1996b, p. 96). *Intertexture* and its relationship to original context centers on the idea of background meaning and memory (Robbins, 2010): exploring ideas, images, patterns, and processes through which groups analyze and interpret meaning. Gowler (2010) defines *intertexture* as such:

> Intertexture designates a text's representation of, reference to and use of phenomena in the "world" outside the text, including a text's citations, allusions and reconfigurations of specific texts, events, language, objects, institutions and other specific extra-textual contexts with which the text interacts (p. 196).

Intertexture analysis passes a pericope through five filters to determine its meaning in its original context. These filters are oral-scribal intertexture, cultural intertexture, social intertexture, historical intertexture, and—an additional filter not in the original conceptualization of socio-rhetorical analysis (SRA)—reciprocal intertexture (Robbins, 1996a, 1996b). It is important to note that every pericope is unique in that each subtexture of intertexture exists to varying degrees. As with inner textual analysis, researchers may not find strong—or any—results in every filter.

It is by systematically exploring the five elements of the original context that interpreters are able to address the interference that occurs from the problem of distance. By examining a biblical text in its original context, researchers are able to apply biblical principles to their contemporary context through spiritual understanding, scientific research, and contemporary application. For these exercises, the English Standard Version (ESV) will be utilized; however, it is important to note that, while most English translations are highly accurate, each provide a nuanced perspective. Given this, it is important for researchers to read multiple translations to ensure that contextual meaning is not lost in translation.

Oral-Scribal Intertexture

The biblical canon, as we know it today, was compiled over centuries. Whether examining the Pentateuch or the Synoptic Gospels, biblical interpreters must be keenly aware of both bardic and written influences. Biblical texts are often highly dependent upon other oral and written sources. This is evidenced throughout the Old and New Testaments. The stories of Genesis were passed on from generation to generation until finally written down and formulated into what is now known as the *Torah*. The historical narratives of the judges, kings, and prophets, as well as the poetic books, routinely reference Levitical law. In the New Testament, the life and ministry of Jesus was grounded in the fulfillment of Old Testament prophecy regarding the Messiah. Beginning with Peter's sermon on the Day of Pentecost, the message of the Church frequently reached back to Old Testament content and the oral tradition of Twelve Apostles. The New Testament epistles are littered with Levitical references, early Christian hymns, and non-biblical references, and the book of Revelation relies significantly upon Old Testament imagery. Given this, when analyzing a biblical text, it is important to give particular attention to outside oral traditions and texts that have influence on a text's content. Oral-scribal intertexture involves considering how a text *configures* these outside sources. There are three forms of configuration to be considered: recitation, recontextualization, and reconfiguration.

Prior to exploring these forms of oral-scribal intertexture, it may be important to define and differentiate the three. Our goal here, however, is to remain as clear as possible: remaining practical in our discussion without becoming mired in the theoretical and methodological implications of configuration. The following provides a plain speech synthesis of how written and oral traditions are replicated in biblical texts (see Table 7.1).

- *Recitation* occurs when a biblical text relies upon other written texts (biblical or otherwise) or oral traditions to evoke meaning. Recitations can contain exact phrases, minor differences, or even substantially change the original text. The defining factor in identifying evidence of recitation is the presence of a **direct or indirect attribution** to an outside source.
- *Recontextualization*, like recitation, relies upon other written or oral traditions to evoke meaning. The key difference between recitation and recontextualization is the **absence of direct or indirect attribution** to an outside source.
- *Reconfiguration* occurs when a text utilizes the recitation or recontextualization of outside written or oral traditions to **establish a new event**. This new event outshines, foreshadows, or replaces the previous event (Robbins, 1996a).

Table 7.1 The Criteria for Classifying Oral-Scribal Intertexture

	Recitation	Recontextualization	Reconfiguration
The biblical text relies on outside written texts or oral traditions to evoke meaning	X	X	X
Phrases replicated with: exact words, minor differences, or substantial changes	X	X	X
Direct or indirect attribution to outside source	X		X
No direct or indirect attribution to outside source		X	X
Creates a new event that is similar to a previous event			X

Note: The grey sections represent the significant differences between recitation, recontextualization, and reconfiguration.

Let us pay particular attention to what distinguishes each. The difference between *recitation* and *recontextualization* at its core is the identification of the source. If the author directly or indirectly identifies the outside source in a pericope, it is a recitation. If not, it is a recontextualization. Reconfiguration, on the surface, will present as a recitation or recontextualization. In this case, however, the difference is not a matter attribution but of purpose. Reconfiguration occurs when a text configures an outside source in a way such that the previous event is replaced with a new event. While working through a biblical pericope, interpreters can use these criteria to determine the type of configuration present.

It is important to remember once more that, just as not every subtexture will be present in a given pericope, not every configuration of oral-scribal intertexture will be evident. Before doing so, however, there are two questions that generally arise here: (a) How do we differentiate between the three; and (b) How does knowing this help us exegete a text? To better understand differences between recitation, recontextualization, and reconfiguration, it is best to see how this works in context. Then we will be better equipped to understand why this is beneficial to exegesis.

Recitation

It may be important to discuss *attribution* for clarity. The distinguishing characteristic of *recitation* is source attribution. This, however, comes in many forms. Of course, the most straightforward version of this is a direct reference: "Moses said, 'The Lord God will raise up for you a prophet like me from your brothers. You shall listen to him in whatever he tells you.'" (Acts 3:22; Deut. 18:15, ESV). In other cases, texts have indirect references to outside sources such as: "as it is written: 'None is righteous, no, not one; no one understands; no one seeks for God. All have turned aside; together they have become worthless; no one does good, not even one.'" (Rom. 3:10–12; Psa. 14:13; 53:1–3, ESV). As seen in Table 7.2, Romans 3:10–18 is an interesting example as the Apostle Paul strings multiple sources together as one larger quote identified under the attribution: *as it is written*.

Table 7.2 Examples of Recitation

	Romans 3:10–18		Examples of Recitation
3:10	As it is written		
3:11–12	None is righteous, no, not one; one understands; no one seeks for God. All have turned aside; together they have become worthless; no one does good, not even one.	Psa. 14:3	They have all turned aside; together they have become corrupt; there is none who does good, not even one.
		Psa. 53:3	They have all fallen away; together they have become corrupt; there is none who does good, not even one.
3:13a	Their throat is an open grave; they use their tongues to deceive.	Psa. 5:9	For there is no truth in their mouth; their inmost self is destruction; their throat is an open grave; they flatter with their tongue.
3:13b	The venom of asps is under their lips.	Psa. 140:3	They make their tongue sharp as a serpent's, and under their lips is the venom of asps. Selah
3:14	Their mouth is full of curses and bitterness.	Psa. 10:7	His mouth is filled with cursing and deceit and oppression; under his tongue are mischief and iniquity.

(*Continued*)

(*Continued*)

	Romans 3:10–18		**Examples of Recitation**
3:15–17	Their feet are swift to shed blood; in their paths are ruin and misery, and the way of peace they have not known.	Isa. 59:7–8	Their feet run to evil, and they are swift to shed innocent blood; their thoughts are thoughts of iniquity; desolation and destruction are in their highways. The way of peace they do not know, and there is no justice in their paths; they have made their roads crooked; no one who treads on them knows peace.
3:18	There is no fear of God before their eyes.	Psa. 36:1	Transgression speaks to the wicked deep in his heart; there is no fear of God before his eyes.

Note: All verses in this table are from the English Standard Version of the Bible.

Recitation comes in many forms. Robbins (1996a) identifies seven kinds of recitation. According to Robbins (1996b), it is suggested that recitation be the first exercise for rhetoricians.

a. Replication of exact words of another written source
b. Replication of exact words with one or more differences
c. Omission of words in such a manner that the word string has the force of a proverb, maxim, or authoritative judgment
d. Recitation of a saying using words different from the authoritative source
e. Recitation that uses some of the narrative words in the biblical text plus a saying from the text
f. Recitation of a narrative in substantially one's own words
g. Recitation that summarizes a span of text that includes various episodes (Robbins, 1996a, pp. 41–43)

Recontextualization

The second type of oral-scribal intertexture is recontextualization. As discussed earlier, *recontextualization* stands apart from *recitation* in that recontextualization presents phrases from other biblical texts without any direct or indirect attribution to the original source. Like recitation, recontextualization can present in many different forms; however, once again the key is the attribution of the source text. According to

Robbins (1996a), there is a lack of an "explicit statement or implication that the words 'stand written' anywhere else" (p. 48). Recontextualization can occur in *narration* and *attributed speech*.

a. Recontextualization in *narration* (allusion) occurs in John 1:1: "In the beginning was the Word, and the Word was with God, and the Word was God" (ESV). This refers to Genesis 1:1: "In the beginning, God created the heavens and the earth" (ESV). John used this recontextualization to establish the idea that the Word existed at the beginning of creation. In this case, the recontextualization of Genesis 1:1 is used as a foundational theological description of Jesus.

b. Recontextualization in *attributed speech* occurs in John 2:16: "And he told those who sold the pigeons, 'Take these things away; do not make my Father's house a house of trade' " (ESV). While John attributes these words to Jesus, there is no indication that Jesus was referring to Zechariah 14:21b: "And there shall no longer be a trader in the house of the Lord of hosts on that day" (ESV). This statement both served to challenge the actions of those in the temple while also alluding to the coming of the Messiah.

Reconfiguration

Reconfiguration stands apart from *recitation* and *recontextualization* in that reconfiguration "makes the later event 'new' in relation to a previous event" (Robbins, 1996a, p. 50). A reconfiguration can present as a recitation or recontextualization. The key difference is with the purpose of the author: to establish a new event in such a way that the previous event served to foreshadow the new event (Robbins, 1996a). One example of this occurs in the sermon of Peter on Pentecost: "he foresaw and spoke about the resurrection of the Christ, that he was not abandoned to Hades, nor did his flesh see corruption" (Acts 2:31, ESV). This is a recitation of David's words: "For you will not abandon my soul to Sheol, or let your holy one see corruption" (Psa. 16:10, ESV). Luke uses Peter's attributed sermon to argue that King David prophetically spoke of the resurrection of Jesus Christ. In actuality, Peter's sermon on Pentecost contains a total of three reconfigurations as Peter leans heavily upon the Old Testament as support for (a) the baptism of the Holy Spirit (Acts 2:16–21; Joel 2:28–32, ESV); (b) Jesus' resurrection (Acts 2:31; Psa. 16:10, ESV); and (c) Jesus' Ascension (Acts 2:34–35; Psa. 110:1, ESV).

Narrative Amplification

While *oral-scribal intertexture* presents mostly as recitations, recontextualizations, and reconfigurations, there are two less common forms of oral-scribal intertexture. The first of which is *narrative amplification*. Narrative amplification is fairly nuanced and may be difficult to distinguish in the interpretative process. Interestingly, Robbins does not always identify narrative amplification as a type of oral-scribal intertexture;

suggesting that recitation, recontextualization, and reconfiguration represent the full range of oral-scribal intertexture (Robbins, 1996b). Narrative amplification is a specific derivation of the aforementioned types of oral-scribal intertexture that expands, or amplifies, a narrative by utilizing recitation, recontextualization, and reconfiguration of multiple portions of a source text.

To better understand *narrative amplification*, it may be beneficial to return once more to Romans 3. As discussed in our examination of recitation, Romans 3:10–18 contains a series of quotes individually that exist as recitations; however, when considered together present as a narrative amplification. Notice that the Apostle Paul begins with a thesis: "Then what advantage has the Jew? Or what is the value of circumcision?" (Rom. 3:1, ESV). He then uses a series of recitations from verse 4 through verse 18 to make the case that all people are under sin; whether Jew or Gentile. While narrative amplification is difficult to deduce, it is helpful to consider a text in its entirety. If there is evidence that the quotes work in conjunction with one another to build or *amplify* upon a stated thesis, then it is possible that the author is utilizing narrative amplification.

Thematic Elaboration

As with narrative amplification, *thematic elaboration* is a nuanced rhetorical technique that is often difficult for interpreters to distinguish. However, unlike amplification, thematic elaboration occurs as a narrative is built upon a *chreia*, or theme, at the beginning of a unit (Robbins, 1996a). Rather than expanding a narrative, thematic elaboration occurs when an author makes a statement, called the theme, and then offers a rationale to support the theme. Robbins identifies four major argumentative figures: (a) argument from the opposite or contrary; (b) argument from analogy; (c) argument from example; and (d) argument from ancient testimony (p. 54). Elaboration is a common mode of argumentation "central to early Christian discourse" (p. 58). As seen Table 7.3, thematic elaboration is present in Paul's instructions to Titus.

Table 7.3 Thematic Elaboration of Titus 1:5–16

Argument	Scripture Reference	Scripture Quotation
Theme	1:9b	so that [*the elder*] may be able to give instruction in sound doctrine and also to rebuke those who contradict it
Rationale	1:5	This is why I left you in Crete, so that you might put what remained into order, and appoint elders in every town as I directed you.

(Continued)

(*Continued*)

Argument	Scripture Reference	Scripture Quotation
Confirmation of the rationale	1:6–9a	if anyone is above reproach, the husband of one wife, and his children are believers and not open to the charge of debauchery or insubordination. For an overseer, as God's steward, must be above reproach. He must not be arrogant or quick-tempered or a drunkard or violent or greedy for gain, but hospitable, a lover of good, self-controlled, upright, holy, and disciplined. He must hold firm to the trustworthy word as taught.
Argument from the contrary	1:10	For there are many who are insubordinate, empty talkers and deceivers, especially those of the circumcision party.
Argument from example	1:11	They must be silenced, since they are upsetting whole families by teaching for shameful gain what they ought not to teach.
Argument from ancient testimony	1:12–13a	One of the Cretans, a prophet of their own, said, "Cretans are always liars, evil beasts, lazy gluttons." This testimony is true.
Argument from analogy	1:12	Cretans are always liars, evil beasts, lazy gluttons.
Synthesis of the argument	1:13b–14	Therefore, rebuke them sharply, that they may be sound in the faith, not devoting themselves to Jewish myths and the commands of people who turn away from the truth.
Conclusion	1:15–16	To the pure, all things are pure, but to the defiled and unbelieving, nothing is pure; but both their minds and their consciences are defiled. They profess to know God, but they deny him by their works. They are detestable, disobedient, unfit for any good work.

Note: All verses in this table are from the English Standard Version of the Bible.

How Does Oral-Scribal Intertexture Help Interpreters Exegete a Pericope?

As discussed before, the layers of SRA provide depth and texture to the analysis of a given pericope. Oral-scribal intertexture, specifically, helps the interpreter to better understand the place of a given text in the broader context of oral and written history. Oral-scribal intertexture provides an additional layer to inner texture by identifying the original location of specific content in the passage. By locating the original source of content, interpreters are able to more effectively explore the original meaning of a given text. By identifying the oral-scribal sources from which a given text draws its content, interpreters can explore the similarities, differences, and contextual applications.

Cultural Intertexture

The Holy Scriptures are rich with cultural context. *Cultural intertexture* allows the interpreter to explore the cultural knowledge of the people. Cultural knowledge is "insider knowledge" (Robbins, 1996a, p. 58). Cultural intertexture offers the opportunity to better understand the cultural underpinnings of the Greco-Roman world. According to Robbins, cultural intertexture appears in a text "either through reference or allusion and echo" (p. 58). It is through cultural intertexture analysis that interpreters are able to uncover cultural patterns, configurations, values, scripts, codes, or systems (Robbins, 1996a).

At this point, it may be necessary to address a point of confusion that may arise as we continue the discussion of the textures of SRA. A common interpretative error occurs when the line of distinction between cultural and social intertexture (a subtexture of intertexture) and *social and cultural texture* (discussed in Chapter 8) is blurred. In reality, exploration of these subsets of SRA will lead to an overlap in data, and this is expected as a goal of qualitative research is to reach data saturation (Creswell, 2009; Fusch & Ness, 2015; Mayan, 2016). It is important, however, to recognize the distinguishing point here. *Social and cultural texture* is utilized to interpret the social and cultural "location" of the language and the world it creates (Robbins, 1996a, p. 71). Social and cultural texture is more than the social and cultural background of a text. Robbins brings clarity with the following question: "What kind of a social and cultural person would anyone be who lives in the 'world' of a particular text?" (p. 71). Herein, we discover the points of distinction for *social* and *cultural intertexture*. We will examine social intertexture in the next section, so we turn our full attention to the distinctives of *cultural intertexture*: references, allusions, and echoes. *Social and cultural texture* explores the sociological and anthropological theories of exegesis that examine the sociological and cultural realities of biblical passages (Bauer & Traina, 2011; Robbins, 1996a). *Cultural intertexture* examines how meaning and memory are conveyed through the text as it appears either through references, allusions, and echoes. Robbins (1996a) defines each as follows:

- A *reference* is a word or phrase that points to a personage or tradition known to the people on the basis of said tradition.

- An *allusion* is a statement that presupposes a tradition that exists in textual form, but the text being interpreted is not attempting to *recite* the tradition.
- An *echo* is a word or phrase that evokes, or potentially evokes, a concept from a cultural tradition generally in a subtle, indirect way such that no words or phrases indisputably come from only one cultural tradition (pp. 58–60).

The key difference between *cultural intertexture* and *oral-scribal intertexture* is that cultural references, or allusions, and echoes do not recite, recontextualize, or reconfigure any actual text. Rather, they point to, and interact with, "cultural concepts and traditions" (Robbins, 1996a, p. 59).

References and Allusions

When we talk about *cultural references* in the Bible, it is important to consider that Judaism, like many religions in Greco-Roman society, was both cultural and religious. Given this, references to Old Testament characters such as Abraham, Moses, and Elijah carry with them deep cultural connotations. For example, the Pharisees come to Jesus with a woman caught in adultery: "Teacher, this woman has been caught in the act of adultery. Now in the Law, Moses commanded us to stone such women. So, what do you say?" (Joh. 8:4–5, ESV). Notice first, that there is no direct or indirect attempt to *recite* any particular text. There are, however, two references to the Law that those Jews to whom this speech is attributed would have been keenly aware. The first reference is to Leviticus 20:10: "If a man commits adultery with the wife of his neighbor, both the adulterer and the adulteress shall surely be put to death" (ESV). The second reference is to the act of stoning as seen in various passages throughout the Old and New Testaments (Num. 15:36; Jos. 7:25; Act. 7:58). While Mosaic Law makes no direct reference to the act of stoning as a punishment for adultery, the presence of the reference to stoning provides the interpreter with a deeper appreciation of the common cultural understanding of the practice of stoning in 1st-century Judaism. Further, there is a cultural allusion embedded within the text that comes forth from the use of these cultural references: the religious hypocrisy of the Pharisees. According to the Law, both the man and the woman were to be put to death; however, the Pharisees failed to follow the very precept with which they challenged Jesus. The cultural allusion to religious hypocrisy is further played out in the narrative as Jesus states: "Let him who is without sin among you be the first to throw a stone at her" (Joh. 8:7, ESV).

Another example of cultural intertexture can be found in Acts 2:29–31. This is an excellent example to help differentiate between *cultural intertexture* and *oral-scribal* intertexture. As previously discussed, and, as illustrated in Table 7.4, Acts 2:31 is a *reconfiguration* of Psalms 16:10. Remember that in this text, Luke uses a recitation of David's words as a prophetic utterance directly pointing to the resurrection of Jesus. He, however, set the stage for this reconfiguration with a series of cultural references and allusions. There are three references and one allusion present in the text. The first two references directly point to the person and tomb of King David. The last reference points back to the Old Testament prophecy of Nathan that a descendant of David

Table 7.4 Cultural Intertexture of Acts 2:29–30

Cultural Intertexture of Acts 2:29–30	
"the patriarch David" (Acts 2:29a)	*Reference*: The Jews of the time would have an extensive knowledge of David as their patriarch and King.
"his tomb is with us to this day" (Acts 2:29b)	*Reference*: The tomb of King David would have been a historical treasure for the Jews.
"being therefore a prophet" (Acts 2:30a)	*Allusion:* There is an allusion here to the Jewish belief in the prophetic office of King David even though there is no such account in the Old Testament.
"knowing that God had sworn with an oath to him that he would set one of his descendants on his throne" (Acts 2:30b)	*Reference*: This is a direct reference to Nathan's prophecy that Israel would have a descendant of David on the throne forever (2 Sam. 7:11–13).
Oral-Scribal Intertexture of Acts 2:31	
"he foresaw and spoke about the resurrection of the Christ, that he was not abandoned to Hades, nor did his flesh see corruption." (Acts 2:31).	"For you will not abandon my soul to Sheol, or let your holy one see corruption." (Psa. 16:10)

Note: All verses in this table are from the English Standard Version of the Bible.

would be on the throne of Israel for eternity. The singular occurrence of an allusion here is distinctive and helps us better differentiate between references and allusions. As discussed earlier, cultural references directly or indirectly *point* to something. In this case, it is clear that Luke is pointing to the personage of King David, his tomb, and 2 Samuel 7:11–13. There is, however, an *allusion* to a common understanding that King David was also a prophet. Was there a common belief that David was a prophet? In fact, the answer is yes. David is listed among the prophets of Judaism (Noegel & Wheeler, 2002). Through this series of cultural references and allusions, Luke is able to establish his argument that David was prophetically speaking of Jesus' resurrection in Psalms 16:10.

Echoes

Cultural echoes are subtle, and their identification is often in the proverbial eye-of-the-beholder. This is why, as Robbins (1996a) points out, there is often disagreement regarding the presence or absence of cultural echoes. Given this, a word of caution and encouragement can be given here. Nuanced elements of biblical interpretation such as this often require of the researcher a level of experience that can only come with time and through practice. In cases such as these, researchers should heed the warning of Bauer and Traina (2011) that sociological and anthropological exegetes can arrive at two errors when exploring historical backgrounds: *overinterpretation* and *underinterpretation*. As researchers with the ultimate goal of practically applying biblical principles to social-scientific contexts, do not become bogged down by the desire to find the ever-elusive hidden meaning in a text, but also be careful not to miss important cultural details that will be invaluable data for interpretation.

Echoes are difficult to discern, because, if it were indisputable, then it would be a reference or an allusion. With that said, there are examples throughout Scripture. One common example of a cultural echo occurs in the phrase *Jesus Christ*, or more specifically, *ho Christos* (Wright, 2013). According to Wright, Pauline theology of Jesus' Messiahship was an echo that carried specific connotations in the Greco-Roman world. According to Wright, the Christian conceptualization of the Messiah was quite different than Israel's as "Paul's Jewish contemporaries could not believe that Israel's Messiah would be crucified" (p. 816). Robbins (1996a) concurred, writing: "The Messiah of Israel in Christian discourse is neither the traditional sufferer nor the traditional king" (p. 61). Further, Witherington (2006) asserts that Paul's statement in Titus 1:15, "all things are pure" (ESV), seems to echo Romans 14:20: "everything is indeed clean" (ESV). It is fairly evident that none of these examples are *indisputable*; however, each of these examples serve to illustrate how the people represented in any given text may derive meaning based upon their specific cultural location.

Social Intertexture

While *cultural intertexture* examines the insider knowledge of people who have interacted with a particular culture, *social intertexture* broadens the interpretative scope to consider social knowledge "commonly held by all persons of a region" no matter their cultural location (Robbins, 1996a, p. 62). Robbins identifies four categories of social intertexture: social roles, social identities, social institutions, social codes, and social relationships. The data gleaned from social intertexture provides a framework for further exploration through the later textures of SRA.

- *Social roles.* Roles such as slave, steward, shepherd, and king were commonly understood by the people. With each social role came certain social expectations.
- *Social identities.* Like people in modern society, social identity was essential to understanding the cultural, religious, and sociological development of the people of a region. Identities such as Jews, Gentiles, Romans, and Pharisees are essential to understanding the social relationships and interactions of the people located within a particular text.
- *Social institutions.* Miller (2010) defines a social institution as "an organization or system of organizations *that* consists of an embodied (occupied by human

persons) structure of differentiated roles" and having had four salient properties: structure, function, culture, and sanctions (pp. 24–25). In biblical times, social institutions included, but were not limited to, institutions such as empires, the synagogue, the Sanhedrin, and the School of the Prophets.

- *Social codes*. Social codes include both written and unwritten rules for behavior, relationships, and appearance that were widely understood by the people of a region. In biblical times, as in contemporary society, social codes came in many forms: honor, hospitality, differences in public and private attire, public and private social interactions, and, from a Greek perspective, *paideia*. *Paideia* is the Hellenistic understanding of education and training (Jaeger, 1939).
- *Social relationships*. The general understanding of social relationships in biblical times is essential to understand as there is a significant gap between contemporary and ancient social relationships. These social relationships can come in many forms: husband–wife, parent–children, master–slave, master–disciple, elders, friends, enemies, and family.

Returning again to Acts 2, we can see evidence of social intertexture. This is an excellent opportunity to return to Osborne's (2006) spiral of *text to context*. In our exploration of cultural intertexture, we focused on Acts 2:29–36. Upon first glance, it may seem like the passage is lacking a strong social intertexture; however, as we have learned from Osborne, it is often necessary to examine the surrounding context of a selected pericope. Social identity is an essential component of properly discerning Peter's message on Pentecost. Notice that Luke is careful to identify who hears the message of Pentecost: "both Jews and proselytes, Cretans, and Arabians" (Acts 2:11, ESV). Given this, the original hearers of the Gospel message on the Day of Pentecost were both Jews and Gentiles from throughout the Roman Empire who came to celebrate the Jewish Feast of Pentecost. There is a rhetorical progression that is utilized by Peter in his sermon that is used to grip the hearts of his Jewish brethren: "men of Judea and all who dwell in Jerusalem" (Acts 2:14, ESV); "Men of Israel" (Acts 2:22, ESV); "Brothers" (Acts 2:29, ESV). The progression of social identity called upon Peter's audience to shed their differences and to recognize that he was not speaking as an enemy, but rather, as family. In the text, there is also one significant social institution that is essential to both Jewish and Christian eschatology: the patriarchy (Acts 2:29, ESV). From here, Peter establishes that Jesus is King: "God has made him both Lord and Christ who you crucified" (Acts 2:36, ESV). Further, the social code of *swearing an oath* is present in the text (Acts 2:30, ESV). It is through the reference to God's covenant with David that Peter identifies Jesus as the fulfillment of God's oath. Last, there are multiple social relationships present in the pericope: brothers (Acts 2:29, ESV); the master–servant relationship in "the Lord said to my Lord" (Acts 2:34, ESV); and the house of Israel (Acts 2:36, ESV). By examining each of the four categories of social intertexture, we are able to better interpret the social knowledge shared by the author and the audience.

Historical Intertexture

Historical intertexture involves researching specific events that are referenced or alluded to in a text. Referencing historical events is a typical rhetorical device used by authors to provide a contextual background. As with major events today, historical events were often culturally and socially transformative. From a rhetorical perspective, it makes sense that an author would only reference an event if it had significant meaning to the people of the region. For instance, it is common for books or speeches in contemporary society to reference events like World War II or the 9/11 terrorist attacks, because these events evoke meaning and memory. The same is true of ancient times. We return once more to Acts 2 as Peter identifies two historical events: the crucifixion and resurrection of Jesus. Interestingly, these were recent events; however, the rhetorical intent of evoking meaning and memory still remain. Peter wanted his audience to know that they crucified the King of the Jews. The images of crucifixion would have come to the fore of their thinking as they considered the words of Peter. The Resurrection is the event that, for Christians, changed everything: the King of Israel is not dead, He is alive (Acts 2:24). There are also more traditionally understood historical events present in the text as well. The Day of Pentecost was the celebration of the giving of the Ten Commandments. On the day that the Jews celebrated the institution of the Mosaic Covenant, Peter told the people of a New Covenant in Jesus Christ (Mat. 26:28; Jer. 31:31–34).

The use of historical intertexture is sometimes used to place the narrative of a text at a specific time and location. An example of this is found in the birth record of Jesus: "In those days a decree went out from Caesar Augustus that all the world should be registered. This was the first registration when Quirinius was governor of Syria. And all went to be registered, each to his own town" (Luke 2:1–3, ESV). From this historical record, we can pinpoint the exact time of the birth of Jesus Christ. Other examples of historical intertexture occur when the author seeks to remind the audience of an event that may not have large-scale historical significance but was meaningful to the audience. Paul utilizes historical events of varying degrees in his letter to the Galatians: (a) Paul's personal history of persecuting the Church (Acts 8:3; Gal. 1:13); (b) Paul's first visit to Jerusalem (Gal. 1:18); (c) Paul's second visit to Jerusalem (Acts. 15:4–21; Gal. 2:1); and (d) Paul's disagreement with Peter (Gal. 2:11–14). These events were personal in nature; however, they were significant to Paul's personal story and were used to provide context for the following theological discussion about faith and works.

Reciprocal Intertexture

At this point, we have explored the four original subtextures of intertexture: oral-scribal, cultural, social, and historical intertexture. As illustrated in Figure 7.2, the flow of the interpretation has been unidirectional as we considered how the author drew upon outside sources to develop the content of a text. For instance, from previous sections, we know that Peter's sermon in Acts 2 draws upon the prophecy of Joel 2:28–32 as a form on oral-scribal intertexture. Now reverse the order here: What happens when we are researching Joel 2? Acts 2 does not occur as an oral-scribal intertexture in Joel 2, because it is impossible for Joel to draw upon an outside source that does not exist and will not exist for hundreds of years. With that said, it feels unnatural to research Joel 2 without looking to Acts 2. So, how do we rectify this? After much consideration, we feel that it is important to add a subtexture to the original intertexture methodology: reciprocal intertexture.

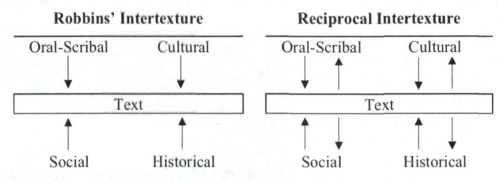

Figure 7.2 Reciprocal Intertexture

Source: Joshua Henson

Moving from a unidirectional approach to intertexture, reciprocal intertexture views the flow of interpretation as bidirectional. Rather than focusing on the individual text in question, the researcher now considers the text's place in the wider canon of Scripture (McConville, 2002). Bauer and Traina (2011) give considerable insight to the need for reciprocal intertexture:

> The principle of the canon of Scripture implies that the Word of God is not reducible to individual passages or books read in isolation from the rest of the Bible. Rather, one encounters the Word of God as one studies the entire Bible in its dynamic complexity . . . These considerations suggest that the concept of *sensus plenior* (fuller/deeper meaning) may have value. *Sensus plenior* is the notion that God uses the interconnections between passages in the Bible to communicate a fuller meaning than the biblical authors themselves knew or intended (p. 342).

Robbins (1996a) presumed this connection in the Divine History subtexture of Sacred Texture discussed in a later chapter. However, when one views God as the ultimate author of Scripture and that the Scriptures are more than the act of human will (2 Pet. 1:21, ESV), it is essential to give considerable care to how a given text is positioned in the greater revelation of Scripture.

Returning for the last time to Acts 2, one should consider the words of verses 1–4 as both an oral-scribal and historical intertexture. Luke points back to the *event* of God establishing the Mosaic Covenant (historical intertexture) as recorded in Exodus 19:16–19 (oral-scribal intertexture). However, when examining either of these texts, the greater context of the canon is essential. Luke used this intertexture to argue that the New Covenant, prophesied by both Jesus and Jeremiah was established by the Holy Spirit in the Church (Jer. 31:31–34; Luke 22:20, ESV). So then, as interpreters, it is necessary to explore each of these passages in relation to the larger story of God's redemptive plan as they are all interconnected. Further, an analysis of Exodus 19 causes us to ask in what ways the giving of the law was to be fulfilled in the giving of the Holy Spirit on the Day of Pentecost. Thus, understanding what was to come helps us to better understand what has been. Therefore, reciprocal intertexture allows the interpreter to move forward and backward through Scripture to better understand the location of a given text in the canon.

Conclusion

Oral-scribal, cultural, social, historical, and reciprocal intertexture work together to aid the researcher in better exploring the textual, cultural, and social world around a text and the way that the author engages said world. Careful consideration of the intertexture of a text allows the researcher to better understand a text's location within the oral and written history of the social, cultural, and historical context of the original author and the original audience.

Chapter Seven Reflective Exercises

1. The original conceptualization of SRA did not include reciprocal intertexture. Why do the authors insist upon the necessity of reciprocal intertexture in intertexture analysis? What is an example in Scripture in which being able to freely move forward and backward through the canon of Scripture is helpful in the interpretative process? Please explain.
2. The sermon and subsequent stoning of Stephen in Acts 7 is structurally similar to Acts 2. Given this, using the principles learned in this chapter, conduct an intertexture analysis of Acts 7 following the reflective guide in the following:
   a. Are there any quotes within the text? Does the author attribute these quotes to another source? How does the author treat these quotes? Identify the recitations, recontextualizations, and reconfigurations in the text.
   b. Are there cultural references, allusions, and echoes present in the text? What about references such as inheritance, covenant, and circumcision? Stephen makes the statement that the Law came by angels (Acts 7:53, ESV). Could this

possibly be a cultural echo? Conduct research on these topics. What can learn from exploring cultural intertexture?

    c. There are multiple occurrences of social intertexture in Acts 7. Identify as many as possible. Classify each occurrence according to the categories discussed in the chapter.

    d. Stephen's sermon tells the story of the Jewish people. Given this, what historical events are present in the text? What can we learn from these occurrences?

    e. Reciprocal intertexture may be helpful in interpreting Acts 7:58. Why would reciprocal intertexture be helpful to the interpreter in this case?

3. Admittedly, intertexture analysis is easier in the New Testament than in the Old Testament. The simple reason for this is that the New Testament draws from the Old Testament. You may wonder: What do I do if I'm researching the Old Testament? Using the principles learned in this chapter, conduct an intertexture analysis of Psalm 142 following the reflective guide in the following:

    a. The title of Psalm 142 says that David was in a cave. To what situation in David's life does this psalm refer?

    b. Are there any quotes within the text? Does the author attribute these quotes to another source? How does the author treat these quotes? Identify the recitations, recontextualizations, and reconfigurations in the text.

    c. Are there cultural references, allusions, and echoes present in the text? What is the trap of which David writes? What is refuge? What is "my portion in the land of the living" (Psalm 142:5, ESV)? Are these cultural terms necessary to the meaning of the text?

    d. Is there evidence of social intertexture? Any roles, institutions, relations, or codes present in the text? How do these help in the interpretation process?

    e. There is a significant historical event in this passage. What is it? How does this help the interpretative process?

    f. Why would reciprocal intertexture be helpful to the interpreter in Psalm 142?

Chapter 8

Working Through Socio-Rhetorical Analysis— Social and Cultural Texture

Socio-rhetorical analysis (SRA) is a multifaceted approach that approaches the text of Scripture from several different perspectives by focusing on different aspects of the reading of the text of Scripture. It interacts with in the text issues as well as behind the text and in front of the text issues. In the text, it deals with words and sections of the text. In dealing with behind the text issues, it addresses background, cultural, and societal issues that are the context or the foundation of the activities and worldviews that are found in the text. In addition, it deals with in front of the text issues as in what the message says to the reader. Life is not one-dimensional and neither are texts, this method allows, even presses for a full examination of the text for it to give its full expression for life. The process of SRA is a system of interpretation that moves from a focus on the words and forms of the text to the interaction of the text with other texts and issues surrounding it and then in this section, it moves to interacting with the world or society of the text not just in societal roles but more to the point of views and ways of life that defined the cultural interactions of the day. Analysis of the social and cultural texture of a text explores the social and cultural location of the language and the type of world the language evokes (Robbins, 1996a). With this focus on language, this gives the researcher the ability to examine this aspect of the texture through the implications of the language used in the text. In the language of metaphor if Scripture is a person then this texture is the culture of the person. This texture deals with the impact of society and culture on the text just as society and culture impacts a person. This section deals with the social and cultural texture analysis of the text as a method of hermeneutics. According to hermeneutic principles, a text cannot be interpreted with any degree of certainty without historical–cultural and contextual analysis; therefore, one must study the historical–cultural milieu in which the author wrote (Virkler &

Ayayo, 2007). This is an important process in the study of Scripture or hermeneutics.

The first step in this process is to discuss and understand the difference between the social and cultural texture and social or cultural intertexture of the last section. The issue here is not the intertexture of a text but its social and cultural nature as a text and it answers the question of the kind of social and cultural person that lives in the "world" of this text (Robbins, 1996a). Intertexture examines issues of connections between persons and culture or society. Cultural intertexture deals with references or allusions that are culture bound and societal intertexture deals with social roles, institutions, codes, and relationships (Robbins, 1996a). Whereas social and cultural texture looks to discover the social and cultural location, view and habits of a person who inhabits the time and space of the original text.

Social and Cultural Texture Method

Social and cultural texture differs from intertexture by its use of anthropological and sociological theory to explore the nature of the voices in the text and it sets forth a set of strategies to pursue, test, and enrich earlier research in these areas (Robbins, 1996b). This is a view from within the text that asks questions about issues that have always existed, yet newer understanding of these theories broadens our understanding of texts and contexts from antiquity. The three aspects of this texture are found in specific social topics, common social and cultural topics, and final cultural categories. These different aspects of this texture hear the voices in the text with different interpretive matrixes that yield insight for interpretation especially in the area of understanding context. Life is full-orbed and full of nuanced meanings and the more that is known about the present the more these nuances can be seen, interpreted, and addressed. So, it is in Scripture in that it reveals full-orbed lives, situations, and interactions that many times were understood by those involved in the original activities, however, are lost on us. When statements are made in the context of Scripture for the most part everyone in the room understands clearly all of the implications. The problem is that we were not in the room. We are outside observers, which has advantages and disadvantages. The advantage comes from objectivity, but the disadvantage comes in easily misunderstanding the message. This message in the text is deeply impacted by the worldviews involved, some common issues that everyone knew about their culture and time and their particular place in culture. They were particular people with particular issues and views that impacted the message. We have these same issues today. A contemporary example is the use of the word tolerance in our contemporary society. In the 1960s tolerance was a way of saying that a person was less important or even bothersome. In the 21st century, the same word is a word of relationship and trust building. What changed? Worldviews have changed as well as some common experiences in our culture and there is more sensitivity now to people in different strata of society. To read a text from the 1960s that uses the concept of tolerance it would be easy for us to misunderstand the word even if we looked it up in the dictionary. The word has not changed we are the ones that have changed. To understand this change, cultural anthropology and sociology offer insights for these complex issues. These are the insights we now apply to Scripture.

These insights can be applied to both Old and New Testaments, but this must be done carefully. These insights can be applied in these different contexts but there will be different issues in the different areas and eras of the text of Scripture. Sacred texture is looking at the view from above while the inner texture is a view from the text, but the social and cultural texture is a searching for a view from the author and audience of the text. The question here is not *what do we see or hear* but the question is *what did they see or hear* in the moment of writing or hearing. We cannot enter their minds and know every detail, but we can find clues to these realities in what we have in the text and what we can know about them in their society and culture from other sources. This is not only a hedge against wrong interpretation, but it also builds a foundation for a carefully nuanced interpretation and understanding.

Each of these three areas has different components for research and some will require different methods and resources. Therefore, each of the three aspects of this interpretive method will be examined separately for insights into the method and practical ways to apply the method. The goal here is the practical application of these insights in the search for authorial intent in interpretation. It is not to create some new ideas that use the text. Instead, it is to research Scripture to be able to hear and see the text clearly with all of the nuances that would have been seen or heard by the original audience. The text cannot mean what it never meant. However, it is much more textured, rich, and nuanced than has been seen in the recent past. This is a close examination of the text in searching for clues about the people of this text. A good interpretation of a text will survive a close reading of the text. This is the process of this close reading to enter not just the social and cultural world of the author and hearers but to hear their voices from their particular location in society and culture.

Specific Social Topics (Worldview—From Conversionist to Utopian)

Texts with a substantive religious texture contain certain ways of talking about the world and each kind of response creates a kind of culture that gives, meanings, values, and actions to people (Robbins, 1996a). These ways of talking about the world can be seen in the text in the way life or spirituality is discussed. In essence, these are different types of religious worldviews or worldviews that could be unique to Christians and people of other religious traditions like Judaism. These specific social topics have been divided into categories to give clarity to these differences and to facilitate the understanding of these distinct ways of viewing the world, spirituality, and life. These classifications were first developed by Wilson (1973) and applied to the study of Scripture by Robbins (1996a). The first process in this category is to define and understand these different classifications. There are seven classifications. An adaptation of Wilson's sociological definitions of different types of religious discourse produces the following seven major responses to the world (Robbins, 1996b).

There are several concepts that need to be noticed before moving on to these seven definitions. First, notice these are based in discourse so the different categories can be recognized by the discourse or interactions in the text. Second, these are ways that a group of people responds to the world around them; it is how they see life and priorities. Third, it is religious discourse in that it is about how they talk about issues that are important to spirituality and the interaction between God and the world. Fourth, these are sociological definitions. These come from the discipline of sociology. Sociologists observe interactions between people and groups. When they recognize patterns and repetitions, they can begin to give it definition. These definitions help us understand and relate to other people. It helps us to understand their messages clearly.

An example of this issue is found when I went to teach among a group of newly reached indigenous peoples. On the third day of the meetings, three of the leaders from this group came to me and wanted to speak to me. They sat in a neat row in front of me with two translators beside me. There were two translators since the translation of everything that was said had to be translated from one indigenous language to another more common indigenous language then to a common Latin American language then finally to English. The first one spoke and invited me and others to come and teach them how to take this new gospel they had heard to other new tribes that needed the gospel but were different culturally. I wanted to hear what the second person said before I responded. The second leader asked the same questions almost verbatim.

I thought maybe there was a problem in communication. However, I went on to hear the third person. He said the exact same thing. I understood the message, but I did not understand why they repeated it three times. So, I asked the translator whether they thought North Americans were not very bright and needed the message repeated. He replied that this was their way of communicating that this was very important to them. This was based on their worldview that viewed the realm of spirituality as very important and their suspicion or fear of outsiders. They wanted to communicate very clearly what they wanted and how important it was to them. In addition, since I was an outsider their fear was alleviated by speaking to me together with one voice. The problem is that we do not have a translator to ask the important question of context instead it must be seen in the text, in the discourse and other information we are given in the text.

This first step in the process is to visit the definitions of these seven classifications. Nevertheless, definitions are not enough without some discussion of how to recognize them in the text and the discourses. This will be part of the discussion. Then there will be some practical applications as well in finding these classifications. It is important to note here at the onset as well that many discourses can have two or even three of these classifications at work at the same time in the discourse.

Conversionist

This perspective can be characterized by a view that the world is corrupt and so are people and the world can be changed when people are changed by salvation through a transformation with a new self and a new orientation toward the world (Robbins, 1996a). The central issue here is that of conversion to bring change to self before addressing the issues of the world. It takes no interest in programs of social reform or politics while it encourages revivalism and public preaching and it encourages emotional but not ecstatic experiences (Robbins, 1996b). The way of change seen in this worldview is through conversion and transformation of the person. It is God dependent while in the world.

Revolutionist

This perspective declares that only the destruction of the world in the natural and social order will suffice to save people and supernatural powers perform the destruction though people can assist in the process (Robbins, 1996a). The central issues here are the ultimate destruction of the world and though it is supernatural there are some ways that people can be involved in this end of the world scenario. It is not the fear of man destroying the world. It is just the opposite in that God will destroy it as the solution to the ills of the world. This argumentation is hostile to social reform and instantaneous conversion and it is occupied with prophetic exegesis with its contemporary fulfillment with the members being God's instruments waiting for the decreed moment (Robbins, 1996b). This is the prophetic and eschatological view that looks forward to the end of this world and the beginning of a heavenly one. The focus is on the future and on the destruction of this present evil world.

Introversionist

This perspective views the world as irredeemably evil and that salvation can be obtained only by the fullest possible withdrawal from it with purification coming by renouncing the world and leaving it and establishing a separate community (Robbins, 1996a). Withdrawal is seen as a response to the evil in the world where the goal is not conversion or outreach but the purity of the individual as gathered in a community of others on the same journey. The overarching motive is purity with the only solution as withdrawal. This is more concerned with deepening rather than widening spiritual experience and it views community as supporting the individual and does not encourage mission in the outside world (Robbins, 1996a). This withdrawal is their strategy for purity which is the goal of life and community for them. This can be seen in early monasteries, but it can also be seen in contemporary churches wherein the people believe the pastor is there to just care for them and not engage the world.

Gnostic–Manipulationist

This response seeks only a transformed set of relationships and this is a transformed method of dealing with evil, but salvation is possible if people learn the right means to address problems in overcoming evil (Robbins, 1996a). This view focuses on relationships and learning how to deal with problems in overcoming evil in the world. It is not a removal from the world, but it focuses on transformations in relationships and in how to address evil. In this view is the claim that the only way to overcome evil is through the special knowledge taught by the movement and the important thing is for people to acquire spiritual attitudes through this process of knowing and understanding (Robbins, 1996b). The focus here is on gaining knowledge, a special knowledge in being transformed and overcoming evil through this transformation. The focus is on knowledge and knowing rather than conversion or social reform or even the end of the world.

Thaumaturgical

This view focuses on the concerns of individual people for relief for present, specific ills and salvation comes in the form of healing, assuagement of grief, restoration after loss, reassurance, the avoidance of calamity and the guarantee of eternal life after death (Robbins, 1996a). Most of the areas of this category are concerned with specific present needs that are met through supernatural provision. The exception is the guarantee of eternal life. So, there is consideration of the life to come but the emphasis is on present relief in many different forms. This argument insists that it is possible for people to experience the effect of the supernatural in their lives and it affirms that normal reality and causation can be suspended for the benefit of special and personal dispensations and these benefits come through other spirits and supernatural powers in miracles (Robbins, 1996b). This is the worldview that sees the supernatural and the power of God at work miraculously in people and events beyond the natural cause and effect of God's sovereignty.

Reformist

This view sees the world as corrupt since its social structures are corrupt and people can create an environment of salvation by using supernaturally given insights to change the present social organization into a system that functions toward good ends (Robbins, 1996a). Here salvation is present on the earth as the oppressive corrupt systems are changed and God works through revealing new ways to address social issues to people who are spiritual. This argumentation endorses a role of social consciousness and being in the world without becoming part of the world but to engage the world by the doing of good deeds (Robbins, 1996b). The focus here is on the change that can be wrought in the world through social change and development for the good of people here on the earth.

Utopian

This response seeks to reconstruct, not just reform, the entire social world according to divinely given principles where evil is absent and people must take an active role in replacing the system (Robbins, 1996a). This is an active response to the evil of the world in people totally rebuilding a new system or a new world order. This new order is perfect in that it is based upon divine principles, but it is built by the imperfect people of the world. It argues that people should inaugurate this new system free from evil and corruption and the whole system must be changed since the system is the source of evil and not the people in the system (Robbins, 1996b). Since the system is the source of evil when it is changed this evil will disappear. It is social evil that is the problem here not personal depravity or evil. Therefore, the pursuit of this utopian solution becomes all-encompassing for solutions and for the future.

Application

Then the first step in the application of specific social topics or religious worldviews is a general read through of the pericope to be studied. In this read through the researcher will need to look for clues as to worldview concepts in the text. These could be very overt, and glaring uses of a certain worldview or they could be more covert particularly since the researcher is so far removed from the cultural context of the text. For example, conversionist language in the text will focus on preaching or conversion or transformation of the person. This is very gospel-centered language, and this is one of the core issues of Scripture in the New Testament. This can be found in the Old Testament as well in discussions of conversions or transformations through divine encounters such as when Jacob wrestles with the angel and sees the face of the Lord in Genesis. In this encounter Jacob's name is changed to Israel which means Prince with God rather than Jacob which can mean deceiver. This is a clear transformation. There are other conversion issues like this in places like the Psalms as well. Look for words or concepts that indicate a clear transformation or a call for a conversion such as when Peter calls for the Jews to repent and turn to God in Acts 2. Remember the first step in this process is to recognize or to gather data; it is not to interpret it at this point. Many times, in the rush to application researchers miss the bigger picture of the pericope or of the complexity of the issues at work in the text. In passion for practical application at times, interpretation is overlooked and thereby misses the intent of the message of the text.

In the revolutionist worldview, the focus is on the future and the destruction of this evil world. It is to be noted though that this is not the only worldview that is focused on the future. However, the uniqueness to this view is the focus on the destruction of this evil world. This can be found in the New Testament concepts of the second coming and the destruction of this present world with the beginning of a new age. Many New Testament writings use this worldview in the discussion of the end of the age including the classical texts about the second coming in the gospels and the book of Revelation. However, there are others as well in the other New Testament writings when Peter discusses how the earth and its elements will melt or when Paul comforts the Thessalonians by explaining the truth about the second coming in relationship to those who believe. However, these concepts can be found in the Old Testament as well in places like Isaiah 61 in the discussions of the day of vengeance of God. In similar ways, the prophets discuss the day of judgment in the destruction of certain Gentile nations to destroy the evil in these nations. In this search for this worldview look for words or concepts like this evil world or the destruction of the world or discussions of the future age when connected to divine intervention and change. Another word or concept that can be seen with a revolutionist worldview is that of judgment when it results in destruction. These concepts can be found in the macro area of the pericope or in the micro areas as well in some statements inside one of the sentences.

The introversionist worldview also views the world as evil with no human solution available. However, the answer for those with this worldview is withdrawal from the world and by renouncing the world system. This view is not focused on the future as much as it is on the present and it looks for a present solution to this evil world. For this worldview look for words or concepts of withdrawal or keeping away from the world. These can be negative instructions like do not do this or that and they can be concepts like keeping yourself unspotted from the world or do not touch. These can be found in the New Testament in instructions to be separate from the world and its pollutions. It can also be found in exhortations about false teachings that instruct about not tasting or doing. In the Old Testament in one sense the nation of Israel was introversionist in being instructed about laws that would separate them from other societies like some of their purity or Sabbath laws. However, in the Old Testament, it can be found that Israel is instructed to go among others as in the blessing of Abraham. In Genesis 12, Abraham is told that he and his offspring would receive blessing from the Lord but that ultimately, they were to bring this blessing to the nations. This is an example of a misunderstanding from the perspective of worldviews. Many later Jews had an introversionist view with a focus on being separate from the Gentiles and the Gentile world. As a result, when they heard or read this blessing to Abraham, they saw the blessing that would come to Israel but they failed to see the mandate for Israel to bring this blessing to the nations. This going to the nations flew in the face of their introversionist mindset and therefore it became almost invisible until Jesus reinstituted this concept in the Great Commission.

The gnostic-manipulationist worldview is focused on learning or knowledge in an effort to bring transformation in relationships or in overcoming the problem of evil. The sense of this view can be seen in the name with gnostic from the Greek language meaning to know and manipulationist which means one who brings change to others through various means or methods. The focus here is on gaining knowledge with the purpose of bringing change. The conversionist seeks change through individual supernatural change, while the revolutionist wants change in society but through destruction of this present world, the gnostic manipulationist seeks change through knowledge and human involvement, while the reformist seeks change through changing society with human aid and the utopian wants to totally reconstruct society according to divine principles. The introversionist does not seek change but desires and pursues withdrawal. All of these views have to do with how to deal with evil. Some look to God for divine intervention while others look for divine insight with action from human aid in the process of dealing with evil. All these views have this core issue in common in dealing with evil. The difference is found in how each view decides to deal with evil that is present in this world. In some ways, they even define evil differently ranging from personal sin to societal sin, to dealing with the results of sin or evil.

In looking for this view in the text look for words or concepts that have to do with learning as a means for change or help or divine aid. Key words can be listened or instruction or learn. In addition, look for instruction from arguments with words like therefore or concepts of if–then construction. In the New Testament, many examples can be found in the epistles or in the teachings of Jesus. Paul tells the Corinthians that he does not want them to be unlearned about spiritual gifts. He gives them instruction to bring change in their worship and spiritual lives. In this same letter, he rebukes them for missing some of the issues of the Lord's Supper then he instructs them so they can change. They were misapplying spiritual gifts as well and both issues were causing division. He corrected them then he instructed them. This view is often found in the Old Testament as well where the reader is told to listen to my words or to listen to the words of your father or mother. It is also found in the prophets as they instruct Israel or individual kings. This view can also include rebukes in the Old Testament as when the prophet Nathan rebukes David for his adultery but then gives instruction to David who repents, and this is a conversionist issue as well. Remember two or three of these world views can be found in close proximity to each other.

The thaumaturgical view looks to relieve the results of evil in this world for individuals. It concerns issues of healing, comfort, restoration, or overcoming disaster. This one is personal and up close in human lives and suffering. It is concerned with dealing with not so much the force of evil in the world but the plights of individuals who live in this evil world. It is also concerned with looking forward to eternal life where these issues will be permanently resolved. Thaumaturgy is a word used for being able to bring change in the physical world many times through a saint or a magician. The thaumaturgical worldview sees the need for change in people's lives that can be changed by divine intervention. This intervention comes in the form of healing or comfort or supernatural help in the times of trouble. In looking for this view in Scripture look for words or concepts having to do with healing or comfort. This can be seen in the New Testament in places like Jesus comforting the sisters after Lazarus had died. He even wept with them. Why did He do that when He knew He was going to raise him from the dead. It had to do with comfort. In another place in 2 Corinthians 1 Paul talks about how he had suffered and then was comforted by the Lord but part of the reason this had happened was so that he could learn how to comfort others in their suffering. Then in the Old Testament this view can be found when Moses provides Manna for the Israelites or water from the rock. There is also a thaumaturgical concept in Psalm 23 wherein the psalmist finds comfort from the Lord who leads him beside still waters. In addition, there are many issues and discussions of healing in both the Old and New Testaments. Jesus and the apostles heal many and even discuss healing as in when Peter says that there is healing through the cross and the stripes of Christ. In the Old Testament is seen healing in the ministry of Moses and later in the prophets. Then finally, there are discussions about the comfort that comes from the coming of the Lord or the eternal future. This is healing or deliverance from these present ills and there are many places that discuss this reality from the book of Daniel to the Thessalonian letters.

The reformist view sees the world as evil due to its social systems therefore the solution is through changing the social systems. This change is brought through social change through human agents though it is motivated by finding a social system that is after a divine pattern of justice. This view is focused on changing the present and it is not so much an individual change that is desired as much as the change is sought for the systems of society. Those who brought change into the church in the 1500s were called reformers. They reshaped the culture of the church but even more they reshaped society. Church and society were much more enmeshed at the time. This view focuses on the systems of the society that were changed even though there were many other issues that changed as well. This view does not look to the future for answers but looks to bring tangible changes in the present through human agency. An example of this is found in history when William Carey went to India in the late 1700s. He went to preach the gospel and his world view was conversionist. Yet when he arrived, he was shocked by the tradition of widow burning. The men in India would marry several wives over many years so some of their wives were much younger than they were when they died. When the husband died, his body was burned but so were all his living wives at the same time. He was horrified! He fought through government systems to have this tradition outlawed. He succeeded before he died. He was a gospel preacher, but he was also a reformer or a reformist. When looking for this worldview in the Scripture look for words or concepts that have to do with changing some activity or system of activity that is unjust. Look for words like just or justice and concepts of change that are focused on present systems. Peter was a reformist in the sense that he changed the status of women in society. The women were taught that they were to adapt to their new husbands in every way, in habits, in friends and even in religion. In 1 Peter 3, he told the wives to win their unbelieving husbands over to the Lord. This was a radical departure from societal norms and part of a reforming movement for women and children in the early church. In addition, there are places in the New Testament where the reader is told not to participate in societal norms and instead of withdrawal the exhortation is to live or speak differently. These concepts are found in the Old Testament as well in the Lord giving new norms or ways of living to the Israelites. Sometimes the issue was withdrawal but other times the issue was for a different more just society. Israel was taught to treat strangers and the poor differently. This was not an issue of withdrawal from society it was in forming a different more just society than had been seen up to that point. The rich were not held up as godly (even though that concept found its way into the culture of the day) nor were they rebuked for having too much. Instead they were instructed to not reap all of the fruit or grain from their farms and they were to allow the poor and foreigners to come in after their reaping time. This was a societal issue, a godly way to deal with the poor without excessive administration that could be abused. This is the reformist worldview and it is found in many places in the text of Scripture. The kingdom of God does belong to the casual observer but to those who seek. These issues may be difficult to see at first but once these concepts are developed and searched out, they can be clearly seen as a help in understanding the text and the context of Scripture. The goal is to hear the intended message but to hear it well we must see the context well of their culture and even some of the finer nuances of their cultural interchanges. These nuances are readily available in modern conversations but when the conversations are in antiquity everyone in the room at the time understood the implications of the message. The problem is that we were not in the room and we are still not there. Nevertheless, through these interpretive methods is an endeavor to rebuild the complete room almost as a virtual room with all of the little nuances and implications of the message so it can be just as clear as it was to those who were in the Old Testament or New Testament room.

The utopian view sees the world in need of being totally rebuilt after a divine design, reform is not sufficient. In this view, the system is the problem not the people therefore there must be a totally new system and people must initiate and build this new perfect system. This utopian system becomes the answer to the present evils. Therefore, society must be rebuilt in this worldview. This view can be seen in the discussions of the perfect future in the new heaven and earth once the discussion moves past the second coming and the destruction of the world. This perfect world is pictured in both Old and New Testaments though it becomes clearer in some of the New Testament writings. An example of this would be in 2 Peter 3 where the reader is told to look for a new heaven and a new earth where there will be righteousness. This can also be found in the Old Testament in places like Isaiah 65:7 where it talks about a new heaven and new earth. There are some forms of thinking and worldviews in this utopian category that would look to build a utopian society here on this side of the coming of Jesus and Scripture warns against this kind of thinking, but it can still be found in the discussions in Scripture. As mentioned before there can be two or even three of these views interlinked or in opposition to each other in one pericope in Scripture. However, once these views are seen the question is how they help in interpretation?

Interpretation

It has already been seen how a particular religious worldview can hinder a person from seeing the truth or a divine message. The researcher needs to know these views to be able to see the different aspects of all these views in the message of Scripture. To limit the knowledge of these worldviews is to limit the ability of the researcher in seeing that which really resides in the text. Israel could not see the mandate to bless the nations because they only allowed one worldview in their understanding of the message from the Lord. This is a warning to the modern researcher to see the text broadly while allowing understandings from these different perspectives. To miss seeing the message is to miss being able to possess that truth. For Israel, this had serious ramifications for generations. Another example is found in the ministry of Jesus. He came into Jerusalem on Palm Sunday to the shouts of adoration for the people yet when He had entered Jerusalem He wept. Why did he weep? According to Luke 19 because they had missed the time of their visitation from the Lord. They were accepting Him now. How had they missed it? They had a revolutionist religious worldview of the coming Messiah. Therefore, they thought he was coming as a military king to set up a world kingdom and that this Messiah would violently overthrow Rome. They had read in Amos 9 about the Messiah who was going to destroy the enemies of Israel. From their worldview, they thought it meant Rome. However, that was never the intent. The intent was to destroy the enemy of sin for Israel and all nations. They could not see through a conversionist worldview to see this reality, therefore, they missed God in the flesh when He came and dwelt among us. What a tragedy. In this story are seen these conflicting worldviews helping the researcher understand the message in this event in Jerusalem. The message on the surface would seem like this is where they recognized the Messiah. The real message though for this day is how they missed the Messiah. Then what is the application? There are many ways this can be applied but the general application is that human ability to understand God is filled with roadblocks and pitfalls and one of these is our limited view of reality and of God Himself. What is the message for leaders? Be careful not to lead in the wrong direction because of your limited view of God and reality. Israel missed God's message to them twice when it was clearly right in front of them. They were blinded by their own self-focus and ethnocentrism. Abraham's children should have seen it but they did not, and the Pharisees and the disciples should have seen it, but they did not. Thankfully, the disciples saw it clearly after the day of Pentecost and this was supernatural intervention but somehow it involved the disciples seeing God and reality differently.

Interpretation in this section proceeds directly from what is found in the observations that come from the pericope being studied. Not every pericope will have multiple worldviews and some pericopae will be clearer about worldview issues than others. Once the researcher has gathered data from the observations the first question to ask in the interpretive stage is if the understanding of these worldviews helps in the process of understanding the text more clearly. As has been seen though this question must be considered carefully since there are different ways that these views can impact and interact with the message. The first question is the observation question in what is there in the text. The second question is, if there is more than one worldview, how these views interact. Are they in the text together and combined closely like revolutionist and utopian in the discussion of the second coming and the new world or are they in opposition like conversionist and revolutionist? Once this is determined then the process moves on to the more complex stage of implication.

The issue of implication can be viewed from different perspectives. One perspective is from the issue of understanding the message in a straightforward manner. In other words, this thaumaturgical view brings the message of the miraculous to the forefront of this message. It can help the researcher to see an emphasis in the text. Another perspective is from seeing this text from a new view since this text is normally seen from, say, a conversionist point of view but the worldview of this pericope is thaumaturgical. What are the implications of this change? A perspective can be from finding the worldview of the implied readers and yet the worldview of the message is different as in the example of Palm Sunday in the previous section. Did Israel or the Jews or even the disciples misinterpret a message that needs to be more clearly understood? Finally, it can be seen from the perspective of opposition. Are there two or more views in conflict or are there two or more views that seem to be in conflict that are being brought together in this pericope?

Once the implication questions are addressed the interpreter can go on and interpret the message in light of the answers to these implication issues. What is the message of this pericope of Scripture to the original readers? Was this a straightforward message or was it a message inside a story or event. Since the Scriptures were addressed to the original hearers in an oral culture there are many oral culture methods used in communication. One of the methods was the use of a story to communicate truth. These were true stories, but they were communicated deliberately in such a way to communicate a message with intentional implications and nuances inside of the story. This is the hard work of interpretation and is much like the work of translating a text from one language to another language. However, with practice, this ability to analyze and interpret the text improves. This is why there is a need to do  interpretation in the context of the community. Interpreters help one another and it is in the context of the dialogue in the church that we discover Scripture as we move from observation to interpretation to application to interaction around the text. The researcher moves from the analysis of the text and interpretation to application or appropriating the message of the text into the present context.

Application

Application is taking the message to the first recipients and then appropriating that message to the present context. The researcher does not want to read into the text preconceived ideas. In addition, the researcher does not want to just apply the message in any way that is convenient for the modern context. Instead, the researcher needs to draw out from the text the message that is timeless to be applied in the present context. Once the interpretation has been made clear the next move is to decontextualize it and then recontextualize it. In other words, the process is to take the message without any cultural baggage that is not part of the message then to put it into the present context making allowances for those in the modern context in how they would understand the message. It needs to be the same message but in a way that is clearly understandable in the present context. An example is found in the story of Jesus on Palm Sunday. There was a message in the story. The message is all of the leaders and people who should have seen Jesus as the real Messiah saw Him but with erroneous understandings that had huge implications. Then moving to application for the present context in that this is a warning to us. Today leaders and believers must carefully understand God and His direction for them. It is quite possible to be sincerely wrong due to preconceived ideas and a worldview that is limited. This wrong view can have serious ramifications for generations. Leaders must lead carefully in having a big enough view of God and His work without which leaders and followers can miss their time or their call or an important moment.

Example

There have already been a couple of examples of this process in this section. However, one more will be developed. In 1 Peter 4:12–19, Peter is exhorting his hearers about an issue that continues throughout his epistle. It is the issue of suffering and Peter begins to take up this topic early in this writing in 1 Peter chapter 1 and continues intermittently to discuss and reconfigure suffering through the end of 1 Peter chapter 5. However, in the middle of this discussion, Peter focuses on this issue in 1 Peter chapter 4 begins with an exhortation to arm themselves with an understanding of suffering. Much of this discussion will focus on leadership as an example of exegetical study for the social sciences; however, the principles can be applied to various constructs.

First, since the researcher will have already addressed intertexture issues it would have been seen that Peter has reconfigured suffering in 1 Peter. It was assumed by good Jews that suffering was a sign of the displeasure of God and prospering was a sign of God's approval. This is the reason that the disciples were troubled in the gospels when Jesus said it was difficult for the rich to enter the Kingdom of heaven (Matthew 19:23). At that point, they were mystified and asked Jesus who then could enter the kingdom. However, Peter takes this concept of suffering and based upon the suffering of Christ turns it around and reconfigures suffering as part of the life of the believer in knowing and following the Lord. In 1 Peter, it is found that suffering is part of the development of our faith and it is a place of rejoicing. It shows God is at work in us and it is not God's displeasure but God's work and connection to us.

In 1 Peter 4:12–19, English Standard Version (ESV) there are interpretive issues to be found in Inner Texture and intertexture analysis. However, social and cultural texture analysis is also instructive. The first step is to look for the words or concepts for each of the views from the special topics or worldviews (Table 8.1).

Table 8.1 1 Peter 4:12–19 Social and Cultural Texture

Worldview	Key words	Key concepts	Intensity
Conversionist	–	–	N/A
Revolutionist	Judgment		Brief
Introversionist	–	–	N/A
Gnostic-Manipulationist	Therefore, Do not	Words of instruction	High
Thaumaturgical	Testing, suffering, suffers	Comfort to those that are suffering	High

In this analysis is found three worldviews but only two with high intensity. The two of Gnostic Manipulationist and Thaumaturgical work together in this pericope to develop a clear and surprising message about suffering: how to be comforted in the midst of inevitable suffering.

Now the researcher must move from observation to interpretation. What was the message to the 1st century recipients of this text? Then what was the message surrounding the instruction about suffering and how to respond and even be comforted in the midst of suffering? Based upon this teaching concerning responding to suffering it will bring comfort and even joy here in this present life (Table 8.2).

Table 8.2 1 Peter 4:12–19 Instructions About Suffering

Verse	Words	Instructions
4:12	Fiery ordeal, testing	Do not be surprised, this is not strange
4:13	Share, sufferings	Share sufferings of Christ—rejoice (present imperfect tense)—future rejoice at revelation of His glory
4:14	Reviled	For the name of Christ—blessed Spirit rests on you
4:15	suffers	Not self-caused suffering
4:16	suffers	As a Christian no shame but glorify God
4:17	Judgment	Begins in the household of God
4:19	Suffer	In the will of God—entrust souls to creator in doing what is right

These concepts are set in the context of verse 10 that is an instruction on how to be a good steward of the many-faceted grace of God. A steward was a head servant or the leader of the servants in a particular context or household. Then Peter gives instructions to stewards about speaking and serving then moves into this extended instruction about how to deal with suffering.

The servant leader is being instructed by Peter to speak well, serve well and suffer well. There is an extended section on suffering since this is reconfiguring a deeply embedded concept in their cultural thinking that is incongruent with God's way of thinking and action concerning suffering. There are different kinds of suffering here in general—suffering which could include many different aspects of trouble—however, it is clear that it is not to be suffering caused by the believer; it is not to come from the results of sowing ungodliness. Instead, this suffering is the result of life and even of being a Christian. There are fiery ordeals that would be difficult circumstances that come from life or the pursuit of God and these can also be trials that test. These events can come from the Lord as in Deuteronomy 8 when the Lord tested Israel by causing them to hunger in the wilderness and then feeding them with manna to see if they would follow the Lord in this situation. Suffering can also be found in the form of being reviled by others for doing what is right or for following the Lord. However, there is also a judgment aspect here as well. Judgment is not always a negative outcome—a judgment can also be to press someone to change or grow. Suffering can come from others; it can come from our circumstances or it can come from God as well.

This pericope also gives instruction to bring change in the life of the believer. This is a change in perspective, actions and outcomes. First it is a change in attitude or perspective in that the believer is not to be surprised by these sufferings this is part of the process of life and of spiritual life as well. The attitude during suffering is to suffer with Christ and in the name of Christ. In other words, even suffering is Christ centered, it is an issue of faith not just the natural life here on earth. These sufferings are part of being in the household of God and part of the growth process as a believer in the purposes of God. There are also changed actions here for those in suffering. The new action is the opposite of traditional actions in suffering. Instead of sackcloth and mourning, the believer is to rejoice, to find joy in the midst of the suffering. This joy is not just future joy, though that is included, it is also present joy. It goes on to instruct the believer to not be ashamed but instead give glory to God—give honor to God in the midst of this suffering in that God is working and the believer is entrusting self to God who is working for good. There are different results then as a result of these changed perspectives and actions. The new results are the presence of the Spirit resting on the believer and instead of a life of shame in suffering now it is a life in bringing honor to God.

The application of this text is rather straightforward. Leaders must learn to speak well, serve well and suffer well. Why suffer well? There are several reasons. One is to be able to embrace the process of suffering and spiritual growth for the process of becoming more mature as a believer. This process in the life of the leader becomes an example for others to follow since this concept of suffering well is for all believers. Then for the leaders to provide comfort for those who are suffering they must first get comfort in suffering for themselves. This would become part of their speaking and serving well to help others understand this process so that they will not be surprised by suffering. Many new believers think that when they get saved that suffering is over because they are right with God. However, this is based on a faulty premise that needs to be explained by leaders as they comfort those who are in trouble or suffering. How does one receive comfort in suffering today? This comfort comes from a change in perspective and actions with changed results. Today, the believer is to respond to suffering by first understanding that this is not unusual; that this is suffering with Christ and in the name of Christ. Having the understanding that this is not abandonment from God, but it is the work of God in bringing change and this brings comfort as well. Therefore, the believers now entrust themselves to God to bring good change and for good in their future. Then there are new actions that seem counterintuitive. The primary action is to rejoice and to find joy in the midst of the trouble in one's connection to God and His work. The believer is to glorify God, to honor God help others to see God's work in this situation as well. The results are a life of rejoicing both present and future, with a life that honors God and a life that is changed by God. It becomes a life that is focused on the Lord and not shame with the Spirit resting upon this believer. Leaders need to learn this truth, embrace this reality, live this process and comfort others by instructing them in this process.

Common Social and Cultural Topics

Common social and cultural topics address the overall environment in a text and knowing these common topics helps the researcher avoid both ethnocentric and anachronistic interpretations (Robbins, 1996a). Discovering and understanding these common topics of the people of the original text shows where a distinction needs to be drawn between contemporary culture and 1st century modes of behavior and understanding. A dimension of the social and cultural texture of a text concerns the social and cultural systems and institutions that it presupposes and evokes, which in rhetorical terms is analyzing common topics that began in New Testament studies using cultural anthropology as a major source (Robbins, 1996b). These systems and institutions are those that would be common knowledge to the people in the world of the text, but they are not familiar to those in the 21st century context. In addition, a great amount of material has been applied to this area from the New Testament context but more needs to be done concerning the Old Testament context for this area of study.

An anachronism is imposing the cultural meanings and behaviors of your own period on the people of the past and the way to avoid misinterpretations through such ethnocentric anachronisms is to understand the culture from which the foreign writings come—and it would be good to understand our own cultural story as well (Malina, 2001). This understanding of the culture and the cultural story is what this section of interpretation addresses. It is different than social or cultural intertexture in that social inter texture addresses how the text interacts with some of the common knowledge of the world of the day in areas like roles and institutions. These common topics deal with the areas of relationships. Cultural intertexture is more about a reference to something in the culture that would be understandable only in that culture like an allusion or an echo. Whereas social and culture texture is more about the connections between people and how they work out. Social or cultural intertexture is information that was readily recognizable by those in the culture. Social and cultural texture is there in the culture and could be discussed by insiders in the culture, but the definitions are clearer from an outside perspective. For example, we live in an urban independent context but without some training in this area, it would be difficult for us to define this concept and understand it though we live in it every day. In addition, it deeply impacts our priorities and communications in ways that often go unexamined by us. Social scientists examine it and help us understand it. In Scripture study we are those social scientists. Social and cultural texture has specific areas of inquiry that can help the researcher find specific areas for important research in common topics.

There are several studies and books that can help in this area of research for both Old and New Testaments (Malina, 2001; Yamauchi & Wilson, 2017). Research in this area will yield rich rewards for the study of social and cultural texture. The following are areas of research that can help in the examination of common topics.

Honor, Guilt, and Rights Cultures

In the male-dominated cultures of the time of Scripture, honor is marked by boundaries of power, sexual status, and position in society and it is related to the social acknowledgment of worth (Robbins, 1996a). This concept of honor brought certain rights to those who were higher on the social ladder and the way of society was for men to promote and pronounce their honor to others and try to move up this social ladder. The female aspect of this kind of society is called shame and this refers to being sensitive to what others think, say and do with regard to his or her honor (Robbins, 1996a). The male place is aggressive in seeking honor while the female place is more passive in being sensitive to others rather than trying to displace others through accumulating honor. The young men that were written to in these texts in Philippians as new leaders were probably tempted to seek to make their own way in the Greco-Roman world and to establish their honor and honor claims in public (Witherington, 2009). Therefore, when Peter writes to leaders in 1 Peter 5 to not seek personal gain or dominance through leadership but instead lead by example and care while developing humility instead of honor, this is clearly in the opposite direction of societal norms. So it is today in that training for leadership that is biblical is actually countercultural pointing leaders in the direction of humility. The leader is to seek to help elevate others by providing an example and in humility considering others first with a desire to do the will of God instead of a focus on self-will.

In the story of the woman washing the feet of Jesus and anointing Him with perfume is seen the interactions of this culture between honor and shame (John 12). Mary comes and pours expensive perfume on Jesus and washes His feet with her hair. She is thinking in terms of shame based in her cultural thinking. She is being sensitive to the honor due to Jesus. She expresses it in ways that would be found to be repugnant or outright immoral today. Jesus does not stop her. However, Judas objects; he thinks the money should be used for the poor. However, this is only a ruse since he wants more money to steal since he was the treasurer. The motives of Judas are seen to be impure. He was seeking to establish his honor by enriching himself. His motives were clearly wrong but who would steal from Jesus. Even if Judas only thought Jesus was a great earthly messiah, he would need an overriding reason to steal. He was trying to build his own honor. This was a cultural priority—almost a mandate—for men in the Roman and even the Jewish culture of the day. This is a warning to us today to weigh carefully our priorities. Do we have cultural priorities and motives that are contrary to the purpose of God but they are so embedded in us that we cannot see them? What was the root issue here even behind the issue of honor? It was self-exaltation. Modern culture still adopts these concepts of self-exaltation but not under the guise of seeking honor instead it comes under the guise of identity and being your own person and even self-reliance in creating your own way. These are not necessarily innately bad, but the question is whether these can distort our motives to the point that we are willing to steal from the Lord for our own gain. This is not necessarily about taking money, but it could be taking time or special gifts that are meant for the Lord in some way and instead focusing on self-exaltation instead of God's purpose and glory. You may not be called to buy perfume for the Lord, but you could be called to give of self in some way that may even be sacrificial so that someone else can buy the perfume.

Dyadic Agreements

In a world of limited goods, these are informal reciprocity agreements that are initiated by means of positive challenges, invitations, or gifts that were to be met in an ongoing reciprocity relationship (Malina, 2001). Once a person gives these gifts to another person it sets up an imbalance that must be met in kind. It is never fully balanced in a back and forth giving and receiving situation between the two people. These informal contracts can be between equals (colleague contract) or different statuses setting up patron–client contracts in this latter case and these contracts are the glue that hold individuals together for long or short terms (Robbins, 1996a). There are no free gifts— just gifts that mark the beginning of an ongoing reciprocal relationship and in the case of a patron–client contract it can tie people together from significantly different social statuses (Malina, 2001). These relationships are understood in the context of this worldview along with the unspoken relational implications. Malina (2001) gives an example of this implicit understanding in that this sort of dyadic contractual relationship is what bothers Jesus' critics when he eats with sinners and tax collectors. This implied that Jesus was in some type of reciprocal informal contract of give and take with this group of people who were considered extremely evil. Even the relationship with God was considered in this light as God as the patron therefore repayment was considered important for gifts received from the Lord (Malina, 2001). This type of relational contract permeated the thinking of the people of this society in ways that went unnoticed as they were part of the habits of relationship. Therefore, when these interactions are viewed from the context of contemporary society some of the nuances that are obvious to those of the culture of the day are missed or even misread.

An example of this type of thinking is found in John 13 when Jesus washes the feet of the disciples. The teacher disciple relationship was a patron–client contract and the patron was to offer the one of lower status a favor that could not be received another way (Malina, 2001). This is what was expected. Instead, Jesus as the patron offers a common service that should have been a client offering to a patron. This is one of the reasons that Peter is bewildered and would not let Jesus wash his feet at first. Jesus is indicating not only a change in normal leadership concepts; He is also indicating a change in relationships and how relationships are developed. Normally this patron–client relationship would always be among those not equal. Jesus was teaching them how to have relationships even as leaders. Leaders are not patrons to offer favors, but they are equals to offer service and love instead of reciprocity. This is seen in other places in Jesus allowing even the unclean to touch Him and then he goes further in touching dead bodies. These do not make Him unclean; instead, He makes them clean. To the 1st century mind, this paradoxical mindset taught about love expecting nothing in return in sharp contrast to giving for the sake of reciprocity or getting something back. The power of Jesus' position and life as Messiah did not come from the reciprocal relationship but instead from the power of love which is giving without expectation of return. This message permeates the gospels, but it is brought into sharp focus once it is seen against the backdrop of the expected dyadic contracts of the society of the time.

Dyadic personalities are those that need another person in order to know who they are, and their self-perception is formed in terms of what others perceive of them (Robbins, 1996a). This way of thinking is quite distinct almost opposite from the current individualistic mindset. This is not to say that modern individuals do not struggle with issues of self-perception and identity. The modern person has these same struggles but views the way of dealing with them differently. The modern person may take comfort or even find identity in being different or independent or innovative. These were not positive concepts in the 1st century. Something that was novel, or an innovation was considered wrong or even evil. This is one of the reasons that Christians tied Christianity to Old Testament Judaism but also to some Greek philosophies in showing that Christianity was not novel or new but tied to historic religious issues and ideas. Identity among the peoples of this time was usually connected to the family history and who they were related to or their genealogy and this was true even in Old Testament Judaism. Robbins (1996a) gives an example of this kind of personality in Pilate who was concerned about his status with both Jesus and the crowd. This relational dichotomy sent Pilate down a road of decision making that was weak and vacillating. His leadership was not servant leadership in serving others instead it was more like modern leadership that is personality-driven and driven by the latest opinion polls. He was more concerned about others' perception of him than in leading well or making the right decisions. As a result, he becomes an eternal example of a weak insecure leader. Even in his interview with Jesus, he was more concerned about getting Jesus to understand the power that he held over Jesus than at understanding the real situation.

In addition, this is seen in the Old Testament in the ministry of Aaron, the brother of Moses. As long as Moses was around Aaron did fine in his leadership role. He was in a dyadic relationship with Moses who was a strong leader. However, Moses goes up on the mountain for an extended time. This dyadic relationship changes to the crowd or

Israel as a group. They convince him to forge a golden calf for worship. This leads to a major disaster and many people dying. However, Aaron's excuse was that he put the gold into the fire and out came this calf. He was trying to warm up to Moses again in this dyadic relationship. This helps to see the weakness of leadership that is driven even by the best of human relationships. An insecure leader is a dangerous leader. There is a certain independence needed for leaders, but this dyadic relationship of the leader needs to be formed with God like Jesus who only did what He saw the father doing.

Challenge–Response (Riposte)

In this system of honor and shame, honor is acquired by excelling over others in social interaction that is called challenge and response wherein certain persons hassle each other according to particular socially defined rules to gain the honor of another (Malina, 2001). This is a socially acceptable concept for a person with lesser honor in society to gain honor or to climb the social ladder. This is a system of communication done in public so that the sender, receiver and the public can see this process of gaining honor in society. Bekker (2007) declares that the text in Philippians 2:5–11 shows a method of leadership that is opposed to this way of honor, or *cursus honorum*, that was a sequence of public offices as a prescribed social pilgrimage for those aspiring to public offices and acclaim. This way of honor was a very public process of honor for those desiring public leadership. This timocratic leadership was an approach that is focused on honor, power and prestige (Bekker, 2008). This type of interaction has three phases: (a) the challenge which comes through word or deed; (b) the perception of the message by the public and the recipient of the message; and (c) the reaction of the receiver and the evaluation by the public (Malina, 2001). In addition, any of these three phases can be negative or positive. In looking for this concept in Scripture look for the patterns of challenge and response that is public or perceived by the public. These can be seen in many different contexts as in the life and ministry of Jesus or the epistles or in the Old Testament in challenges to kings from prophets.

A good Old Testament example could be found in the book of Job. Job as the main character is challenged by his "friends" while he is in his misery. They are looking for a way to increase their honor at the expense of Job's or in light of his recent mishaps which seems to mean to them that Job has fallen out of favor with God. They are looking for a way to excel over Job at the expense of Job. However, Job responds to their challenge and ultimately God responds and honors Job while bringing dishonor to these "friends" of Job.

In the New Testament Jesus does not always play this social game with those that challenge Him. When Jesus is confronted by Pilate, Jesus for the most part remains silent. In some sense, this could be part of this process. However, it is significant that Pilate is astonished at Jesus' lack of response. Pilate was trying to show himself as superior to Jesus at the trial, but it did not work, and Pilate tried to wash his hands of the whole event. Another time we see Jesus in Mark 2 being confronted by a group of people who wanted to know why His disciples did not fast. The underlying implication may have been that the disciples who fast are better or have more honor than those that do not fast. However, Jesus turns the tables on them by saying they will fast when the Bridegroom is gone inferring that He is the bridegroom. This should have given them pause right there. All good Jews knew that the Bridegroom was a reference to the Messiah and his connection to Israel. He was claiming to be this bridegroom. However, he does not stop here. He pushes the issue even further in discussing sayings concerning unshrunk garments and new wine. He was pushing them to consider new ways of knowing God or of their religion. Scripture does not tell us how the people responded. Nevertheless, in this exchange the people do not gain honor. The goal of Jesus here is not to help the people to gain honor but to gain understanding. Was this a challenge to this system of seeking honor? Nevertheless, He responded in a surprising way that was not the norm.

Even in the following story in the Book of Mark Jesus is challenged by the Pharisees about harvesting grain to eat on the Sabbath (Mark 2:23–24). This was a challenge where the Pharisees were looking to establish their honor at the expense of Jesus and His honor. Jesus pushes back and they do not gain honor here. In fact, they lose honor as they are seen as not knowing the Scriptures as well as Jesus. Jesus proves His position by quoting Scripture like the Pharisees or even Satan would do to Him. However, he does not stop here. He goes on with a new declaration about the Son of Man and the Sabbath. He was pushing to change their thinking about Him and the Sabbath. He moved past the honor issue to an issue of spirituality and understanding of the truth of Scripture not just a battle of Scripture verses. He won the honor game, but His purpose was larger than this issue of honor it became an issue of an understanding or revelation of God and His work. This is more important than honor or prestige and Jesus declared this message in many diverse ways but for the 1st century mind it would have been difficult to receive. Truthfully though the people of the 21st century have different ideas about honor it is still difficult for us to receive.

Economic Exchange Systems

The context of 1st century economic system is agrarian-based exchange systems rather than urban-centered and this is the foundation of many of the statements made during the New Testament period (Robbins, 1996a). Therefore, people in this era would work to maintain inherited social status rather than work to get richer and it was a closed society wherein all goods were considered to be limited (Malina, 2001).

The world was viewed as having limited goods and this permeated the thinking of the people to the point that it impacted not only economics but also other decisions. The honorable person did not strive to accumulate capital since this would do harm to the community (Malina, 2001). Since goods were limited if someone accumulated capital it meant that it had to be decreased or taken from someone else. It was not just an economic issue it was also an issue of honor. This is one of the reasons that tax collectors were disliked in that they were considered as lacking honor. In this system, there was reciprocity in that those in the tribe would freely give to each other and those who were close but for those not in the tribe there was a weak reciprocity wherein exchanges were allowed but it had to counterbalanced with equal gifts in return, but an outsider was fair game for haggling, cheating and lying (Robbins, 1996a). Tax collectors who were from the tribes of Israel acted like outsiders in their dealings with Israel increasing the lack of trust and honor given to them. Money or wealth is not the determinant of social status here, but status comes from birth and being considered poor is not necessarily a declaration of their economic situation (Malina, 2001). The system was set up for people to gain and lose honor not money. Money was part of the system and there are many exhortations about finances in the Scriptures, but it was written into a context that viewed money and goods differently.

An example of this can be found in the agrarian-based system as found in the Old Testament as well. In dealing with the poor and foreigners Israel had a law in Leviticus 19 that forbade landowners from gleaning their fields all the way to the edges of the field. In other words, they were required to leave some corn, grapes, figs, and grain for the poor or foreigners to eat. Jesus and His disciples are seen doing this gleaning and eating from the fields in Mark 2. This was a way to develop a just society in an agrarian-based economy with a limited goods view. Notice here two things. It assumes that there are those who have more than others. In addition, there is no outcry for a redistribution of wealth or for the landowners to give land to the poor. Instead, they are to care for them in this way. This is seen in the book of Ruth when Ruth gleans behind the workers of Boaz (Ruth 2:2–3). It is in this context that Boaz seeks to marry Ruth. There is not a plan for Ruth and Naomi to buy land and to start their own enterprise. Certainly, she had to become part of the existing system of the family in some way since there were no ways to create new resources. The entire cultural world of this limited goods agrarian system played out in this context and God met with them in the context of their culture to provide help for them in their context. However, Jesus did challenge this way of thinking in different ways. When he needed to pay a temple tax, He received money from a fish through the fishing of Peter (Matthew 17:27). This was a miracle, but it was also a challenge to the limited goods view.

Purity Codes

Purity is about boundaries separating certain matters and issues where the impure is something that does not fit in the space in which it is found wherein everyone and everything has a proper place and time (Malina, 2001). In Israel, there were classifications of people by certain classes like Priest, Levites, Israelites all the way down to Gentiles (Robbins, 1996a). However, there were also certain events or activities that would make a person impure. Once someone was impure, there were certain rituals that were to be followed to achieve ritual purity again. This was an issue for both Old and New Testament contexts. These laws of purity are found in several different Old Testament texts such as Numbers 5:2, ESV. Here impurity is explained as being caused by touching a dead body or by leprosy or if someone has a discharge from their body. There are many other examples like this one and there are even time periods or rituals that are mentioned to bring purity back to the person. This was deeply embedded in the thinking and views of Israelites in both Old Testament and New Testament contexts.

A striking example of this reality is found in the gospels in Mark 5:21–43, ESV. Jesus is on His way to heal a girl of her disease in response to a request from her father who was one of the rulers of the synagogue. On the way a woman with an issue of blood that had continued for years came into the crowd around Jesus. This woman was unclean or impure due to the nature of her physical ailment. Those who were unclean knew they were not to touch other people since this would make them unclean as well. This woman goes up and touches Jesus and is instantly healed of her malady. Jesus asks who had touched Him. The disciples told Jesus that there was a crowd and it would be impossible to determine if one person had touched Him. However, this woman came forward and confessed. Nevertheless, instead of her making Jesus unclean, Jesus had cleansed her of her disease. Jesus is so powerful that His power goes beyond resistance to impurity in that He can cleanse impurity. However, the story is not over, this is simply a convenient interruption. Notice how Mark links these two stories together one within the other. This is an intercalation. In our passion to discover timelines in Scripture, we forget that oral cultures tend to link stories together not by time but by internal connections. The story goes on but takes a turn for the worst. The young girl has died. Jesus is not deterred from this healing mission by this seemingly story stopping news. He continues to the house, lays His hands on the dead girl and she rises from the dead. Again, this girl being dead was impure and if someone touched her body that person would become impure. Nevertheless, when Jesus touches her instead of impurity being transferred to Him, she is raised from the dead. Jesus is more powerful than any uncleanness and even more powerful than the ultimate in impurity, death. The power of Jesus to bring purity does not just stop impurity it changes the rules. It changes the recipient of the power; His power is not just stopping disease it is giving life. He is not just the cure to impurity He is more powerful than that and He brings not just purity but new life that is surprising and full. He changes the rules of impurity and moves the focus from dealing with the impurity to a new focus on full life.

Old Testament Law

The Old Testament had not only purity laws but also laws of all sorts having to do with many more issues than that of purity. There were ceremonial laws that were religious, there were laws about marriage, laws about worship, and relationships. There were laws about dealing with theft or murder and there were laws particularly for Levites or priests. There are many more than 10 commandments in the Old Testament. Some see as many as 613 distinct commands in the Old Testament (Eisenberg, 2005). You thought 10 was difficult to keep up with and understand. This is not to say that the believer must go back and discover all of these laws and try to obey them with a new legalism.

The book of Galatians and Romans would prevent us from moving in that direction. However, it is important to see and recognize them to aid in understanding some of the issues of both Old and New Testaments. For instance, the Sabbath and Festival laws are very important laws in the Old Testament. As a result, these become interpretive issues in different texts in both Old and New Testament studies. Old Testament studies become very important in this area of research to be able to see and understand how these laws impact the life, people and culture of both Old and New Testaments.

For example, Sabbath keeping was one of the 10 commandments and there were other laws or regulations that were given in exactly how to keep the Sabbath holy. This concept of Sabbath permeated the culture of the Old Testament and even the land was to keep a Sabbath rest every seventh year where it was not farmed but the people were to live off of the fruit from the previous year (Lev. 25:3–7). This became very important as the people were told when they went into captivity that one of the reasons was that they did not let the land have her Sabbaths (Lev. 26:32–35; 2 Chron. 36:20–21; Jer. 25:11–12). The land would now keep her Sabbaths since the Israelites could not farm the land because they were in captivity. In the New Testament, the Jews are extremely zealous for the Sabbath. The Pharisees consistently questioned Jesus about His interaction with the Sabbath and the Sabbath laws. Then in Mark 2 He tells them that He is Lord of the Sabbath and that they have misunderstood the Sabbath. How is this to be understood? Part of it is that the Sabbath is all about connection to the Lord and this is ultimately found in Jesus not in a religious system. To see this clearly one would need to understand all of the issues and regulations about this all-important Sabbath. The Pharisees missed the point because they really did not understand the Sabbath and its regulations. Let us not commit the same error. In addition, there are festival laws and Sabbath laws having to do with the temple or tabernacle of the Lord. The analogies and issues of the temple are scattered throughout both testaments and good Israelites or Jews caught the analogies and declarations, but they can often be missed if these laws are not clearly in mind and understood in the interpretation of the text. In one book in the New Testament, there are hundreds of allusions and echoes from the Old Testament that are interpretive keys to the book. That is the book of

Chapter 8: Working Through Socio-Rhetorical Analysis—Social and Cultural Texture

Revelation. John the author knew these topics common to the Jewish culture and the people in the church to whom it was written knew them as well. Everyone in the room, the writer, the reader of John's day and the audience of this era all knew these topics and their significance. The problem is that we were not in the room and we are still not in the room. As these topics are rediscovered by the contemporary reader then we are able to come back into the room to hear the message of the text.

Final Cultural Categories

Final cultural categories of rhetoric are those topics that most decisively identify one's cultural location and this concerns the way people present their propositions, reasons and arguments (Robbins, 1996a). These locations show the particular group that the person or group belongs to and how they think in distinction to others. This has to do with social or cultural strata that a person or group belongs to and thereby views reality from this perspective. Analysis of cultural alliances and conflicts in New Testament discourse is in its infancy but a look at different kinds of basic culture can give new insights to some studies that have already been developed (Robbins, 1996b). These final cultural categories examine the connections between those in the text with different areas of culture that can be seen in all different types of culture moving from dominant culture to subcultures including five different types of cultural strata and cultural rhetoric. As the researcher approaches biblical literature cultural topics appear in the form of cultural rhetoric and the sociology of culture provides insight on the different kinds of culture (Robbins, 1996a).

Before moving to the descriptions of these five types of cultural rhetoric it is important to notice several important concepts that will help with research in this area. The answer to the issues of which strata of culture is found in the text is the issue of rhetoric with the arguments or discussions that are formed in the text. In addition, these different ways of argument or discussion can be described by the sociology of culture or by the ways people interact who are from different levels or strata in culture. Defining and describing as well as finding these different final categories in the text will help the researcher understand the nuances of the discussion. In addition, notice that there are different cultural locations inside of any given culture. In other words, a culture can be a system of a certain ethnolinguistic group but inside of that group, there can be dominant as well as liminal cultures or locations of culture. In addition, these dominant and liminal or subgroups can also be

seen in relationships between different ethnolinguistic groups. The differentiation is found in the rhetoric that is used in each group and this differentiation can become clearer as they come into proximity to each other. The clues of these different kinds of culture are in the actions, priorities, and even words of those in the culture.

An example of this differentiation in final cultural categories is found in a story of a missionary. This missionary went from the United States to a Latin American country and began to live with an indigenous group of people. He learned the language and customs. He walked with them, worked with them and in all obvious ways became one of them. He even changed his appearance and looked like them. After quite some time he went into a small area store to buy some food. The lady at the counter called to him with a name that meant she knew he was not one of them. He asked her how she knew he was not one of them. She could not say at first and needed to think about it because it was not obvious to her at first. After some thought, she said it was because of the way he walked. The indigenous people walk with their heads down and shoulders forward as if they are carrying a burden. People from the United States (from a dominant culture particularly) walk with their shoulders back and enter the room as if they own the place. This was so much part of him that he did not know that he needed to work on it but it was obvious to others. So, it is with these different kinds of culture. There are clues that are linguistic and even embedded in the way rhetoric is used. In this story, it was not just his posture, but it was his attitude. The people of the Old and New Testaments did not think in these terms of whether they were in a dominant culture. However, the reality of dominant and subculture existed and can be seen just as clearly. For the researcher though the point is that this helps in understanding the message to understand the perspective from which it comes into the discourse.

This concept of cultural rhetoric is an important one in this research area. Rhetoric is the art of persuasion and Aristotle insisted that rhetoric was so important that it was not fully separable from philosophy (Witherington, 2009). It is using words to convince people of an argument and it is a way to use words. In this way of using words, one's philosophy came through since the rhetoric is founded upon beliefs that need description so others can believe. There are different aspects to rhetoric, but a major part is words and how they were used. Our research in the texts of Scripture works with words and arguments and these arguments can reveal the underlying philosophies of the speakers and this helps in finding the speakers cultural location when the researcher knows the different descriptions of different cultural rhetoric. Rhetoric or the art of persuasion is the method and the language that is used in each different cultural category to explain and persuade others both inside of their category as well as those outside of it. This is the area of final cultural categories.

This first step in the process is to visit the descriptions of these five kinds of final cultural categories or cultural locations. Nevertheless, descriptions are not enough without some discussion of how to recognize them in the text and the discourses. Then there will be some practical applications as well in finding these categories in the text of Scripture in both Old and New Testaments.

Chapter 8: Working Through Socio-Rhetorical Analysis—Social and Cultural Texture

Dominant Culture Rhetoric

Dominant cultural rhetoric is a system of attitudes values and norms that the person presupposes, or asserts are supported by social structures vested with power to impose its goals on people (Robbins, 1996a). These are the people in power or what is called the majority culture not in that they are the most numerous, but they are the ones with the most power in the culture. The dominant culture is designated this way because it controls greater wealth and power and is more able to impose its view of the world on other aspects of the culture while they retain their power through control of institutions and in contemporary society public schools as well as media help to maintain their message (Nanda & Warms, 2018). This aspect of culture brings the message of the prominent ideas of the society and culture in which it resides. These dominant culture ideas tend to permeate the culture. However, this is not consistent in that the other categories push back against this message in different ways or forms. For the researcher these messages are important and even finding the source of these messages in cultural categories helps to clearly understand the message in its context.

Subculture Rhetoric

Subculture rhetoric imitates the attitudes values and norms of the dominant culture claiming to enact them better than the dominant culture whereas an ethnic subculture has its origins in a different language from the dominant group and they attack a few elements of the larger society but not the society as a whole (Robbins, 1996a). This rhetoric is different than the dominant culture in either degree (they do it better) or kind (they have changed it). This difference is seen in their discourse and responses to the dominant culture. An ethnic subculture attempts to preserve an old way of life or system in a dominant cultural system (Robbins, 1996b). This rhetoric is seen in the response to the dominant system by adhering to old ways, which brings them some cohesion or pride in their better cultural norms than the dominant culture. Subcultures are smaller units found within larger cultures and a subculture is different from the larger culture in that it has a cluster of behavior patterns that are related to the general culture but distinct in some ways (Grunlan & Mayers, 1988). A subculture is a smaller culture with some distinctions and though different it is not necessarily antagonistic to the dominant culture.

Counterculture Rhetoric

Countercultural rhetoric evokes the creation of a better society through its rhetoric by providing an alternative with the hope that the dominant society will see this new way of life but allowing the dominant society to go on with their way with the hope of voluntary reform of the culture (Robbins, 1996a). This rhetoric is different than the dominant rhetoric in providing a different way, yet it is also distinct from a subculture in that its goal is not the preservation of old ways but living presentations of new and better ways. The stories that express the worldview of a group provide answers to the questions of identity, environment, evil and eschatology and these worldviews are the precognitive stage of a culture (Wright, 1992). Countercultures have an alternative worldview that creates a different rhetoric. Worldviews include a praxis and the worldview of a person can often be seen in the actions that are performed and the goal of life and to ignore this in the study of culture would result in extraordinary shallowness (Wright, 1992). The rhetoric of countercultures will speak to this difference in praxis and teleology in its rhetoric. Rhetoric is the language used to explain and persuade others both inside of their category as well as those outside of it. A counterculture community will prefer this form of persuasion rather than other forms like withdrawal or violence.

Contraculture Rhetoric

Contracultural rhetoric is a short-lived group culture rhetoric that is primarily a reaction to some form of the dominant culture, subculture, or counterculture rhetoric and so it reacts in a negative way to certain values or practices in another culture (Robbins, 1996a). This is a reaction to existing issues in other cultures and it can be seen in revolutionary movements that are opposed to others but do not have a viable alternative way ahead. The element of conflict is central in the contraculture though the conflict need not be violent, but it will be creative as it develops responses to the dominant culture (Heddendorf & Vos, 2010). This is also known as oppositional cultural rhetoric (Robbins, 1996a). This conflict in this cultural category can be violent in its opposition to the dominant culture as seen in some of the revolutionary movements of the past and the present. The rhetoric in this category is in opposition to other categories of culture to their values, norms, or activities with the goal of creating change and even pressing for change. Rhetoric is used by those in this contracultural category, but it can be used with other means of persuasion or pressure as well.

Liminal Rhetoric (Transitional, Minimal Rationality)

Liminal culture exists in the language it has for the moment and it appears as people transition from one cultural identity to another or with groups who have never been able to establish a clear cultural identity in their setting and it starts and stops without consistency or coherence (Robbins, 1996a). It is the rhetoric of groups in transition or migration. It could be seen as the culture being in fragments from oppression, conquest or suffering especially if these events are long-term situations. Liminality is a term that is used in writing fiction and in anthropology. The liminal narrative brings themes of fear and trembling, and this liminality may be defined as a certain kind of chaos inspiring something akin to fear by its newness and the paradoxically productive absence at its center (Phillips, 2015). This liminal cultural rhetoric is transitional and disjointed to the point of chaos and fear. It is not necessarily focused on productive outcomes as much as on the moment. The attributes of liminality are necessarily ambiguous, and these persons slip through the network of classifications that locate them in cultural space with this aspect of culture being likened to death or being in the womb or even invisibility (Alexander & Siedman, 2000). These are the people at the fringes of society or the invisible people who are at the point of chaos from fear and transitions.

Application

The first step here as in some previous studies is a general read through of the pericope or text to be interpreted. In this read through the interpreter is looking for language or concepts that indicate one of the five cultural rhetorics in this category. These concepts can be either very overt or covert in the context of the discussion or the story. This rhetoric can also be understood by knowing some of the backgrounds of the groups involved in the interactions of the text. It could be a teaching to a group of people and then the rhetoric would be found more clearly in the language itself. The researcher should attempt to determine the rhetorical situation of the unit and in this process should examine the persons, events, objects and relationships involved (Kennedy, 1984). These are the preliminary issues to be observed and documented in this process. Then the researcher needs to ask of who the audience consists, what the audience expects in the situation and how the speaker addresses these expectations (Kennedy, 1984). This process will involve the words of the text as well as some background understanding as well as an understanding of the interaction itself in the text. Generally, the initial observation will consist of the people, the event, the relationships, the words, and the intent of the speaker. Each category will process some of these issues differently particularly the last category of intent.

In dominant culture rhetoric look for concepts of coming from the position of the ruling power, like the Roman power or the Persian power. These would be declarations or discussions about expectations in normal society. In the persons in the text look for people of cultural power like kings or governors. The speaker usually speaks from a position of authority with the ability to enforce the goals or rules that are given in the speech or text. Intent in this category would be to bring conformity to society or culture and its norms. The question of relationship comes into consideration here as well in determining the kind of interaction that is happening here in whether it is between equals or is occurring in some kind of cultural strata difference. For example, in the discussion between Pilate and Jesus in the trial, Pilate is using dominant culture rhetoric in his declarations to Jesus. Pilate seems puzzled since this rhetoric does not have the intended impact on Jesus (Jn. 19:10, ESV). The intent of Pilate here was to invoke fear in Jesus or to show his superiority in the situation. Jesus instead responds to this rhetoric by asking questions of Pilate, which troubles Pilate on some level since he tries to get out of this situation without invoking his dominant culture privilege of the death penalty over Jesus.

In subculture rhetoric, their worldview is not about dominance and conformity but often it is in preserving their ways in spite of the dominant culture. In this rhetoric look for those that are responding to the dominant culture not as a king or person of authority but as those responding to those in authority by declaring that their way is better or just different. Look for those that are withdrawing from society or those who have a different heritage that are trying to preserve a different way of life. In many ways, the Jews had formed a subculture when they were taken into captivity in the Old Testament era. They learned the language of their captors, but they still spoke the other language of Israel. They lived in the cities with their captors, but they were different, and this difference was represented in the synagogues that were built during this period. An example of this subculture rhetoric can be found in the story of the Gentile woman who comes to Jesus for the healing of her daughter in the gospels (Matt. 1:26–27). In this instance, Jesus is speaking from a dominant culture worldview from a Jewish perspective. He initially rejected her request for healing according to normal Jewish thinking. According to this worldview, Gentiles were inferior and not part of the divine covenant. Nevertheless, she appealed to Him using subculture rhetoric. True she was different she confesses and is not worthy from a Jewish perspective. She is not combative and she understands the issues of the dominant culture. She does not oppose the dominant view in fact she agrees with it. However, then she changes the discussion and appeals for mercy by offering a new way to look at the Gentiles. They might be considered dogs but even dogs deserve mercy. She does not directly challenge the dominant view, but she looks at it differently. Jesus responds and heals her daughter. Notice here that Jesus sets her up to be the one who teaches this lesson about mercy on the Gentiles (and others). Jesus helps her through her subculture rhetoric to teach about mercy and overcoming racism and ethnic division. She teaches the lesson, but Jesus endorses it. Jesus' humility shows through here in that as the great teacher He does not have to be the one to teach directly. He uses others to teach eternal truths even though they may not fully understand it.

Counterculture rhetoric will challenge the dominant thinking of the culture by showing a better way. In this rhetoric look for sections that challenge norms or teachings of the other rhetorical cultures. Subculture thinking is different than the dominant culture but is able to move through life in a different way only challenging the dominant culture indirectly. Whereas counterculture thinking is building a better culture that is a direct challenge to the dominant thinking with different ways of living with the hope that the dominant culture will see the light and change. Countercultural thinking is about a different society, which is an intentional challenge to change the dominant society. An example of countercultural thinking can be seen in Daniel when he challenged his captors to let him eat and drink differently and then for the captor to judge the difference (Daniel 1:8–15). Daniel was a counterculture thinker in many ways throughout the scenarios in the book of Daniel. Then in the New Testament, countercultural rhetoric is seen in the instructions to believers. They are to think and live differently and this is a challenge to those of the dominant culture who do not believe. An example of this rhetoric is found in 1 Peter 3 where Peter tells wives to submit to their husbands. This first phrase matches dominant cultural rhetoric. Then Peter changes rhetorical gears when he tells the wives to win their unbelieving husbands with their godly lifestyle so that their new husbands can see and believe the gospel. This might seem normal to 21st-century believers but to 1st-century believers this was a radical departure from the dominant culture thinking particularly of Rome. In the cultures of the time when a woman married, she was to adapt to the lifestyle and ways of her husband including his religion. She was expected to convert to his religion. This was not a discussion it was just the way it was done. However, Peter says no to this norm of society and the dominant culture. He told the new wives to continue in being a Christian and bring your new husband into the church. This could be very dangerous for her, but this was a new culture—the counterculture of the church. In this way and in other places, it is seen that Scripture consistently challenges dominant culture in many ways, especially in the area of the treatment of women. Scripture spoke into the culture of the moment but challenged it on many levels in developing a counterculture. It could be that the church is designed to work best in a countercultural position. The church does not work best in subcultural rhetoric that withdraws nor in a dominant cultural rhetoric that feeds power issues and pride nor in contracultural rhetoric that can become antagonistic and even violent. Countercultural rhetoric creates an alternative society and invites others to come and live in this new way.

An example of contracultural rhetoric during Jesus' day would be the political group called the zealots. Even one of Jesus' disciples came from this group (Luke 6:15, ESV). This is the rhetoric of revolution and change that needs to be sudden. There is no time or concept for the slow incremental change of society by indirect influence. In the book of Judges Israel would often use this rhetoric when a new Judge would arise to throw off the yoke of the oppressors. In this cultural rhetoric, look for those who are in opposition to others in society and usually there are found negative words or concepts in this thinking. Look for concepts of overthrowing or changing society suddenly. Samson is a good example in that his rhetoric tended to be in opposition to the Philistines. He was a judge in Israel and led Israel, but his major area of leadership was in opposition to the Philistines which he did sporadically (Judges 15:15–20, ESV). Nevertheless, his overall rhetoric was contrary to the Philistines and even his final prayer was contracultural. An example of this type of rhetoric in the New Testament is found in 2 Peter 3:10–12 where Peter describes the coming of the Lord from a macro perspective and how the Lord deals with the kingdoms of this world wherein the world will pass away with a roar suddenly and the instructions are to look forward to and even hasten the coming of this day. Another example is found in Acts 1 when the disciples misunderstand the mission of Jesus even after He rose from the dead. They asked Him if He was going to restore the kingdom to Israel at that time and they were looking for a military oppositional response. However, Jesus guided them back to a more countercultural response. In this context is seen that the message, the mission and even the method of Jesus was countercultural. This is not to say that all His words were countercultural, but His overall plan was countercultural. He did not give the disciples a mandate to become the dominant culture neither were they to become an opposition culture. He did not want them to become just a subculture hidden inside of a dominant culture. Instead, He instructed them to be engaged with dominant cultures of the world as a counterculture. They were to become witnesses of Him and His way of life, faith, and leading. Each of these were and still are countercultural. He did not send them to destroy the world, He did not send them to become the world, he did not send them to hide in the world instead He sent them to counter the world with a new way of living and then to invite those in these other cultures into this new counterculture of the Kingdom of God on the earth. Notice here in Acts 1:8 that he includes a different use of power or a countercultural rhetoric of power. In the dominant rhetoric, power is used to make things happen like restoring Israel but in countercultural rhetoric, power is used to be witnesses to give testimony of this new way of life. In this context, power is not to dominate others it is to help others see the new way. It is to help others rather than to use them for personal gain. Power is used here to help others increase rather than for increase in the one with the power. In this section is seen a contrast between contracultural thinking and countercultural thinking and teaching.

Those using Liminal cultural rhetoric could be refugees or people who have been in captivity and they have lost their way culturally where their concepts are focused on today and maybe even survival rather than consistency or any message or agenda outside of the moment. Nations under oppressive rule will develop some form of liminal cultural rhetoric among the people whereas the leaders will use dominant cultural rhetoric. In this rhetoric look for words or concepts of fear or chaos. The people have usually undergone some type of extreme pressure that has impacted their previous worldview or concepts and they are on their way to another view but not there yet. It sounds confusing because those in this cultural rhetoric are often confused. In the Old Testament, this would be found in the book of Judges but not in the leaders or judges of Israel. Instead, it would be found in the people of Israel like Gideon before the Lord changed him into a judge (Judges 6:11, ESV). He was threshing wheat in a winepress. Normal farmers do not thresh wheat in a winepress. He was hiding and fearful. At first, he could not believe that he was the man for the job since he was the weakest or lowest even of his lowly tribe. Israel was in chaos as was Gideon. This changed in Gideon to a contracultural rhetoric and he led some in this manner but after his death Israel returned to liminal cultural rhetoric. In the New Testament, there is an example of liminal cultural rhetoric in the gospel of Luke 24 after the resurrection when some disciples were met on the road by Jesus. These disciples did not recognize Jesus and they begin to explain to Jesus about the confusing or even chaotic situation they found themselves in at the moment. They were hoping that Jesus was the great prophet and Messiah, but Rome had crucified Him and though some women had said they had seen Him risen some of the men found the empty tomb but hey had not seen Him. These disciples were perplexed and even downtrodden, it is as if they had lost hope that Jesus was the one to deliver them. They were in disarray about the situation since they had not seen Him even with some testimonies from others. Then Jesus, without revealing who He was explained the reality of the Messiah and the prophecies to them. This rhetoric was so countercultural that even these disciples did not understand it. This is a countercultural rhetoric answer to those in liminal cultural thinking and rhetoric. Sometimes the countercultural rhetoric of the kingdom of God causes confusion and chaos and even liminal thinking. The answer to fear and confusion over life and life difficulties is not just being miserable. The answer can be found in a different way of thinking or living that is countercultural rather than just being troubled over the lack of engagement with good fortune from a dominant cultural rhetoric.

Example

In the previous application section, there are many examples in how to find, interpret, and apply different cultural rhetoric. These ways of thinking or rhetoric can be found by looking for certain words or concepts associated with different cultural rhetoric. Sometimes it will be found that there is one rhetoric at work in the text while other times there could be two or even more locations at play in that section of Scripture. These could be two cultural locations interreacting or trying to correct one or the other or it could be simply two or more cultural locations side by side in the same text. The first step is in finding the final cultural locations at work in the text. Then the next step is to interpret the message of that day for those involved in the message or the story. The final step is to find how this understanding from the text can be brought into the modern context in how it applies to life, leadership, the church, or relationships.

The example of the story of the exchange of Jesus with a rich ruler in the gospels helps to see this process. First in Mark 10:17, a man comes up to Jesus and asks what he must do to inherit eternal life. He kneels but he is looking for exceptionalism. He asks not about salvation in general but what he must do; he is bold in his approach and we find out later he is rich as well. He believes he has done everything right; he is rather confident, even over-confident. This is dominant cultural rhetoric. Jesus answers him in surprising ways, even in countercultural ways. The man seems to have expected the commandments answer but giving to the poor was a surprise. He could not understand this or fit it into his worldview, so he left. Then the disciples enter the story as Jesus explains to them how hard it is for a rich man to enter the kingdom. They were surprised since in Judaism wealth was a consideration in spirituality. If one was rich it was considered as a result of the blessing of God and if one was poor it was considered the result of the lack of blessing or even a curse from God. Therefore, the wealthy were closer to God. This was their subculture thinking about spirituality. Nevertheless, Jesus brings a totally new perspective to the discussion. This is a countercultural position using countercultural rhetoric. His statement that it is difficult for the rich to enter the kingdom confuses and confounds the disciples. Then Jesus declares new countercultural principles of the first being last. This concept opposes both the dominant cultural rhetoric of the confidence of the rich man and the subculture rhetoric of the Jewish subculture thinking in spirituality (Table 8.3).

How does this apply in the contemporary context? The answers of the gospel today are still countercultural and can be met even by believers today with amazement and astonishment. Especially those that are caught in a subculture of Christianity that is driven by withdrawing from society and having special rules that are assumed but not

Table 8.3 Final Cultural Categories—How Hard It Is for the Rich (Mark 10:17–31, ESV)

Final Cultural Category	Words/Concepts	Person/Section
Dominant	Rich, bold, confident	Rich man
Subculture	Protest, amazed, astonished	Peter/Disciples
Counterculture	New instructions for life	Jesus
Contra culture	–	–
Liminal	–	–

founded upon Scripture. The answers to modern dominant cultural issues are not to form a subculture and circle the wagons and worry. This was the response of the disciples. Instead, the answer is to give an answer from the divine perspective which can be shocking and yet innovative and engaging. This was the response of Jesus. He calls us to lead in the church and in the world by first understanding the gospel in all of its countercultural divine perspective ways. Then He calls leaders to lead by caring for others like Jesus did here and yet by giving answers and direction that have divine perspective in them.

Conclusion

All these categories help the exegete enter the world of the author and the first recipients of these texts of Scripture. There is a divine message here, but it was communicated with human words in particular human contexts. These contexts are vastly different from the contemporary context of the modern interpreter. These gaps in understanding must be overcome to hear well the message from the text and in the text. Some of these are in the text issues and some of these are behind the text issues but they each bring light to the understanding of the message in its original context. Some of these terms that are used in this section would be strange terms to the people of the Old and New Testaments like dominant culture or conversionist view. Nevertheless, these are words that help the interpreter see what is really happening in these different texts and contexts. They are words that help us see the nuances of human reality and the divine message. Life is full of fine nuances and these are seen more clearly as we are able to identify and discuss them. In linguistic theory, it is seen that language helps us see the finer points of reality. The ability to identify something brings it into sharper focus. In this search through cultural and social texture is found contexts and nuances that inform the reader concerning the message of the text that is both human and divine.

Chapter Eight Reflective Exercises

1. Social and Cultural Texture analysis is different than social or cultural intertexture analysis. Explain this difference giving an example of this difference in a particular pericope of Scripture that contains examples of both. Look for a text that has the issue of social or cultural roles in the text and one of the three aspects of social and cultural texture in the same text. Explain the insights from the two different textures clearly noting which interpretation goes with the proper texture.
2. Do a social and cultural texture analysis of 1 Peter 2:1–12 including all three sections of this textual analysis.
    a. Find the prominent specific social topics in this pericope and discuss their implications for the interpretation of the message of this text.
    b. Discuss one of the common social and cultural topics in this pericope and its impact on this text and the larger context of this book.
    c. Do a chart concerning the final cultural categories in this section of Scripture. Then choose one of the categories and discuss the interpretive implications for this text.
    d. Develop a preliminary understanding of this text based upon this social and cultural analysis with a focus on the concept of a holy priesthood.
3. In examining a New Testament Scripture that is impacted by Old Testament, study Mark 5:21–43 and discuss the understanding of this text based upon the interpretation of common social and cultural texture analysis.

Chapter 9

Working Through Socio-Rhetorical Analysis Ideological Texture

If Scripture is a person then ideological texture is the reputation that it has gained with others. Much like a reputation, it varies from person to person. Sometimes this is because of the material within Scripture itself but, at other times, that reputation is gained due to the experiences and biases of those who perceive that reputation. This is why two colleagues in an organization can have an equal experience with a leader but have significantly different perspectives of that leader.

Ideology, then, is concerned with the manner in which people interact with Scripture. Obviously, as shown in the previous texture analyses, how the original author and audience interact with Scripture are critical to its interpretation. However, just as critical is understanding how interpreters have interacted with Scripture throughout history and the impact that has upon the contemporary reader. Being unaware of one's inclination to a particular worldview will lead to either eisegesis or anachronism in their interpretation.

Individual Locations

While inner-, inter-, and social/cultural textures have developed the perspective of the author and original recipients, up to this point we have not established the location of the contemporary recipient and how that fits within the location of the recipient's theological history. Some of that history begins prior to the recipient's existence—all theological perspective is built on something that has come before it. Thus, it would be appropriate for researchers to identify not only their own individual location but the individual location that they grew out of.

Individual location is linked to social–cultural relationship (Robbins, 1996a). Thus, just as the author and audience of a text have been examined in relationship to their social–cultural texture, so also the contemporary recipients need to identify their historical and personal social–cultural texture. This means that the very same elements of specific topics (conversionist, revolutionist, introversionist, gnostic-manipulationist, thaumaturgic, reformist, and utopian topics) and final categories (dominant culture, subculture, counterculture, contraculture, and liminal culture) need to be considered, especially in terms of how that individual location could skew interpretation away from what the original author intended.

For example, in Exodus 17:1–7, we have the story of God commanding Moses to strike a rock for water supply. For the ancient Israelites and the 1st century Christians, their worldview-specific topic was significantly embedded in thaumaturgical beliefs. Thus, for the original author, the original audience, and Christians who adopted the Jewish Scriptures, there was little question as to the veracity of the account. At the time of the striking, the Israelites were in a liminal culture final category as they transitioned from slaves in Egypt to occupying the land of Israel. The early Christians found themselves in a similar final category as they were either coming out of the dominant culture (Roman Christians), subculture (other Gentile Christian groups), or contraculture (Messianic Christians). In all of these contexts, God's miracles would be understood as His provision in the midst of uncertain transition.

Of course, when we consider the specific and final categories, a contemporary identification of a specific ideological location will be deeply dependent on the context. If we consider an individual in North America, then in likelihood, the individual would have a much lower or nonexistent thaumaturgical-specific topic. Science is used to explain much of what happens in the world and the miraculous, while theologically upheld, is not nearly as expected as it would have been for ancient Israel and/or 1st century Christians. Additionally, while Christians in North America might fall within a sub-, counterculture, or perhaps contraculture final category, still the culture as a whole is a significantly dominant global culture. As such, it is possible that a North American approaching this passage might be less aware of the manner in which culture has shaped his/her worldview, less open to varying ideologies, and less likely to listen to representatives from less dominant cultures. Each of these elements could pose exegetical challenges for a North American Christian.

Relation to Groups

Both the ideologies that are represented by an individual as well as how a person is perceived by others are shaped by the relationships that they are associated with. Thus, as interpretation occurs, it is necessary to understand the types of groups that the

Chapter 9: Working Through Socio-Rhetorical Analysis Ideological Texture

original author, original recipients, and contemporary recipients are associated with. Robbins (1996) listed six categories of groups that impact ideology: clique, gang, action set, faction, corporate group, and historic tradition. As might be expected any one individual, ancient or contemporary, might belong to a number of different groups at the same time.

A clique represents a partnership of individuals based on some form of common interest that maintains a shared identity that is bound by, typically, a group of charismatic leadership. Within this group are three primary types of members: core, primary, and secondary. Core members are the inner circle of leadership that have a high commitment and trust. Primary members are those who are willing to go along with clique values but are not as trusted by the clique leadership. Secondary members are those who are trying to move into a primary membership role by effectively meeting the expectations of the clique leaders. Determining the interpretive impact of the clique group to one's exegesis requires a knowledge of what membership the interpreter has with the clique. Additionally, the clique's values can influence the interpretation. As might be expected, one or more cliques can exist within a larger corporate group. Generally, in the North American context, cliques are viewed derogatorily although they may not necessarily be negative to the context.

Robbins (1996) names the next group as a gang. However, that holds such negative connotations in most English contexts that perhaps troop might be a better term.

A troop is essentially the same as a clique but tends to be larger and has a single leader. As such, interpretive elements tend to be similar to cliques with minor caveats. Rather than being group-based values, the values of the troop are defined by the leader. While the same types of members exist, the inner core tends to be those who are most trustworthy to the leader. Troops often do not allow secondary members to become primary members without an initiation to test trustworthiness. The interpretive implications remain the same as a clique.

An action set is a group that is gathered together by a leader to achieve a goal defined by the leader or a group that gathers to achieve a goal and selects a leader to assist in accomplishing that goal. Interpretation by those who are part of this type of group will be swayed by action set values and increase of desirability with the leader. Actions that do not naturally fall within the action set that are described or prescribed by Scripture may have a difficult time being exegeted without bias. Additionally, it is likely for this group to see most of its interpretation of Scripture through a lens colored by its focused action.

Factions are a group that rivals another group in an attempt to subsume the rival group into the faction. It is that "win" that the faction is seeking. Factions can either function like a clique or a troop. However, from an interpretive perspective, its bias lies in focusing on outcomes that will place the faction in a superior position to the rival.

Corporate groups are the longest lasting of the groups and are usually structured around values and norms that establish expectations. Typically, corporate groups will have some form of recognized structure that distributes power among its constituents. Members are expected to relate to one another in specific ways. Corporate groups usually have a clear identity that is memorialized in some type of artifact(s). If there is a group that allows for unique perspectives or even, at times, contradictory ideas, it is the corporate group. Since the principles of the group clearly delineate its parameters, a wider range of ideas can be compared to the principles to identify what would fit into the group expectations. As such, interpreters will find this group the most likely to allow competing ideas to be drawn from Scripture.

The final group is the historic tradition. This group is made up of those who align themselves with a particular theological tradition. That tradition may cut across other types of groups that the individual belongs to. The bias common to this group is to impose theological emphases into the text rather than drawing the original meaning from the text.

Perhaps the easiest example of this type of analysis would be the 12 disciples. Jesus probably saw the group as a combination of troop and action set with Himself as the primary leader, His 12 disciples as the core group, and the completion of the Father's will as the action goal. Of course, at least one of the disciples was a zealot who would be identified as faction, but it is likely that Jesus' entire troop would have been considered a faction by the religious leaders and Romans. This perhaps explains why there was so much confusion—both within his troop and outside it—over what it was that Jesus was seeking to accomplish. Of course, as contemporary readers, once again, we may be part of any number of groups depending on our context. However, the inclusion into that group necessarily causes us to read Scripture from distinct biases—in many ways, it replicates the confusion that surrounded Jesus because of the variety of groups that overlapped with His ministry.

Modes of Intellectual Discourse

When one approaches the unique components of Scripture, with what lens does a contemporary reader interpret Scripture? While strengths and weaknesses can be found in each approach, Robbins (1996) identified five primary approaches: Historical-Critical, Social-Scientific, History-of-Religions, New Historical, and Postmodern Deconstructive. It is unlikely that a contemporary reader will be completely immersed in only one of these discourses, however, it is likely that the reader will have a preference that may color the interpretation that is obtained.

Historical-Critical discourse seeks to reconstruct the ancient context and meaning of a text. This is done through analysis of grammatical, rhetorical, and historical elements presented in the text and their impact on the meaning of the text. While the strength of this approach is that it anchors meaning with the original author and audience and only then applies it to contemporary environments, the weakness of this approach is the gap that exists between contemporary understanding and the reality of the ancient world. For instance, prior to 1901, it was a firmly established fact that gear mechanisms were created in the 14th century, primarily in Europe. However, with the discovery of the Antikythera mechanism, suddenly the knowledge of gear mechanisms stretched back into, at minimum, the 1st century BCE. If the ancient Greeks/Romans were capable of gear mechanism, what other technological advancements were they capable of that are unknown to us? We know that large cut stones existed in antiquity ranging from 500 (Western Wall block) to 1,000 (Colossi of Memnon) tons; but how they were transported can only be surmised. In other words, our understanding of history, while sometimes supported with specific artifacts, should be considered a sketch at best.

The same would apply to Social-Scientific discourse. Certainly, an understanding of the anthropological insights of ancient history contributes to our proper interpretation of Scripture. For instance, we can be certain that in the first century, honor was highly valued and pursued, that shame—especially public social shame—was to be avoided at almost any cost, and that both of these developed into a patron–client relationship. Still, the day-to-day workings of this system and the parameter of expectations are somewhat lost in time. Thus, Social-Scientific discourse that is rooted in artifact support contributes to the *understood* meaning of a text for the original context. However, at the same time, while we can hypothesize about deeper implications, we must be willing to hold those implications loosely—even more so when we are trying to apply those implications to contemporary contexts.

The History-of-Religions discourse, influenced by Historical-Critical and Social-Scientific discourses, seeks to understand the relationship of the biblical text with other existing religions of the biblical era being studied. This discourse then attempts to understand the impact that biblical religion had on those religions or, much more commonly, how the other religions impacted the biblical material. The strength of this approach is to develop a stronger understanding of the biblical material that often times is most disengaged from the contemporary reader. Consider the sacrifices listed in Leviticus 1–7. Clearly the writing of this material is not a step-by-step instruction manual on ancient sacrificial ritual. Instead, much is presumed to be understood by the Levites when reading this. Obviously, future generations of Levites would have the apprenticeship of older Levites to rely on. However, for the first generation of Levites, this material must have been understood and, presumably, based on ritual sacrifices from the ancient Egyptians that the Israelites had lived with for several centuries. Additionally, there is more than enough evidence within Scripture that ancient Israel involved itself with syncretism from surrounding religions. Much less discussed, however, is the influence that Judaism and Christianity had on surrounding cultures. For instance, the fact that wise men from the East came expecting to find a ruler that was born would seem to be something that was ascertained from Jewish writings that they had access to and thus had felt compelled to save at some point in their past. Thus, the strength of the History-of-Religions discourse is in its insights from surrounding cultures on the culture of biblical accounts. Its weakness lies in not expecting the opposite to also be true.

The New Historical discourse tends to view Judaism and Christianity as simply religions among other religions, developed by its practitioners either to establish power over others or as an evolution of various social and cultural influences. Again, one can see that there are strengths to this. Both in the Jewish and Christian Scriptures, there are clear power abuses where religion is used to disenfranchise and dictate others. Additionally, there is a sense of evolution both in the Jewish religion (cf. tabernacle vs. temple worship) and in the Christian religion (initially a Jerusalem temple-based gathering vs. localized synagogue-structured gatherings). However, its weakness, certainly in the context of historical Judaism and Christianity, is the abating of Scripture to purely a social–cultural product rather than a revelatory and inspired text. In other words, the New Historical discourse too often ignores the spiritual and deific contribution to the development of Scripture and the practice that derives from that contribution.

Finally, Postmodern Deconstructive discourse seeks to understand Scripture from the perspective of the contemporary reader. In many ways, this approach is the antithesis of the Historical-Critical discourse. From this approach, it is presumed that the ancient meaning of the text is either no longer obtainable or no longer applicable. As such, it is necessary to apply contemporary values and worldviews that deconstruct the text by identifying aspects that no longer comport with contemporary thinking resulting in a critique of the text. Through this process, the text will provide new insights into contemporary contexts for either the individual or group values providing support and direction. Where the text differs from contemporary norms and values, the contemporary is expected to critique the ancient rather than the other way around. So, for instance, a feminist reading of Scripture would focus on what Scripture has to say about women, the historical implications of those readings, and the manner in which the biblical material can be included or should be rejected in contemporary environments. Since Scripture is not always advocating the actions or outcomes of the characters it records, this can be a helpful approach to avoid injustice. However, this approach can also refuse to allow the historical material to identify contemporary blind spots.

An example of the differing discourse approaches to Scripture can be exemplified in 1 Timothy 2. A Historical-Critical discourse might approach this text to highlight a historical understanding of the commands in the text, unique words used, influences of historical events occurring at that time, and the interaction with other biblical material. A Social-Scientific approach might discuss the social roles of men and women in the Greco-Roman timeframe and how what Paul was writing differed from those roles. History-of-Religions discourse would likely seek to understand the role of men and women specifically within the religious ritual of the time and how that differed from or may have influenced Christianity. A New Historical discourse would seek to understand the evolving role of apostles and local church leaders as a hierarchal power brokers and the impact that has had upon the way that the church understands power throughout history. A Postmodern Deconstructive discourse might approach this passage from a feminist perspective, identifying the ways in which the passage has been used historically to minimize power and authority for women within Christianity. As noted earlier, it is much more likely that the contemporary reader will have a combination of a few or all of these influences on their interpretation. By identifying this recognized bias in interpretation, it assists the recipients of the research to better understand the researcher and the results that the researcher obtained.

Spheres of Ideology

Spheres of ideology analysis, according to Robbins (1996), is a culmination of the other areas of ideological analysis. To complete this aspect of the methodology, the researcher begins with the ideological analysis of location, groups, and discourse for as many of the participants of the text as possible. This includes the actual author, actual audience, implied author, implied audience, historical audience(s), and contemporary reader/interpreter. One can from there envision an almost radar diagram-like interaction between each of these participants and the ideologies of location, group, and discourse. In some cases, there will be overlap between one or more of the participants. Typically, the more overlap, the easier the text will be to interpret since the gap between the contemporary and ancient is narrower. The less overlap, the more difficult the text will be to interpret since the gap will be much wider. At times, there may even be spheres that have no overlap which will require significant reliance from specialized researchers (e.g., interpreting a text on ancient purity laws and applying it to contemporary North American contexts). At times, the ideologies of a participant will be quite explicit. This, again, makes the understanding of the spheres easier and, thus, the interpretation of the text easier. However, more often than not, most ideologies are presumed and as such require an understanding of those presumptions and their impact on the interpretation of a passage. Once these spheres of ideology are identified, the interpreter will typically use them in conjunction with other methodology(ies) to gain a fuller interpretation of the text across time and perspectives.

Seeing the Picture

As each of these perspectives is identified for each interaction with the text, various viewpoints of the biblical picture come to light. Research has shown that people view and perceive material art differently (Vogt & Magnussen, 2007). In the same way, the pictures that represent our perception of the world can differ depending on the individual perspective. If this is the case, then an added component for ideological analysis, not included in Robbins' (1996a, 1996b) original writings, needs to be rhetography.

For most people, experiencing the world is not only an esoteric experience but also a visual experience. What that means is that not only are actual visual experiences processed and placed into a framework, but also nonvisual experiences are often times visualized mentally for the sake of processing within the same framework (Erfani, Iranmehr, & Davari, 2011; Gowler, 2010). When a text is read, it is not simply a matter of determining the meaning of a text through reasoning. While determining meaning, the mind attempts to visualize what is read so that it can be connected with other elements of memory. Rhetography seeks to understand the pictures that have been created in the mind of both the author and recipient based on the shared communication and how those pictures cause different interpretations of the data (Robbins, Thaden, & Bruehler, 2016).

The difficulty arises in the pictorial differences between the author, audience, and contemporary readers. For the people in Jesus' day, the lowering of the lame man from the roof (Luke 5:17–39), while wildly unusual, was quite physically possible due to the common steps to the top of a roof and its flatness. For a North American, where roofs are typically pitched without staircases for access, this is not only an unusual but a dangerous endeavor if the 1st-century mental picture is not available to the reader.

Such images create a conceptual framework for each participant of the text (deSilva, 2008). Continuing with the Luke 5 passage, to the author and initial recipients the faith of the friends is conceptualized as those who would associate themselves with the shame of the lame man by acting on his behalf, persistence in finding a manner to approach Jesus to show Him honor, and personal sacrifice for damaging the property of another that would need to be repaired lest they act dishonorably. Essentially, such a deep trust in Jesus was shown that friends were willing to lose personal reputation in order to show honor to Jesus by presenting Him with the opportunity to heal. The more contemporary picture of faith that is developed from the mental images are friends who love their friend so much that they are willing to take a risky chance to put their friend in front of Jesus for the chance that He might decide to heal him. While overlapping in some ways and having nuanced differences, these are two very different perspectives of the same picture. Contemporary readers do not place the friend or their actions in a shameful light nor do they consider the possible client–patron relationship that either existed or is being offered between the friends and Jesus (Malina, 2001).

Thus, it is important, when considering ideological locations, to consider the rhetography. The pictures that the various perspectives present in the mind of the participant, how consistent those pictures are with each other, and the manner in which the social/cultural context of the participants colors the picture's conceptual framework will determine how dependable are the intended and received meanings of the text. It is also important for the interpreter to provide contemporary pictures when appropriate. For instance, while contemporary readers will be less familiar with the Roman breastplate spoken of by Paul (Eph. 6:14), still, connecting that idea with the contemporary usage of stab-resistant vests would likely create a closer mental and conceptual picture despite the very different technologies involved. The interpreter must not only, then, consider how to present an accurate picture from the biblical times but also translate that picture conceptually for contemporary audiences.

What Is Love? An Analysis of 1 Corinthians 13

To provide an example of ideological analysis, we will use 1 Corinthians 13. It is presumed for this analysis that Paul is both the real and implied author and that the church of Corinth—whether monolithic or clustered in house churches—is both the real and implied recipient. Thus, for this example, using 1 and 2 Corinthians, we will identify the ideology of Paul, the church in Corinth, and the contemporary reader.

When considering Paul's individual location, we might say that Paul presents himself as a combination of a conversionist (change people to save the world—2 Cor. 5:20), revolutionist (supernatural recreation needed—1 Cor. 15, 2 Cor. 5:17), and gnostic-manipulationist (proper thinking will save the world—1 Cor. 1:18-25). While we know that historically Paul was not adverse to aligning himself with the dominant power (e.g., Acts 16 & 22), more often than not, Paul was a combination of counterculture and, due to the burgeoning Christianity, liminal culture. Paul belonged to a composite of multiple groups as well. Certainly, his emphasis on spreading the gospel made him part of an action set. At the same time, Christianity was a faction of Judaism (1 Cor. 9:8–10), from which it had been birthed. At the time of Paul's writing, there was at least some degree of structure both for local gatherings and the church as a whole, making him part of a corporate group (1 Cor. 11–14). As a Jewish man, he also would have identified with the historic tradition of Judaism (1 Cor. 10:1–5).

It appears as though the Corinthian church would have shared gnostic-manipulationism with Paul, however, their emphasis on secret knowledge would have pushed them to a different form of gnostic-manipulationism than Paul was comfortable with (1 Cor. 3:18). Additionally, social structures become considerably important to the Corinthians identifying them as Reformists (1 Cor. 8). Interestingly, it appears as though the Corinthian church saw themselves as a subculture relationship—trying to enact the values of the dominant culture in a purer way (1 Cor. 3:18–22) even though they also seemed to be failing at this due to the countercultural necessity of Christianity (1 Cor. 6). In terms of group relationships, the Corinthian church would have recognized themselves as living in a faction against the culture around them, although, it appears that they wanted desperately to be part of the larger cultural clique (1 Cor. 8).

Obviously, the North American church is diverse and typically the analysis of the contemporary reader would be focused on the researcher. However, for the sake of making this example as applicable as possible, we might consider the early 21st century North American Christian location to be tied to a mixture of gnostic-manipulationist, reformist, and utopian topics. As members of North America, Christianity basks in the glow of the dominant culture and probably mostly lives in the subculture. The group relationship would, by and large, be a combination of action set, faction, corporate group, and historic tradition. North American Christianity runs the gamut of discourse modes dependent primarily on theological historic tradition. Thus, the ideological spheres would look something like Figure 9.1.

Of course, the results listed in Figure 9.1 are arbitrary without a full ideological analysis (although with such analysis, a better representation could be made—content analysis could be used to quantify qualitative results). However, Figure 9.1 shows one possible way of visually representing what is happening in the passage. Paul's view of specific location seems to be strongly revolutionist in that there needs to be a radical recreation of self and the world in order to be saved. Contemporary readers, on the other hand, tend toward a more reformist approach where changes to culture happen through changing the structure of culture. These very different perspectives will create a profoundly different conceptual picture of the manner in which change occurs in ourselves and the world. Interestingly, all three perspectives have a strong gnostic-manipulationist emphasis, although all three are likely quite different from each other, as will be noted in what follows. In terms of specific topics, there is quite a difference between the three perspectives. Paul seemed to believe that change occurred by living in a way that was markedly different from the surrounding culture, although not necessarily becoming cloistered. Given the way that the Corinthian Christians seemed to continue many of the Corinthian activities, it seems fair to say

Chapter 9: Working Through Socio-Rhetorical Analysis Ideological Texture

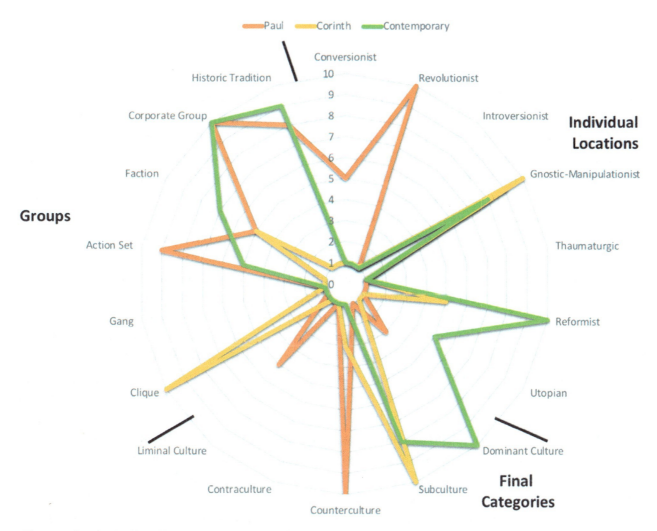

Figure 9.1 Radar Chart of Ideological Analysis

Source: Russel Huizing

that they saw themselves as still related to the surrounding culture, embracing its values and norms while wanting to live those values and norms in a better manner (subcultural). Contemporary Christians are perhaps in a liminal stage shifting from dominant to subculture. However, it does not seem to be truly there yet and American Christians still enjoy many of the benefits of being part of a dominant culture. It is not surprising then that Corinth is cliquish both internally and in its relationship to the surrounding culture. The Corinthians seem to yearn to move from secondary status within the surrounding culture into primary and core positions and, devoid of that goal, to play that struggle out in microcosm within the Christian community. While Paul and contemporary Christians share a corporate grouping, again, they are quite different. For Paul, the corporate grouping is a singular entity wherein everyone is so connected to the other that anything good, bad, holy, or sinful that occurs to one occurs to all. For contemporary Christians, the corporate grouping is far more along the lines of theological distinctives and, too often, a wariness of the intentions of other believers.

Ideological Effect on Meaning

Paul sees love as a Christian who uses their personal abilities, gifts, and accomplishments for the honoring of others. This is not tertiary to the use of these honorable characteristics—rather, it is the purpose and primary goal of their use. Often times, it will mean acting in a way that will be viewed as shameful or self-demeaning to the surrounding culture although recognized as virtuous within the Christian community. Paul's gnostic-manipulationist emphasis is based on a knowledge of Jesus. However, not simply a factual knowledge of Him but an interpersonal knowledge of Him. Why one would ever want to associate with one who has been the recipient of the death penalty of Rome, is beyond the comprehension of the Corinthians, and even somewhat outside the scope of the contemporary reader. In other words, Paul's knowledge does not set one up to be honored among others but rather sets one up to be considered a fool. Thus, the purpose of knowledge is for it to drive one to use it in love toward others, drawing attention away from self, recklessly giving it and its accompanying power away to others, and, in this way, reflecting the life of Christ in the believer. Paul, then, wants to see his readers embrace a countercultural approach where love becomes the defining virtue of the Christian community. While this may have impact upon the surrounding culture, Paul seems less concerned about that as he seems to presume that the "counter" of culture will always exist; there will simply be movement of distinct persons from the surrounding dominant culture to the Christian counterculture through the love that is experienced within the Christian community. All of this leads to Paul suggesting that what holds the Christian community together is, in its simplest form, love. It is love that transcends the differences, that causes believers to plunge into sacrifice for others, and that causes the body of believers to glorify Christ over self and themselves. The conceptual picture of 1 Corinthians 13 for Paul, is that love represents the primary identifier of the new life in Christ, what differentiates believers from the world, and the covalent bond that keeps the body of Christ bound to each other.

The Corinthians desired knowledge and thus were strongly gnostic-manipulationist. Having knowledge that others did not have accomplished two desired outcomes: it honored the one with knowledge; and, the careful distribution of that knowledge to those who would also carefully disseminate it, provided a patron role for the one with knowledge. The Corinthian struggle between subculture and Christian community is perhaps nowhere better seen than in the church's struggle between the incestuous believer and the use of lawsuits. It would seem like grace shown to the sinful believer would be an expression of love, something even the Corinthian culture is unable to do. While Paul will argue that with repentance, the believer can be readmitted to the body of believers (2 Cor. 2:5–11), the rejection of unrepentant sin is the loving response. It is also love that compels one not to follow the culture that would pursue litigious action against another believer. The conceptual picture of 1 Corinthians 13 for the Corinthians is that it likely looked like a stiff rebuke of the life that they had been living. This was a life in which they had desperately been seeking status through any superiority that they could level against those around them in order to Christianize the cultural values and norms. All of this was done so that perhaps they might have standing not only within the Christian community but within the surrounding culture. Second Corinthians 7 seems to suggest that they heard this message.

The contemporary reader would be focused on using divinely inspired insights to change the cultural structures of the world and in this way bring salvation to the world (reformist). While this can have political overtones, the primary structure that the church seeks to change is the family unit. If family units were functioning in the manner prescribed by Scripture, then the culture around those units would change and the world could be changed. Within this conceptual framework, this passage is read as a foundational passage to understanding love within the family, and thus, becomes a widely used marriage passage. As a part of the dominant culture, contemporary readers might use this passage as a means of lowering those outside the Christian community as unvirtuous. At the same time, their dominant power means that a sober self-assessment of their own expressions of love both within and outside the Christian community do not need to go too deep. This is perhaps why this passage is seen in the contemporary environment as primarily a family/marriage passage rather than a church community passage, as Paul's original context clearly places it within. The conceptual picture of 1 Corinthians 13 for the contemporary reader is as a how-to on marriage, a way of showing ourselves as being the most virtuous and therefore most equipped to handle power in our culture, and, ultimately, a finely worded poetic piece on love.

As one can see, these represent very different pictures of the passage that have been developed using the multiple layers of specific location, final topics, and relationship to groups. Together, they assist us in seeing the biases of all the perspectives that approach a particular text. As might already be ascertained, as throughout this book, this example focuses on a Historical-Critical and Social-Scientific mode of discourse. Others approaching from other modes of discourse may bring new insights missing from this perspective. Of course, this is the very point of ideological analysis—allowing multiple, sometimes contrasting, perspectives to contribute to the understanding of the proper interpretation of the text.

Conclusion

The important role that ideological analysis plays for the interpreter is to identify ancient, historical, and contemporary biases that may impact the exegetical results. These biases should not be taken lightly as being blind to them may cause an interpretation that would not be consistent with the message of God through Scripture. Nor should we exclude perspectives that may not completely align with our own. This is not to suggest that Scripture can simply mean anything anyone wants it to mean.

We can draw an analogy from the Rubik's cube. If I were to hold up the cube in between two people looking at different sides of the cube, each would be insistent that the color they see is the correct color of the cube. Neither would be completely right or completely wrong. Their ideology would be based upon the location of their perspective.

Changing their location changes their perspective and allows for something more to be seen than before. Scripture has these ancient, historical, and contemporary perspectives all contributing to an understanding of God's Word—each contributes something to a deeper understanding of God's intention in His revelation. However, this is not to say that any perspective is right. If the people looking at the cube are insistent that it is a sphere, then they would not be looking at the same object. Scripture cannot be interpreted to say anything, but it often says more than our perspective allows. Ideological analysis helps to tease these meanings out.

Chapter Nine Reflective Exercises

1. Choose an aspect of yourself that you might use to describe yourself to someone else (e.g., I am a student, or, my heritage is from a particular country). Using that simple description, write out your individual location(s), group(s), and final category(ies). How might those perspectives bias you against others who would not describe themselves in the same way? How might those perspectives bias you against perspectives presented in Scripture?
2. If you have embraced a particular theological perspective, how might that bias you in your reading of Scripture? If you do not align with any particular theological perspective, how might that change the way you interpret Scripture?
3. Conduct an ideological analysis of Acts 15:1–35. Identify all the characters represented in the text and provide support for the individual locations, groups, and final categories that you would align them with. As the reader, add your own location, group, and final category. Based on that analysis, what do you think Luke was trying to convey to Theophilus by including this story in his book?

Chapter 10

Working Through Socio-Rhetorical Analysis Sacred Texture

Socio-rhetorical analysis is a multifaceted approach to the discovery of the message of Scripture that facilitates both discovery and dialogue. This dialogue concerns issues of the words of the text and its interaction with other texts or issues of society, it concerns the discussion of the kind of person who lives in the world of the text, and it even discusses issues of ideology. Nevertheless, this would be an incomplete discussion without interacting with the divine issues in the text itself. Sacred texture analysis asks this very important question. What does the text say about or how does the text interact with divine issues? How is this message in all of its words, its cultural sensitivity, and its ideology connected to God and His message to humans? What are the divine issues, message, and concerns here in the text of Scripture? Sacred texture analysis looks deeply into the issues of God in who He is and what He says to humans in the text. In the language of metaphor sacred texture is like the spirit of the person. The spirit of the person is the part of the person that connects to God and it is here where the growth or spiritual growth of the person begins through interaction with God. Sacred texture is about the message to humans in knowing God, knowing who God is and in responding to God. This is the ultimate question. It is ultimately left to last in the analysis with the hope that all of the other textures will help answer these ultimate and important questions. These are not only questions about God; these are questions that surround the issues that are important to God like religious community, ethics, and redemption. This is the core of theology or the study of God. The goal is to grasp the meaning of the text God has intended; it is not to create meaning; it is to seek the meaning that is already there (Duvall & Hays, 2012). This is particularly true as the sacred texture of Scripture is approached. The goal is to determine what God has said in sacred Scripture to determine the meaning of the Word of God and it is important that the voice of God is not confused with the voice of man (Ramm, 1999). This study of theology is important then not only for understanding the text but also for knowing God's divine perspective on issues that surround Himself. The big problem with Bible

Study today is that many believe that it should be easier than other things we do, like hobbies or instructions repairing different items (Osborne, 2006). This then becomes a question of priorities and where one is willing to invest the time to become good at something whether biblical study or something else. Scripture needs to become a priority for proper understanding of the text especially in the area of the sacred texture.

Sacred texture analysis looks for insights into the nature of the relation between people and God as well as religious life. Sacred texture is examining the text for insights into the nature of the relation between people and the divine, locating the ways that the text speaks about God and talks about realms of spiritual life. The study of sacred texture of a text has a long history of people who are interested in finding insights into the nature of the relationship between the human and divine and this is a way to guide the researcher in search for sacred aspects of the text (Robbins, 1996). This method is part of a theological method for studying Scripture and is the ultimate reason for studying Scripture, finding teaching or words about God and words from God. Therefore, it is important to determine how God's word is to be understood so that there is clarity rather than confusion that it may be known what God has said (Ramm, 1999). Sacred texture is deeply embedded in the textures of a text. As a researcher works carefully with the nature of language itself in a text, with the relation of the text with other texts, and with the material, social, cultural, and ideological nature of life, a thick description of the sacred texture of the text emerges. Following are the categories of research for sacred texture analysis.

Deity

God may exist in either the background or in a direct position of action and speech in a text and this includes issues of the nature of God and God's revelation in this first step in analyzing the sacred texture of a text (Robbins, 1996). The Scriptures reveal and discuss many different aspects of God and His work among humans. The Scriptures speak of the attributes of God, the relationships of God, the truths of God, the power of God, and the declarations of God. The knowledge of God found in the texts of Scripture is both extensive and profound. Though we cannot know God exhaustively we can know true things about God, but we simply do not know facts about God; we know God himself (Grudem, 1994). The believer knows God through prayer and through Scripture. These are the places of encounter with God though it can take many forms like worship or personal experience wherein God causes His word to come alive in us. The Scriptures answer the question of the ages in showing who God is and who humans are in relation to Him. Therefore, this issue of Deity in Scripture is prevalent, profound, and not just informative; it is also formative.

There can be many aspects of God in the text. God can be speaking or someone may be speaking to God. God can be described or is the one who is worshipped in the text. Sometimes He is represented symbolically in a story or he can be described in a story. In looking for this texture in the text look for words like God or Lord and then go past this to search for God speaking or being described. His attributes many times come out in His actions or His declarations of His design for humans or in particular situations. God is very present in the text of Scripture and these divine realities are clearly implied to the audience.

An example of sacred texture concerning Deity can be found in the first pericope of 1 Peter—1 Peter 1:1–12. In this text, God is described as the Father who chooses and has foreknowledge of the believers, but He is also seen in relationship to the Son and the Holy Spirit as well. In some ways, this is a full-orbed description of God. He is described as the Father of the Lord Jesus in the area of relationship and some of His attributes as well as actions are described. He has great mercy and He has caused us to be born again. Notice in this text God is the initiator. Then by His power He guards the inheritance that has been prepared for the believers. The Son is present here as the redeemer but also as the word of the Lord in the mouths of the Old Testament prophets. Then the Holy Spirit is sent from heaven as the divine proclaimer through human voices of this good news. God is seen here as Father, Son, and Holy Spirit. His attributes, actions, and relationships are seen here as well. It is significant to note His power here and how He uses it, He initiates the plan of redemption, He fulfills the plan in Christ, then He proclaims the accomplished work by the Holy Spirit. He uses His power to initiate salvation in people then He uses His power to protect their faith until they come into the inheritance that He provided. God's power here is related to His mercy and He uses His power to do the work Himself rather than requiring the work from the believer.

Holy Person

Regularly one or more people have a special relation to God or His power and in the New Testament the ultimate holy person is Jesus Christ, and this is an area called Christology or the study of Christ (Robbins, 1996). However, there are other persons found in the text that would be considered holy persons as well (only on a different level) like Moses or Paul. These holy persons are significant in that they tell us much about God in their relationship to Him and in the way that God speaks to them. They also show the way or set the example in following God. They do not follow the Lord perfectly, but the reader gets to see the activity of God in correcting them, displaying his response to them in mercy, grace, and discipline. The reader gets to observe these holy persons and their activities, attitudes, and even their personal issues. These issues are instructive for the believer and they were intended to be instructive. Many times, the Scripture teaches truth in story form of real historical events, but it allows the reader or interpreter to look into the lives of the different important people as if they have glass houses; we can peer into and see the reality of their lives, the good, the troubling, the perplexing, and the bad. These holy persons even speak in the text sometimes directly to the audience. The interpreter gets to hear the words and many times know the inside story of the events in the life of this person. The reader sometimes even gets to hear God's perspective on this person or the activities of the person. These insights are instructive for the interpreter as the reader gets to enter the world of this person. Since Jesus Christ is both divine and human He fits into both categories of Deity and holy person. This is a most amazing miracle that is seen in Scripture in that the infinite, omnipotent, eternal Son of God could become human and join Himself to human nature forever; this is a most profound mystery (Grudem, 1994). This profound mystery is discussed, revealed, and applied in the text of Scripture. Mark's gospel, for example, is especially important in explaining the nature of Jesus' messiahship where He is seen as the Son of God yet this messiahship is kept hidden since only Jesus understands the true nature of His destiny in that of a suffering servant who conquers through death (Fee & Stuart, 2014). This is the role of a holy person. Other religions have holy persons, but Jesus Christ is unique among them all. In this area of study, the interpreter needs to look for Jesus as a holy person as well as other persons that stand out or are distinguished as special though imperfect people.

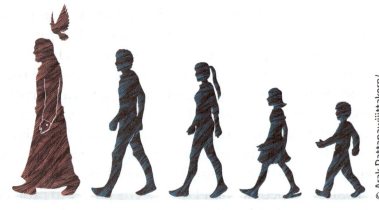

A good example of this texture can be seen in 1 Peter 1:1–12. It has already been seen that God is present in this text as Father, Son, and Spirit. Jesus Christ is a prominent holy person in this text as well. In this pericope, Jesus is seen as the son of God the Father. Jesus is the one who fulfilled the activity or the actions of redemption through His resurrection from the dead. Notice here His death is only mentioned in connection to the resurrection; the focal point is the resurrection. Then there is coming a moment of revelation of Jesus wherein the believer's faith will be shown as genuine. In this context is found that Jesus is the One who is the focus of love, joy, and faith of the believer. Then Christ is the one who is preached and the one who suffered according to the words of the prophets. He is the fulfillment of the prophecies of redemption then He came and redeemed believers through His resurrection. Now believers place their faith in Him while they look for their eternal inheritance. In addition, joy, faith, and love are found in relationship to Him. Jesus is no ordinary holy person. He is the divine holy person, but He came to us and though divine He suffered then died but He rose from the dead. This is the central issue of the faith; it is a mystery, but it is revealed in Scripture and history for us to understand and be changed by its reality. It is found in 1 Peter that Jesus is this incredible divine human person that actualized redemption and yet becomes the example for us to follow in suffering and living. In this text is found the work of Christ but also the truth that in Him is found, faith, love, and joy. Possibly many today are looking in all of the wrong places for these profound experiences.

Spirit Being

These spirit beings are divine or evil beings who have the nature of a spirit; these are referred to in places in Scripture as angels, Holy Spirit, demons, unclean spirits, or the devil and these often emerge in the context of battle between good and evil (Robbins, 1996). At other times, these beings are described in certain activities or actions. In some places, they can even have doctrines or teachings. These beings can be found in the text as they are mentioned by the author as being present or in describing them in some way. These beings are all spirit beings, but they are in three distinct groups. First the Holy Spirit is divine, a person of the Godhead and He is unique. He is manifest in many places in both Old and New Testaments from Genesis 1 in creation to Revelation 22 where the Spirit and the Bride say come. Angels are spirit beings, but they are sent to minister to the heirs of salvation and they are seen in Scripture as active in the world but mostly behind the scenes. Angels are created spiritual beings that worship God and serve Him but without physical bodies though they can take on physical forms (Grudem, 1994). Then there are evil spirits, demons, and the devil. The devil is a distinct person among this group of evil beings. He is known as the opposer of the Lord and of the believers. He is known in Scripture by several other names like Satan or the Serpent. In addition, there is a grouping of evil spirits or demons who are the ones who oppose that which is good, God and His people. These different persons are often named in the text when they are there and active in the story or the instruction. Look for them in the text and how they relate to the others in the story. Sometimes there can even be interaction between two of these groups in the text.

An example can be found again in 1 Peter 1:1–12. In this text, the Holy Spirit is seen in connection with the Father and the Son as the one who sanctifies the elect and the one through whom the human messengers preach this truth about redemption. He is the one who applies the work of the Son in redemption in sanctifying, bringing internal formation and change in the believer. In addition, He is the one who activates this message of the gospel in the preacher. The message is preached through Him. Then there is another Spirit being mentioned, which is the Spirit of Christ. Is this the same as the Holy Spirit? This is really not the issue of the text here. However, it is curious that the author would use the Holy Spirit in activating the message of the New Testament messengers while it is the Spirit of Christ who activated and gave power to the message of the Old Testament prophets. One is a message about the future and the other is a message about the past with implications for the present. The message is similar, but the time context is different. Paul in Romans 8:9 uses the terms Spirit of God and Spirit of Christ closely together. This is the same Spirit whether He is called Holy Spirit or Spirit of the Lord or Spirit of Christ. Why the different terminology though? This is a bigger question than cannot be answered from this one text. The interpreter would need to examine several texts on their own merits then look for connections or implications for answers to this question. For this text, the Spirit of Christ was in the prophets showing them and speaking through them about the person and work of Christ. However, there is more here.

Angels are also part of this pericope. These things that have been preached to you through the Holy Spirit these angels desire to see it to understand it (1 Peter 1:12, ESV). The angels are servants to God and yet they do not fully grasp redemption. It is not for them though they work with those who are redeemed. The Spirit works in ways that are often unseen and not easily understood. Yet this internal work is important and present in Old and New Testaments and today. Part of this work is internal change in the believer; He is the agent of transformation. Another aspect to the work of the Spirit is in revealing and inspiring the message of the Lord though His messengers to others, He is the agent of proclamation. The believer today needs to find new levels of dependence upon the work of the Holy Spirit. This is an internal work that manifests in real change in the believer and through the delivering of the message of redemption.

Divine History or Eschatology

As God directs historical processes and events toward certain results this salvation history is God's plan for humans that works itself out through an ongoing process that moves slowly toward God's goals (Robbins, 1996). This texture examines the events in this process whether they are past or future or even present from the perspective of the writer of the text. In this context, history moves toward the time of the last things and issues of the last times are made known before they occur (Robbins, 1996). These occur in apocalyptic sayings and books, but they are also found throughout Scripture. This divine history can be seen in the Old Testament in Abraham sacrificing his son

Isaac, in a type (Gen. 22). This is foreshadowing the ministry of Jesus in His crucifixion and resurrection, which is the pivot point of divine history. This includes eschatology itself or the events of the last days as well as the early prophetic issues of moving toward this conclusion. In the Old Testament, this would include the feasts that are prophetic events as well as the events like Abraham and Isaac on the mountain. It is divine history, but it may not be history yet. Once the eschaton has happened then it will be history.

Peter makes an interesting statement in 1 Peter about this divine timeline from divine perspective. In 1 Peter 4:7 in the midst of exhortations about people giving account to God he says that the end of all things is at hand. Then he followed it by exhorting the believers about self-control, love, and the proper use of their gifts. Was he saying that the eschaton was imminent in his day? In one sense, the eschaton is imminent, but this was not his message. This is the same language that Jesus used when He told a crowd that the Kingdom of God is at hand. He did not mean it was coming soon, He meant it was already here. It is so close if it was physical you could reach out and touch it. The same idea is found here in Peter. The last days are not coming they are here. Truly if it was physical you could reach out and touch it. The last days began when Jesus died and rose from the dead. These are not days of the ultimate fulfillment, but it is last times. We are not to go looking for last days they are already here. We obviously are not in heaven yet and the return of Christ has not happened. However, we live in the era of the last things. This is part of God's timetable and it is important that we understand our own context. In these last days, there is a heightened sense of urgency in living as stewards of God's grace.

There is also a good example of divine history found in our example text of 1 Peter 1:1–12. Verse 5 talks about a salvation that is ready to be revealed in the last time. There are two senses to this timeline here. One is the salvation that is being presently revealed through believers being born again and they are in the process of this salvation in sanctification, in the process of refining faith and living in joy. In the past, the prophets wanted to understand this but it is now revealed to the believers. This then looks forward to the conclusion of the eternal inheritance in heaven. First Peter is rich in oral-scribal intertexture with the Old Testament as well as with allusions and references to Old Testament stories and figures (deSilva, 2000). These connections to the past are drawn upon here to connect salvation history to the present and even the future. This pericope draws a timeline from the angels in the past to the prophets who wandered at this redemptive plan. Then the timeline moves to the present revelation of Jesus Christ and His work of redemption that is now being lived out by believers through the work of the Holy Spirit. This is founded upon two realities. One in the past, the election of the Father of these believers before time and then the fulfillment of eternal heavenly reward. God is always working in His timeline and history is moving toward this conclusion and no event or disaster will change this reality. This is the revelation of the power, mercy, and love of God toward us.

Human Redemption

There is a transmission of benefits from divine to humans as a result of events, rituals, or practices and through divine powers these will transform human lives resulting in an immortal nature or liberation from powers that are destructive (Robbins, 1996). This complex set of events and correlations with certain cause and effect implications are examined in this concept of theology from the text. The doctrine of redemption is deeply embedded in Scripture. There are events in the Old Testament that are redemptive in concept and many are symbols or foreshadowing of the spiritual redemption that is revealed in the New Testament. There are many textures to this concept of redemption, and it can be found in various places in the Scriptures. The truth of human redemption is both profound and nuanced and this depth can be found in the many texts and types and implications when Scripture discusses redemption. Often blood is associated with redemption and different festivals have the message of redemption in them as well like the feast of Passover. This feast is full of redemptive language like blood and sacrifice and being set free from an old life. The actual feast is filled with redemption language that Israel understood because of their deliverance from Egypt (Exodus 13:3–16). This is correct and this deliverance from Egypt was an act of redemption by God for the people of Israel. Jews still celebrate this deliverance today though they have other more contemporary reminders of God's deliverance. Yet Jesus takes this feast in the New Testament and fills it with new meaning by becoming the Passover lamb that was a fulfillment of this feast, but He points it toward eternal human redemption for all peoples (Luke 22:15–20, ESV).

Is there the texture of human redemption in the example text of 1 Peter 1:1–12? Yes, in several parts of the pericope. It talks about the sprinkling of the blood of Jesus, which was a concept for redemption and purification from the Old Testament. Here is seen how the different textures can overlap and help each other. Intertexture of this text is important in understanding the concept of blood sprinkling as found in the Old Testament (Ex. 24:6–8; Lev. 1:5; Lev. 9:12–15; Heb. 9:18–23) and it became part of the cultural understanding of Israel. The believers are told that they are born again by the resurrection of Jesus Christ from the dead. This is the central redemptive event of Scripture. This redemption then brings an inheritance that is undefiled (pure) and unfading (eternal). In addition, this salvation for humans has puzzled the prophets of the past and still makes the angels want to look into it. This redemption is rooted in the activity of God and is so amazing it mystifies prophets and angels. Human redemption is the core message of the Scriptures and it is an act of God that has made this possible and the result for believers is an eternal inheritance that is kept for them through God's power. This redemption needs to be looked into and believers can understand it and proclaim it. It has become part of who we are or our human identity. It is more than an event it is a miraculous intervention that changes everything including how the believer lives today.

Human Commitment

This texture of a text regularly includes a portrayal of humans who are faithful followers of the Lord and supporters of people who play a special role in revealing the ways of God to others and the issue is the response of humans at the level of their practices, it involves humans in their commitment to divine ways (Robbins, 1996). These followers have certain commitments to the Lord and to each other and this texture can involve divine calls to be disciples or descriptions of how they live out these commitments. This is still part of theology in that it is teaching about God and his relationship with His people and how they are to live out their commitment to Him.

In the example of 1 Peter 1:1–12, there are some issues of human commitment like the response to the various trials that are spoken about. The believer responds in such a way that it brings praise glory and honor at the revelation of Jesus Christ. The response of love to the Lord causes the believer to do well in these trials that bring glory to God. However, a further example is found in the next short section of 1 Peter 1:13–19. The text specifically calls the believer to thoughtful action. The first commitment is a soul issue of setting the mind and setting hope on the grace given in Jesus. This is a commitment of faith and an internal issue of motive. The second call is a call to obedience to holiness since the believer lives in exile. This is a call to action but also a call to understand that this earth is not the real home or the ultimate goal. The third call is a call to remember how redemption came with a focus on Christ and to remember that the believer's faith and hope are to be in God. Notice that this call to holiness is sandwiched between two calls to faith and it is God who has done the work of redemption so the believer can give glory to God and live by faith. Notice these calls to commitment begin with grace and end with faith. Also notice that it is God's work that makes this call to holiness possible. This holiness is not a call to new regulations or ceremonies. It is an internal call of motive, faith, being mindful of grace and of redemption in Jesus. This quote from the Old Testament about holiness is from Leviticus 11:44 that classifies holiness as obedience to certain regulations. This concept of commitment does call the believer to obedience but not an obedience that has to do with regulations and foods but having to do with faith, redemption, and soul issues like motive. This is a new kind of holiness. Israel could not fulfill the law of externals, but this new kind of obedience is given power by redemption, this power impacts the life of the believer.

Religious Community

An aspect of this texture is the formation and nurturing of religious community in the text that is bigger than human commitment in that it is a matter of participating with other people in activities that fulfill commitment to divine ways or ecclesiology the church in the wilderness (Acts 7:38, ESV). There are texts that specifically give instructions to the church about being the church as in 1 Corinthians or Ephesians. However, there are many other places where Israel or believers are called to religious community. Just as the people of God were called to follow the Lord, they were also called to form community and these communities functioned in many different ways as places of exhortation, comfort, insight, or even direction. They also provided a place for the believers to live their lives in obedience to God in the

way they connected to other people in love and care. In looking for this texture, find ways that people are called to gather to interact with each other or how they are to come together for worship or other functions. In addition, look for instructions that are clearly for the group or when they are called together.

Though this first pericope of 1 Peter is focused on God and his work of redemption and the response to this work by the believer, there is a brief reference that implies community. This reference is found in verse 1 where Peter calls the people to whom he is writing the elect exiles or aliens of the dispersion. These were those who were chosen and then called out of the dispersion to live a different life than where they came from. This was a corporate call. This would call to mind in the Jewish heart how Israel was still in many ways scattered in the dispersion among the Greek world leftover from the conquests of the foreign powers of the Old Testament. Many in this Jewish dispersion had gone back to Jerusalem to form the community of Israel there again. Peter was calling this picture to their mind. They were called out of the foreign places to come together to form a community around God and his word only not as Jews but as believers. The focal point was not Jerusalem and the temple, but it was the true source of God's presence—Jesus and His work of redemption. There are other places in 1 Peter where religious community is found like later in 1 Peter 1 chapter 1 when the believers are called to love one another in verse 22. In 1 Peter 2, the believers are called to religious community in becoming a spiritual house and a holy priesthood. It is not a focus on one individual as a priest but to be a community of priests together or a priesthood. This was a new kind of community not based on birth or geography but based on new birth and a common experience in redemption. Then becoming disciples of Jesus Christ together the believers form new community in exile. When Jerusalem was destroyed by the Babylonians, they also destroyed the temple worship for all of the exiles. They became foreigners. Their way of community was gone. They formed new communities based upon their common heritage and the word of God. They met together in buildings that became the center of the community and these were called synagogues. They formed community in exile. Even when worship at the temple was restored to them, they kept the synagogues that were based in community.

There is power in this community; even today Jews meet in synagogues. Peter was calling them to form this kind of exile community again but based in the redemption for Jesus, the true temple.

Ethics

Ethics concerns the responsibility to think and act in certain ways in both ordinary and extraordinary circumstances that are motivated by commitment to God and answers the questions about the things that are the will of God (Robbins, 1996). These are issues of how one responds to God as the result of knowing Him. The question is what is in the text about how one is to respond to God, and this can include issues of ethics in God's way or according to life in the Kingdom or rule of God. Normally, ethics would be defined as doing the right thing or the moral thing or making the right decision for everyone. However, in this case, ethics is about doing the right thing in response to God or according to the will of God. In looking for this texture look for how one should respond as a result of a relationship with God. This an issue uniquely suited to Scripture. The original issue with ethics began in the garden. Adam and Eve were told not to eat of the tree of the knowledge of good and evil. This is ethics at its core in the ability to see good and evil and to decide for the good. Adam and Eve were tempted by Satan telling them that their eyes would be open knowing good and evil. They really wanted this ability, so they bit the fruit. The problem is that human ability to determine right and wrong has been distorted from the first moment our eyes were opened since it was rooted in sin and actually the source of depravity. The irony is that in our zeal to know ethics we destroyed the foundation for ethics by disobedience to God. Therefore, humans have a hard time seeing right and wrong clearly even with ethical rules and systems in place. It is here that Scriptures can help us by giving us the divine perspective on right and wrong even though it may be difficult to see it clearly since our ability to discern this is distorted and broken.

In 1 Peter 1:1–12, there is found a section that describes a right response to a situation that seems awkward and even opposite to what would be right or normal. The text talks about being tested by fire and being grieved by trials. First, it is important to see the purpose here in that these trials are not random nor are they part of disfavor from God. They are part of the development of faith and the response is rejoicing and joy. This seems odd but Paul tells the believer the same thing in rejoicing in suffering because of what it does in that it produces perseverance and character. Humans misjudge events and issues because the full character of the issues is not clearly seen. Then the human's inordinate focus on self, distorts the truth of that which is occurring. The result is glory and refined faith and the response is joy. This is counterintuitive but it is the right way ahead. This position of joy prevents unethical conduct such as blame-shifting, anger bitterness, or playing the victim. The believer must relearn how to think about life and circumstances and against all training learn to respond in joy to suffering.

Application

In this texture, there are many different facets of the sacred and there are many places that this sacred texture can be seen. These can be held together as different aspects of this sacred texture. Many of the textures interact with and even overlap each other. A table or chart can be used to display and compare these different parts of this texture (Table 10.1).

All verses have sacred texture and there are more of this texture in these verses that were not discussed. The individual issues were discussed in each section for interpretation and application. However, the question is whether an overview of this texture gives insight to the interpretation of this pericope. There is a great amount of material and insight concerning Deity, divine history, and redemption with a counterintuitive turn in ethics and several exhortations in human commitment. The overall message appears to be in forming a divine community based in redemption and a new place in divine history or the narrative of God's story with His people. This new community has a new sense and a new way of obedience founded in grace and faith that is initiated by God's work rather than human work. In this new community, the human response of holiness is based in grace and faith and based upon God's power to elect, preserve, and to change the believer. Since this is the introduction to the book, this could set the pace for the rest of this book.

Conclusion

Sacred texture is an integral component of effective biblical exegesis in that Scripture speaks clearly and definitively and broadly about the issues of the divine. It is important that these issues are not missed in the study of the text of Scripture. The goal of exegesis is to draw out what is there in the message of the text of Scripture. There are many textures that are involved in this process, but sacred texture is a foundation for all textures that hold all of the other issues together. At one time in human history theology or the study of the sacred was considered the queen of the sciences. In other words, it is what held all of the other sciences and disciplines together it was considered the foundation to truth. The teachings about God, His ways, and His instructions are truly the foundation to truth and reality. It is what holds everything together. The interpreter therefore must examine this texture with a heart to learn, to understand, and to be directed by the sacred texture of Scripture. This is not for the casual observer, but it is for the diligent researcher and interpreter. However, it is not just about understanding Scripture, as important as that is, it is about understanding self, God and life itself. Scripture is the key of knowledge and as we hold the key, we must learn to use it well and then give it to others as well. Learning this process of interpreting the sacred texture of Scripture is not just so that the student can become a great interpreter, it is also so that the researcher can teach others to become great researchers, which will impact their lives and their teaching.

Table 10.1 Sacred Texture of 1 Peter 1:1–21, ESV

	Deity	Holy Person	Spirit Being	History	Redemption	Human Commitment	Community	Ethics
1							Exiled community	
2	Father, Son, Spirit	Jesus	Holy Spirit		Sprinkling blood			
3	Father	Jesus		Resurrection	Born again			
4				Inheritance				
5				Salvation revealed, last time				
6								Rejoice in suffering
7	Jesus	Jesus		Revelation of Jesus				
8						Love Him		
9					Salvation of souls			
10					Prophets desired			
11	Spirit		Spirit of Christ		Sufferings of Christ			

(Continued)

(Continued)

	Deity	Holy Person	Spirit Being	History	Redemption	Human Commitment	Community	Ethics
12	Holy Spirit		Angels Holy Spirit					
13	Jesus Christ					Sober-minded		
14						Obedient children		
15						Be holy		
16						As I am holy		
17	Father					Conduct self with fear		
18					Ransomed			
19	Christ				Blood of Christ			

Chapter Ten Reflective Exercises

1. Sacred texture is about discovering the theology or the teaching about God in the text. However, sacred texture is much broader and deeper than simply the words about God just as theology is more that the study of God. Explain how sacred texture examines the breadth and depth of divine issues in the text in its examination of theology or the teaching about God.
2. Do a sacred texture analysis of 1 Peter 5:1–11 including all eight sections of this textual analysis.
   a. Examine the text for the expressions of Deity, holy person, and spirit beings and discuss the implications of this data for the interpretation of the text.
   b. Study the text and note the areas of divine history and redemption with their implications for interpretation of this text.
   c. Find the human response issues in this text of commitment, community, and ethics with a discussion of how they connect to the other issues found in this text.
   d. Develop a preliminary understanding of this text based upon this sacred texture analysis with a focus on the concept of the person of and work of Christ with the desired human response as connected to leadership.
3. Examine Philippians 2:1–11 through sacred texture analysis. Then explain the connection between the holy person here and the human response or human commitment based upon the divine example.

Chapter 11

Treating the Text as a Data Source

We can be honest. Treating Scripture as purely a combination of symbols that are presented by the original authors and interpreted by contemporary readers seems a bit sacrilegious. Certainly, the words of Scripture, presuming they are guided by the inspiration of the Holy Spirit, carry something more than just any other human writing. However, the qualitative method necessarily reduces that text to personal, cultural, as well as rhetorical components of communication, which seems to rob the text of its divine nature. This is not the intention of exegetical analysis.

However, at the same time, we want to structure exegetical analysis in a manner that allows multiple researchers to speak into any one specific analysis. That goal necessitates methodology, which requires us to develop steps to interpretation that multiple researchers can both agree upon and follow in order to provide an objective perspective to the unique text that is at the heart of exegetical analysis.

Should Scripture be treated as sacred or as data? There is in that question, of course, a significant tension in values. On one hand, Christians would agree that Scripture needs to be approached as something more than a collection of words or the experiences of individuals in history. The true experience of Scripture is an encounter that includes the work of God and as such goes beyond a simple equation of the words that make it what it is. On the other hand, most agree that Scripture is written in a dizzyingly number of genres over the course of centuries and, thus, by its very nature must be considered as something that needs interpretation lest the original message be misinterpreted. Qualitative analysis explicitly wrestles with both of these tensions of experience and meaning.

The Use of Qualitative Analysis

Qualitative analysis allows the researcher to understand recorded experiences and apply the descriptions of those experiences to contemporary fields of study (Patton, 2002). Starting with individual experiences, qualitative analysis seeks to inductively synthesize themes within the data that holistically describe contexts (Patton). Due to the subjective interjection of the researcher's bias, qualitative analysis also is well aware of the analyst's own perspective (Patton). Essentially, qualitative analysis consists of the recollection of an experience that is then analyzed for themes that emerge throughout the data (Patton).

Three perspectives are always at work in qualitative analysis (Patton, 2002). The first perspective is that of the original author/audience. This requires an understanding of the original culture, values, worldview, and presumptions that dominate not only the author but the world around the author. The greater the distance in time between the original author and the researcher, the deeper this analysis needs to be. The second perspective is that of the researcher. Everyone approaches data with a bias and perspective that needs to be taken into account when proposing results. The third perspective is that of the reader. Those who will be the recipients of the research will also have their own perspectives. While the researcher cannot be expected to address all possible interpretations of the research, it should be written in such a way so as to minimize misunderstandings that could creep in based on differing perspectives.

To accomplish this, several methods of qualitative analysis have proven effective in determining the meaning of qualitative data, including Scripture. While the specific methodological steps may vary based on the unique elements of divine material, still, these steps are drawn from more broadly established qualitative research analyses.

Types of Qualitative Analysis

The types of qualitative analysis available to the exegetical researcher are quite varied yet align well with the search for meaning within a text (Patton, 2002). Phenomenological analysis (Patton) focuses on how the experience of the passage contributed to changing the original author. It is presumed that a component of the original author of Scripture is that the divine experience that they had assisted in changing them to such a degree that it changed their perspective of God and/or the worldview that they have. In other words, the motivation for the original author to scribe what occurred to them was a significant enough experience for them based on their interaction with the divine.

Qualitative heuristics (Patton, 2002) focuses on the manner in which the text has changed the experience or worldview of the author or other recipients. This particular type of exegetical study focuses on the manner in which Scripture causes motivational changes in followers of Scripture.

Ethnomethodology (Patton, 2002) focuses its research on determining the assumptions within a writing or culture that are so deeply embedded that the original author/audience would not have understood their perception as anything other than *a priori* understanding. When compared to other worldviews, the weakness of this position becomes quite clear. An example from Scripture could be its embracing of slavery despite the clear narrative of freedom throughout Scripture. Later worldviews that embrace freedom over slavery are an advancement over the scriptural perspective. Still, lest one become proud too quickly, there are likely scriptural positions that speak into contemporary worldview. In other words, contemporary does not trump ancient any more than ancient trumps contemporary. Ethnomethodology seeks to understand which worldview is closer to a comprehensive biblical worldview.

Hermeneutics, the most commonly associated qualitative analysis with biblical analysis, seeks to determine the proper interpretation in the original author/audience's culture and how that interpretation bridges to a contemporary application (Patton, 2002). Duvall and Hays' (2012) Interpretive Journey, discussed earlier in this book, is an excellent example of this.

Narrative analysis studies stories to gain a deeper understanding of the culture in which the story originated (Patton, 2002). While this may seem straightforward, it is important to understand how stories are structured within a particular culture. For instance, is the moral of the story embedded in the ending of the story, within each of the major characters, or in the metaphorical elements of the story? Each of these could suggest very different interpretations of a story and as such narrative analysis becomes an important tool in interpreting the accounts of Scripture.

Finally, qualitative analysis can be pursued through grounded theory (Patton, 2002). This form of analysis seeks to develop new theory based on qualitative analysis. This, ultimately, is the goal of a Christian social science theory development. While Christians can appropriately draw upon the development of non-biblical theory, ultimately, it is seeking to develop a unique theory of the world based upon the analysis of Scripture. As such, grounded, theory will be an important first step to Christian theory development.

For instance, Noblit and Hare (1998) combine qualitative analysis research studies to reveal consistencies across studies to create meta-categorization. When put to use in exegetical study, this methodology allows the biblical researcher to draw upon many different passages on the same topic to understand its many facets. For example, God's sovereignty can be found in many different passages. However, drawing together analysis of all those passages allows for a much richer understanding of God's sovereignty. Another form of qualitative analysis that would be beneficial for the exegete would be qualitative meta-analysis (Timulak & Creaner, 2013). This form of analysis seeks to combine multiple studies in order to reveal new conclusions that cannot be obtained by any one of the studies. An example of the use of this research for the exegete would be showing a biblical basis for the doctrine of the Trinity. No one single passage adequately gives a complete picture of the doctrine. However, when combining the analysis of multiple passages, the historical Trinitarian statement becomes clear.

Results of Qualitative Analysis

Through all these possible methodologies, exegetical research, as a subset of qualitative research, has the same goals as qualitative research. Ultimately, the purpose of exegetical research is to develop possible theory that is tested through summative evaluation that results in action research (Patton, 2002). This begins with identifying an appropriate research question (Denzin, 2002) that will provide direction and perspective to the research. The data is deconstructed, and its raw parts analyzed to understand their relevance to the whole (Creswell, 2009; Denzin, 2002). This is done by reading carefully through the data and providing some form of coding that assists in identifying underlying themes and descriptions within material (Creswell, 2009). Coding typically progresses in three steps. The first step is open coding (Seale, 1999). During this step, the researcher moves through the text and highlights anything that might stand out to the researcher. This could include repetitions, unique words or phrases, social/cultural clues embedded in the text, the use of other sources, and rhetorical structures. The results from this coding may require the researcher to dig further into supporting research to provide meaning and context to what has been coded. The second step of coding is axial coding (Strauss, 1987). The open codes already identified are gathered into categories and the text is reanalyzed with these axial codes in mind, allowing other portions of the text to either support or negate the category. This may require the researcher to adjust the axial codes until they match the totality of the text as best as possible. After this analysis, the data can be reconstructed into a whole and coded selectively. This selective coding allows for the combination of the axial codes into meta-themes of the text and contextualized to the contemporary world (Creswell, 2009; Denzin, 2002; Patton, 2002; Strauss, 1987).

While qualitative analysis is typically thought of as purely textual analysis, it is quite possible to quantify results through content analysis. Thus, for text that includes frequencies, attributions, or qualifications, these can be measured as indices within the text to provide quantitative perspective (Krippendorff, 1980; Neuendorf, 2002). These results can then be used to provide a measurement of the text. For instance, Huizing and James (2018) took all instances of the Greek word for *teach* in the New Testament and then compared every pericope in which the word appeared to see if there was a more likely usage of apprenticeship word domains or pupilship domains. The results suggested a stronger relationship to apprenticeship words, which has an impact on the way that teaching should be understood in Christian disciple-making.

In addition to this, software can be used to assist with the research. Of course, software is incapable of identifying the meaning of the text or results. However, software can be used to assist in retrieving specific textual instances, coding, code linking, conceptual visualizations, and, to the extent that qualitative data can be quantified, statistical analysis (Denzin & Lincoln, 2000).

Obviously, a single study does not establish fact. Rather, multiple studies from multiple methodologies and varied sources assist in building a stronger grasp on the true outcomes. Typically, this process of using multiplicity to strengthen analysis is termed triangulation (Seale, 1999). Historically, four types of triangulation have been recognized. Data triangulation seeks to draw results from diverse sources in order to find confirmation of anticipated outcomes (Seale). Investigator triangulation purposely uses different researchers studying the same phenomenon in order to indicate similarities from different perspectives (Seale). An often overlooked, yet critically necessary, component of proper investigator triangulation is identifying researcher bias (Creswell, 2009). All researchers, perhaps doubly so for biblical researchers, approach analysis with some form of bias based on their theological worldview, culture, experience, as well as socioeconomic considerations (Creswell). To assist with investigator triangulation, researchers should be clear about how their own biases may have impacted the results of the study. Theory triangulation attempts to apply diverse theories to the study in order to identify the strongest working theory (Seale, 1999, p. 54). Finally, methodological triangulation will seek to use varying methodologies on the same data to confirm that similar results can be obtained from varied approaches (Seale).

Another aspect to consider when trying to strengthen results is to pursue disconfirming evidence (Seale, 1999). For the biblical researcher, this will mean not only studying portions of Scripture that provide the expected outcomes of the research but purposely studying other portions of Scripture that would not seem to confirm the research. So, for instance, if we were trying to identify the leadership style of Jesus as a servant leader, we of course would go to Matthew 23:1–12 but also to the narrative of Jesus cleansing the temple in Matthew 21:12–17. Additionally, it is important for the researcher to include perspectives that counter their own in a fair and balanced manner (Creswell, 2009). Doing so assists in establishing the results of the study in the complexities of the original and contemporary contexts.

As this research accumulates, it is moving toward saturation or redundancy (Patton, 2002). In other words, qualitative analysis seeks to continue its analysis until it reaches a point where any additional analysis will likely repeat what has already been researched. Certainly, a single analysis does not accomplish this. So, while theological approaches to a specific passage might support foundational truths of a theological position, a truly qualitative analysis will allow for other perspectives to add insights that may or may not cause tension. Presumably, when describing a God that is beyond human description, this is a necessity of theological pursuit. Ultimately, we must feel tension in our theology, or we have not reached its edges.

Ultimately, we are not God who has an infinite parameter. We are finite and we should expect certain aspects of our theology to be finite as well. Thus, our research should have certain parameters that measure the effectiveness of research. Typically, in qualitative analysis, this has been identified by four parameters: credibility, transferability, dependability, and confirmability (Denzin & Lincoln, 2000). Typically, credibility is recognized when the qualitative research has reached a point where the original author would agree with the outcome (Denzin & Lincoln). Transferability occurs when the specified outcomes can be applied to new environments (Denzin & Lincoln). Dependability occurs when the researcher can expect that certain variables/outcomes can be anticipated across many different contexts (Denzin & Lincoln). Confirmability occurs when there is corroboration across multiple studies on the same material (Denzin & Lincoln). Of course, all of this is dependent on a consistent, descriptive, interpretive, theoretical, and evaluative outcome (Maxwell, 2002).

The Holy Spirit in Interpretation

So far, so good. If all we are studying is a contemporary theory, a Renaissance poem, or a late Spring Chinese writing, then certainly these tools work. However, with Christian Scripture, there is an expectation from its followers that there is something more—another facet to interpretation that adds a tension between past meaning and present application. Often, this tension requires an added step for Christians to the data analysis.

Pinnock (1993) noted that Scripture is not so easily interpreted solely through qualitative methods. A tension arises for those who see Scripture as not only representing an ancient, original meaning but also a contemporary application. For the Christian, both require guidance by the Holy Spirit as we seek to consult the Author of Scripture rather than simply analyzing His meaning (Hart, 1987). This is where it is possible to focus solely on the rational components of qualitative analysis to the point of demystifying the work of the Holy Spirit in interpretation (Hart). It is here, perhaps, that we see the unity in diversity that is so often illuminated in Scripture: the layperson will be strengthened by scholarship while the scholar will be challenged to deeper receptivity of the Holy Spirit's work through the layperson (Hart). Thus, the church does not move toward either anti-scholarship or hyper-scholarship. Rather, it recognizes that both those gifted in scholarship and those who are impacted by that scholarship are in a symbiotic relationship that results in greater maturity and fruitfulness in both (Hart).

More is at stake here than might at first be realized. Ignoring the meaning in the past leads to heresy while ignoring the application to the present leads to dead orthodoxy (Pinnock, 1993). The Holy Spirit is involved in both determining the original meaning in its original context while at the same time restating the meaning to a new context (Pinnock). Of course, if the Holy Spirit is involved in both these activities, then not only is the original inspiration considered spiritual, but also the proper interpretation of Scripture is spiritual (Breck, 1983).

Nebeker (2003) makes a compelling case that proper interpretation of both the ancient and the contemporary contexts require an understanding of how God is intending to transform humanity into the likeness of Christ. If this is the case, then veracity goes beyond simply lacking falsehood and instead is measured by the person of Jesus (Nebeker). This is an uncomfortable place for most scholars. It suggests that truth is not simply reasonable but necessarily relational (Luke 24:27; John 5:39; Nebeker). In other words, if we treat Scripture as purely data, then we have missed an important component of interpretation. While interpretation does include scientific methodology, it must also include a Holy Spirit component of illumination that challenges us to be transformed into Christlikeness (Nebeker). Thus, while we use the tools of interpretive methodologies to increase our understanding of the text, that interpretation necessarily requires additional steps not taken for other texts. Breck (1983) provides a helpful outline that includes understanding the original text in its original context, indicating the way in which salvation through Christ is expressed through that writing, and, finally, the application of that salvation to contemporary contexts (p. 90).

The interpretation of Scripture, then, will necessarily have an effect on our understanding of Scripture itself. Obviously, Scripture never sets out rules for its own interpretation. Nor, should we expect that the Holy Spirit is going to provide new revelation (Zuck, 1984). Rather, the Spirit allows Scripture to be understood and applied to a bevy of contexts (Pinnock, 1993). We have received Scripture in our own day through a fivefold process: "revelation, inspiration, canonization, preservation, and translation" (Hart, 1987). Thus, anytime one is interpreting Scripture, it is required to ask how this interpretation fits into the overall meaning of the original revelation (Dorman, 1998). While we anticipate the Holy Spirit's role in interpretation, it does not mean that we are going to equally understand all parts of Scripture (Zuck, 1984). Additionally, as Christians, we would expect the apostolic testimony to the interpretation of Scripture provided in the New Testament to have a unique insight that cannot be superseded by any other testimony (Pinnock, 1993).

Surely, this allows that there will be interpretations that are fallible. This is true—simply because the Holy Spirit is part of the illuminating process does not necessitate that believers will comprehensively and completely understand the implications of Scripture (Zuck, 1984). However, this does not reduce all interpretation to invaluable (Dorman, 1998). Rather, all interpretation of Scripture from a Christian perspective requires a deeper understanding of Christ (Nebeker, 2003). Certainly, we can misinterpret texts because we import truth that has been rightly ascertained in one text into another in a way that does not reflect the character of Christ (Nebeker).

In this instance, the interpretation is correct in the overarching biblical meaning but is incorrect in the particular text being interpreted (Nebeker), which can result in a misinterpretation at the micro-level while still allowing for Christ-like transformation because of the macro-interpretation.

Interpretation's Effect on the Interpreter

All this being the case, the interpretation of Scripture will also have an effect on the interpreter. The primary goal of interpretation should be that the interpreter is changed in such a way that they align with the Gospel message of Christ that the Holy Spirit seeks to communicate (Dorman, 1998). This is the crux of the difference between inspiration versus illumination. Inspiration represents the initial revelation of God and His will within a specific context. Illumination represents the application of that revelation to new contexts. Inspiration states from the perspective of the ancient world that there are certain activities that are inconsistent with Christian living (Gal 5:19–21). Illumination recognizes that certain contemporary activities, such as smoking, would align with the destruction of the temple of God. Illumination never unravels inspiration but rather applies the original meaning to new contexts that did not exist at the time of the original revelation (Keener, 2016, p. 12). In this way, historically, it has been difficult to distinguish between inspiration and illumination (Pinnock, 1993, p. 4).

This illumination necessarily changes the interpreter. While typical qualitative analysis does not require spiritual disciplines, the illumination of Scripture necessarily requires, at the very least, a discipline of prayer (Dorman, 1998). It is in that prayer, guided by the timeless Holy Spirit, that the gap between inspiration and illumination are bridged and God guides us just as relationally today as He did with the original writers of Scripture (Pinnock, 1993). This is not to suggest that interpretation of the biblical data is not work . . . in fact, just the opposite (Pinnock). It is the work of the Holy Spirit, as one submits to His guidance, that directs the interpreter (Pinnock). Of course, this is then the reason why new realities can be seen in the application that would have been invisible to the original author or recipients (Pinnock). Thus, we would speak of the interpretive process as revealing revelation in a new light rather than a new revelation (Pinnock).

Once this revelation has been understood by the interpreter, their job is not done. Instead, interpreters stand between the ancient world and the contemporary and bridge the chasm between the two (Hart, 1987). Some interpreters seek to transform the passage for elements that may be untenable for contemporary contexts (Hart). Others will translate historical interpretation for contemporary relevance (Hart). In either case, personal relationship with the Holy Spirit is needed. This is why it is possible for those who are not Christ followers to perceive the meaning of the text and yet not understand the truth that it holds (Nebeker, 2003). One must have a relationship with the truth in order to understand what is being said.

Conclusion

We can then establish that the Christian interpreter must have an understanding of Christ and a willingness to be changed into the likeness of Christ irrespective of the implications that may have upon their individual spheres of influence (Nebeker, 2003). In other words, the Holy Spirit is involved in both the theological development and the transformation of the individual—both the reason and the experience (Nebeker). At the same time, it needs to be recognized—perhaps even embraced—that we are part of the broken world that sin effects. As such, we realize that interpretation is not infallible (Zuck, 1984) and is quite likely to be "vulnerable to lust for recognition, arrogance, vain assertiveness, hasty defensiveness, incredulous denial, provincialism, egotistical opportunism, as well as other subtleties of the flesh" (Nebeker). While we may comprehend Scripture, we may still not welcome or even apply the truth that we find there (Zuck). While the Holy Spirit has an essential role in interpreting Scripture, still, this does not happen without the interpreter disciplining themselves to hear and follow the Holy Spirit's prompting, lest our lack of preparation hinder our interpretive endeavors (Zuck). It is in this way that we do not negate diligent study, commentaries, and other biblical resources in our pursuit of meaning (Zuck). Nor do we eschew reasoning or anticipate epiphanies of insight (Zuck).

Essentially, Scripture can and should be read rationally. It also can and should be read experientially. The first keeps us from allowing our subjectivity to overwhelm the objective truth contained in the inspired word. But the second allows us to avoid the cold callousness of reason. Instead, we see in our experiences a comradery with the experiences contained in Scripture—ultimately, God Himself entering our experiences through the experiences of others. The first makes sure that we place our faith in what is true, the second makes sure that we place and act our faith in relationship with someone (Keener, 2016). Such a reading allows a faithful imagining of the text that helps us suspend reasonable disbelief and allows faith to bridge the chasm between what we know and what we experience with great expectation (Keener).

If interpreting Scripture changes the way we think of Scripture and changes the interpreter, then, naturally, we should expect it to change the way in which Scripture is applied across time and contexts. Surely, we focus on the meaning of the original authors, yet, still, we realize that Scripture has a unique way of allowing a broader interpretation than what the original authors intended (Dorman, 1998). We see this in the way that New Testament writers use the Old Testament and we can expect the same in how the New Testament writings are applied to our current day. In other words, the Holy Spirit is at work in the midst of interpretation to illustrate the original meaning in contemporary terms (Dorman).

Still, one of the invaluable assets of the universal church is its interpretation of Scripture throughout time. While not all interpretations will be applicable to all times, seeing how the church has interpreted Scripture throughout time provides a road map for contemporary interpretation. While ecclesial tradition does not determine the interpretation, still, it is a guide in the process of interpretation (Dorman, 1998). Thus, proper interpretation happens within the community of the universal church (Dorman). While not jettisoning the consensus of the historical church (Dorman), nor is application to contemporary complexities as easy as making one-to-one parallels between the text and contemporary thinking (Pinnock, 1993). For instance, it may be possible that contemporary thinkers place an undue emphasis on individualistic thinking/spirituality while ignoring the contribution of community interpretation (Pinnock). At the same time, the calls for a dissolution of denominations for a universal "whole" may be seeking support for their own interpretations rather than allowing their unique insights to be judged by the church (Pinnock).

Ultimately, the pursuit of what is "true" requires an openness to changing norms that is guided by the Spirit that is not bound by either human reason or culture (Hart, 1987). Interpretation and application are so interconnected that the Holy Spirit is needed in both (Nebeker, 2003). Thus, interpretation must include, "hearing the text, understanding it, and allowing the text to change us not only individually but corporately as well" (Nebeker). This does not mean that interpreters of Scripture are given a superhuman ability to ascertain truths that others cannot see (Zuck, 1984). Rather, it means that identifying the intended truth from Scripture is open to all those willing to submit to the guidance of the Holy Spirit. While this process is not mystical in the sense of having no parameters, at the same time, it is not simply a set of steps that if followed will bring everyone to the goal of "truth." Ultimately, if we are to approach Scripture as data—which qualitative analysis rightly demands that we must—then we must also understand that for the biblical scholar, there is an influence of the Holy Spirit that must be ascertained as supported by the wider Christian body.

Chapter Eleven Reflective Exercises

1. Choose two of the six types of exegetical analysis listed in this chapter. In what ways could those analyses be applied to the study of Scripture? In what ways would they be a useful tool in analysis and in what ways might they limit the analysis?
2. What are some of the unique ways that a relationship with the Holy Spirit assists in data analysis of Scripture?
3. How do we distinguish between what the Holy Spirit is illuminating to us and our own personal biases?

Part 4
Addressing the "So Whats"

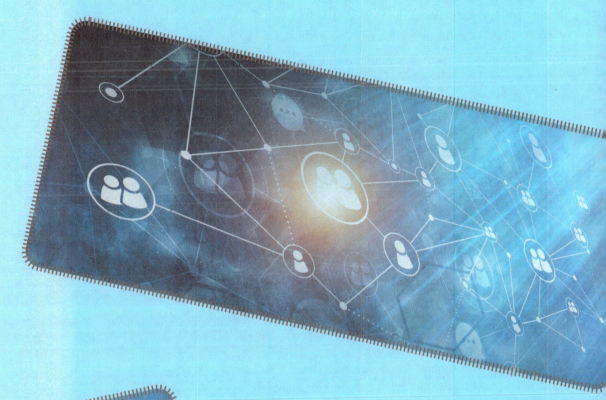
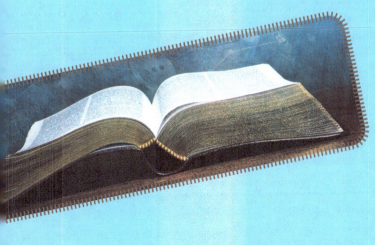

Chapter 12

Moving from Interpretation to Application

In the final stage of understanding the message of the text, the researcher must move carefully through a process from interpretation in all its complexities and nuances to application to the present context. The message of the text must now be understood from the message to the original audience to be appropriated into the present context. This appropriation looks for the transcendent truths that can now be recontextualized into the current situation and cultural setting. The process of interpretation recognizes the cultural issues for understanding, in essence it is decontextualized then this message must be recontextualized into the contemporary moment, but it must be applied to a genuinely comparable situation (Fee & Stuart, 2014). In other words, this process must be done carefully with wisdom, not haphazardly or with wrong motives. Meaning refers to what the author intended to communicate through the text, but application refers to the response of the reader in answering the question of how to live out or apply this meaning to the current situation and to grasp His Word by understanding it and living it (Duvall & Hayes, 2012). This final process is for more than understanding it is for application and the point is to know God who He really is and to follow Him in ways that He really desires.

This final process helps the researcher move past interpretation for the original audience to understanding the meaning for the present realities of life. Vanhoozer (1998) asks this question of whether there is meaning in the text or if it can simply mean what we want it to mean for our moment and particular situation. Yes, there is meaning in the text of Scripture and it is found through this nuanced process of interpretation through observation and interpretation and even effective questions for research. The meaning then is seen and heard in the text that can then be moved into several different situations for application. This meaning is important in that without it there is no way ahead for life and godliness. Nevertheless, there is a way ahead, but it is available to those who seek and search not to the casual observer.

As the researcher enters this realm of inquiry, there are several issues that must be addressed. It must be remembered that interpretation of Scripture is a spiritual exercise as well. In this process, the reader struggles with historical distance, with themselves and the matter of the text as the reader seeks to appropriate its meaning and the text aims to transform the person into the image of the Word and the goal is embodiment for the reader (Vanhoozer, 1998). This process is formative through encounter in the Word and with meaning from the Word. Therefore, this process must be completed with care while remembering that the process is part of the goal as well. So, in pursuit of this meaning, the research question or questions need to be revisited. This is to help bring clarity and focus to the application process. Then the biases of the researcher need to be revisited. In some interpretative processes, this will already have been examined but they need to be brought to the forefront again for this movement toward application. Finally, the text must be considered in the new context. Just as the original context must be clearly understood so the new contemporary context needs to be clearly seen in its own right and as compared to the original context.

Biblical interpretation entails a spiral from text to context from its original meaning to its significance for the church today and this task of exegesis is not complete until one notes the contextualization of that meaning for today (Osborne, 2006). Then the answer to the question of meaning in the text is not only answered but it becomes a place of insight and even power for life and godliness for the believer and for the church.

Revisiting the Research Question(s)

The research question is an important component in the analysis of the text in that it is important in moving from data gathering to interpretation to know the focus of the analysis. Then it is important again when moving from interpretation to application. It is important to learn to ask good interpretive questions in the analysis of the text of Scripture. Good interpretive questions come from the text. Nevertheless, even before this process the researcher needs to have a research question to give focus to the study as part of good qualitative analysis. In qualitative study, researchers develop research questions for the study—not objectives—and this asks the broadest question possible for the exploration of the central concept in the study as a general issue to be examined (Creswell, 2014). This central issue is the crux of the research question.

Then this research question begins to drive the examination on several levels. The central step is how to formulate the research question, and this is an issue for the beginning or the conceptualizing of the study and in several phases of the process including the process of collecting data and in conceptualizing the interpretation (Flick, 2009). Therefore, here at the end of the process, the researcher must revisit the research question for clarity for interpretation in answering the original question of the study though other issues may fight for ascendancy in this final process. The less clearly a research question is formulated, the greater the danger of too much data that the researcher will helplessly try to interpret, and the researcher must develop a clear idea about the research question while remaining open to new results (Flick, 2009). This question is not a hypothesis looking for an affirmation instead it is a clear concrete question about the data and its implications for a particular issue. The research question must have an open-ended design to be able to discover, understand, explore a process, describe an experience, or to report a story from the area or phenomenon that is studied (Creswell, 2014). This is a search for meaning for "what is actually there" concerning this issue in the data, the story, or the process. The truth is out there, but it needs to be explored and discovered and this process of discovery is focused by the research question even in the final stages of interpretation.

Once the data has been collected and a beginning interpretation has been made from the text of Scripture, then the question must be asked again to keep the focus of the study on track. At this point, it is easy to forget the origin of the study considering new discoveries made in the research process. In addition, it is easy to simply go on to application without first developing the initial interpretation of the data and what it means in the original context for the questions that will be asked in the application stage. It is at this stage that interpretive questions can be asked for clear and nuanced interpretation based in the information found in the research and the research question. To do exegesis well, the secret lies in learning to ask the right questions of the text (Fee & Stuart, 2014). The answers to these questions help to develop the message and even the nuances of the text. It is very tempting to move off in new directions or to jump too quickly to application without due consideration of what was found in the text.

So, then what is the researcher to do? The first issue is to reexamine the data and initial interpretation to develop the connections between the original question and the interpretation. How does this data and initial interpretation answer or address the research question? This needs to be developed with good connections between the interpretation and the beginning answer to the research question. Then once these connections are made explicit then the researcher can form interpretive questions that are connected to the data and the original broad research question. The answer to these questions could call for more research as well. Finally, the researcher will need to summarize the findings of how the interpretation of the data and the interpretation answered the research questions along with noting any surprises or new insights. Qualitative research is to discover what is there not to create new issues nor is to ignore unexpected results. These anomalies are not to be discarded but addressed and even pondered in this stage of the study.

The research questions set the agenda and the other questions later refine and help with interpretation from the observations from the different textures. An example of a research question for exegetical study in the area of leadership is seen here for the examination of the text of 1 Peter. What leadership style and practices were developed by Peter in 1 Peter and do these practices negate or support contemporary models of leadership (Crowther, 2012)? This question is broad enough to discover truth in the process of the search that is surprising and unexpected. Yet it narrows the field to ask only questions having to do with leadership.

Then once the different textures are examined considering this question different issues begin to come to the surface of the study. These issues need to be pursued. One way to pursue them is to ask good interpretive questions of the text. These questions do not need to be stated in the study, but they can be implied by the answers to the issues. Once the texts of the early verses of Peter are examined several textures of socio-rhetorical analysis (SRA) become relevant in this question about leadership. In the verses of 1 Peter 1:1–12, there are several aspects of inner texture as well as intertexture and even a concept of ideological texture that all present themselves. The observations from this thick description of the text bring several issues to the forefront for consideration. One question concerns the discussion of suffering and power and the message to the believers and even leaders. The answer to this question has to do with a reconfiguration of suffering from judgment to an issue of transformation for real change in believers and this is needed in leaders as well. Then another question is to consider the importance of Peter as a leader who is called an apostle. Who were these apostles and what was their role as leaders (Crowther, 2012)? These and other questions come to the surface and the answers provide some interpretive work and development. However, it is important to note that these questions are interpretive, and they have not moved to application at this point. So, the question is not what this means for leadership today. Instead it is a question of the significance for leaders in Peter's era and context. Application or moving the message into a new context comes later.

Recognizing Our Own Biases

Before moving to the stage of application or bringing the message into the current context, the researchers must consider their own biases or even their own agendas in this interpretive process or in this subject. Often in zeal for pragmatism, the researcher will be tempted to rush to application even before interpretation and this shortened process lends itself to a biased view of the message. Along the way for understanding of the Scripture, the researcher must pause and ponder first interpretation then even before moving to application consider the ever-present threat of an ego centric or even an ethnocentric interpretation. Each researcher enters the business of interpretation with a set of preconceived ideas about reality, relationships, and righteousness or ethics and morality. We tend to think that our understanding is the same as the Holy Spirit's or the human author's intent, but we bring to the text all that we are, with all of our experiences, culture, and prior understandings of worlds as well as ideas that can cause foreign ideas to be read into the text (Fee & Stuart, 2014). These come from our own particularity as an individual, in our place in history or even our place in economics and culture. There are many areas where these differences in understanding can occur, which emphasizes need for the process of hermeneutics. In reading Scripture, the researcher will view the text from one's own particularity. Most of these differences are not normally recognized since this is simply how one does life from the settings and preconceptions of one's particularity. Nevertheless, these differences are very real, and they have real impact on worldviews and bias impacting interpretation.

Some of these areas are addressed in ideological texture in examining cultural location and similar issues. However, there is more to be seen and addressed here. There are several obstacles or gaps in understanding that need to be overcome including historical, cultural, philosophical, and linguistic gaps, which can block an accurate understanding of Scripture (Virkler & Ayayo, 2007). Some of these issues are also dealt with in the areas of intertexture or social and cultural texture. Nevertheless, bias goes deeper than the issues covered in these processes. Every reader brings to this task a set of preunderstandings from one's background and paradigm community and these preunderstandings too easily become prejudice that can place a grid over Scripture to make it conform to these conceptions (Osborne, 2006). In this way, the text can be used to confirm ideas and concepts of the reader rather than to give new understanding and insight to the reader. The reader must be placed in front of the text to be addressed by the text instead of behind the text where the reader manipulates the text so that meaning is understood rather than created (Osborne, 2006). The bias of the reader can force the text into a mold that was never intended. This misshapen message can then be understood to be divine guidance or directive causing great distortion to the message of the text of Scripture. Many of the textures used in SRA and in other methods are designed to address this issue as part of the process of interpretation. This is very important in the doing of hermeneutics. However, ultimately the researcher must address this self-focus and self-identity issue directly. It is not only the broad worldview differences that trouble interpretation it is also some that are very personal and close to the individual doing the research. Some of these would include issues like gender or even socioeconomic class. Then there are the issues of personal passion and a personal sense of justice or the particular wrongs in society that are more troubling from the particular place of the interpreter. These personal issues of particularity cause miscommunication in discussions that are contemporary. How much more problematic are they when the communication participants are separated by so many other issues that are complicated and intensified by the addition of time. These personal issues give nuances to the worldview of the researcher that are not covered in general hermeneutics. Hermeneutics is the study of how to determine what a discourse means using exegesis that is the bringing to expression of an interpreter's understanding of an author's intended meaning of the text (Cotterell & Turner, 1989). In this process to bring the intended meaning, the interpreter must deal with the issues of the text in all of its nuances as well as deal with self and its nuances as well.

How can this bias be addressed in the process of interpretation? The immediate questions are whether this bias can be eliminated even for the lofty goal of biblical interpretation to find the divine perspective. This problem has some similarities with crossing cultures for ministry. The one who did this perfectly was Jesus Christ. He crossed from the culture of heaven, eternity, perfection, and immortality to the culture of earth that is filled with temporal realities, imperfections, and desperate needs brought in by mortality and sin. He came from the infinite totally present to the finite totally linear filled with brokenness and desperation. Scripture says he did not grasp equality with God (Philippians 2:6). He never ceased being God, but He became human and even embraced death. He became bicultural. He was from one culture, but He became incarnated into another, foreign culture. He became the ultimate bicultural missionary. He is fully God and fully human. He did not cease one but became the other. Nevertheless, in some senses this made Him very unique. He did this perfectly and we cannot do this perfectly, but it gives us an example to follow. As humans cross over to new cultures and become bicultural, it gives them new insights and perspectives even in reference to the first culture. This cross-cultural perspective has several benefits including a new understanding of self in the original sociocultural matrix and a new understanding of others in the new sociocultural matrix (Kraft, 2007). This new perspective is a bicultural one with new insights into both worlds. By analogy, this can be applied to the current issue in this discussion about bias. Can the researcher cancel all bias for the sake of interpretation? Probably not. However, it does bring new insights almost suspending the bias of the first world perspective for a moment. The missionary can live in this new world relatively well, but they are still from another world. This is the same with scientists, though they are searching for unbiased repeatable truth they still bring themselves into the equation. They cannot take themselves out of the scenario, but they can make allowances for this reality. How do they do this? One way is by keeping notes that show their process so others can repeat the process and note the findings of the new research. In other words, it is a process that is continuing not a onetime event and it is done in a community.

Humans interpret but they interpret in relation to themselves and seem to be incurably subjective (Kraft, 2007). Humans see through the subjective eyes of self. How then does the researcher overcome this interpretive bias? There are several general ways to overcome these deep personal biases in interpretation. The first way is for the researcher to find her or his personal areas of bias—like gender and whether married, single, or divorced, passions, special areas of justice issues—and become like the bicultural missionary. This means that though the researcher does not change themselves, this researcher suspends those as best as possible for the moment. The researcher brackets these areas or suspends them for a moment for the process of interpretation. The researcher cannot become someone else, but they can suspend or bracket the issues for a moment. The researcher becomes bicultural in particularity for a moment looking at it from the perspective of one who does not have the issues impassioned by the text. Second the researcher needs to keep good detailed notes of the process and the results so that others can critique nuance or challenge the research. This can happen in the publication of research for others to see, study, and critique. This is part of the academic process yet there are few who enter this public discussion compared to the number who could be part of this nuancing of the understanding of Scripture. Then third the researcher is to do this in community asking for insights not just in the results but also in the process from other researchers. This community broadly is the church both present, past, and future. However, the researcher needs to have a community of peers, mentors, and students who can enter the process together for effective understanding of the text of Scripture. These communities exist in formal and informal groupings from local churches and bible colleges or seminaries to groups of friends who have worked together or studied together. These three processes do not destroy bias and prejudice, but they minimize the impact and as the process advances through time and with more research, this process is refined for better insights from the text. It is like a hermeneutical spiral a term used by Osborne (2007) in moving from interpretation to contextualization of the message. However, this picture of the spiral is relevant here as well. As these texts are searched for meaning in a way that can be discussed with others, there is a spiraling effect not of the meaning spiraling out of control but of the spiral narrowing toward a finer point or truer understanding of the text and its meaning.

Applying the Text to the Context

How does this meaning of the text then move from meaning for the original audience to significance for the contemporary audience or context. This is the process or the movement of decontextualization to recontextualization of the eternal truth of the text and the message of Scripture. The difficulty of this task has already been seen in all of its complexity and even its complications from subjective human involvement.

Nevertheless, this is the goal of hermeneutics. Part of the task of hermeneutics is the bringing to expression of the interpreter's understanding of the significance of the meaning of the text to the world of the interpreter (Cotterell & Turner, 1989). This meaning of the text is then to be appropriated into a new context, the context that is pertinent to the researcher. Biblical interpretation entails a spiral from text to context from its original meaning to its contextualization or its significance for today and in the process of refining the hypothesis, there is a spiraling nearer and nearer the text's intended meaning (Osborne, 2006). The result is this intended meaning then is brought to bear upon the new context with more clarity and impact.

As has been seen so far good application to a new context must be founded upon good interpretation for the original context. The only proper control for application is to be found in the original intent of the biblical text, this is the objective point of control, therefore a text cannot mean what it never meant (Fee & Stuart, 2014). Contextual application is taking a message or concept and appropriating it into one's context or a desired context different than the original one. This contextual application can be directed by several questions or steps to facilitate the process. The first question asks for the function of the biblical instruction in its original context. Virkler and Ayayo (2007) in discussing steps for translating biblical commands from one culture or time to another say that the initial step is to discern the principle behind the command. So, the first question is what it meant to the original audience but in that process the researcher is looking to decontextualize this meaning. The original message was clearly written to a different culture and societal context. Can those particularities be removed to find the timeless message? At this point, the researcher must discern whether the principle is timeless, or time-bound or even culture-bound (Virkler & Ayayo, 2006). This is part of the reason for the use of intertexture, social and cultural texture, and ideological texture during the interpretive stage. In addition, this takes an understanding of the new culture or context into which the message is to be sent. This becomes more problematic the more rapidly culture changes. As a biblical scholar, the researcher must have one foot firmly planted in the biblical world and one foot planted in the contemporary world. This is not to imitate or become the world but to be able to understand how to communicate with people in this new world. The biblical message needs both revelation and relevance. Revelation in that it must be a divine message and relevance so that it can be an understood message.

Then the question at hand is how this new context is the same or different than the original context. This area of application is one that still causes controversy in the Body of Christ. The question concerning the part of the message that is culturally contingent needs to be discerned to be separate from the message that is eternal. The place where the researcher makes this separation matters. This is the reason that the interpretation phase must be done deeply and carefully. In addition, this is why the issue of bias needs to at least be noticed before entering this area of application or appropriation from one culture to another one. This must be done carefully so that the eternal message of the gospel is not damaged or partially discarded. Additionally, this must be done carefully so that there are not additions made to the grace of God as found in the gospel and the text of Scripture. There are no culturally neutral messages. Each message has a context even in contemporary conversations. This is an area of great misunderstanding between people even today. People are formed by their culture and this is usually unnoticed by the individual. Therefore, individuals think they are correct in their thinking since it makes sense to them. However, when there are people from different cultures and generations in serious conversations, there are many disagreements. Many times, it is the result of not realizing the problem of different cultures. Even simple words like justice or fair or even love have different meanings and practical applications in each of these groups. So, what is a researcher to do? In this place of application, the researcher must become the anthropologist, sociologist, and a social worker to begin to bridge these two worlds. Actually, it is three worlds. First there is the eternal realm or world from which the message originated then there is the world of the original message wherein the eternal message had to be enculturated for it to be understood. Then the message must be decontextualized and recontextualized or enculturated into a new culture. This must be done intentionally, carefully and with helps from other sciences, researchers, and communities.

The final question is how this message can function analogously in the new context. Augustine said that in his study of God that language fails us. However, it is what we have therefore we use language by analogy. In this discussion, he was talking about the concept of the Trinity as found in Scripture. He was trying to explain this eternal truth in language that could be understood by people of his day. This eternal truth is found in Scripture, but it is communicated in a way that 1st-century believers could understand. He had to work with this material to apply it. He helped develop the economic doctrine of the Trinity that we discuss today as God being one in essence but three persons. Today in application, we look for the way that the message can be applied or how it can be discussed or done analogously or how this can function analogously in the new context. If a principle is transcultural or transgenerational, the researcher must study the nature of the application in the new culture (Virkler & Ayayo, 2006). In other words, the concept cannot simply be dropped wholesale in the new context since the way or the understanding of the message must be developed to be understood or even used in the new context. The researcher does not canonize the cultural particulars in which the biblical instructions were given but neither does the researcher acquiesce to the sinful issues of the new context. Nevertheless, the message must wear the clothing or the words or the understandings of the new culture. It is an exercise in analogy moving from one culture to another with a message that is superior to both and even transcendent over both. The researcher must move from thick description and interpretation to appropriate the eternal message to the new present context without addition or loss of the eternal nature of the message. The key to the process is to move slowly, to move intentionally, to do so in the context of more research and in the context of community.

In this process, here are some questions for engagement:

1. What is the function of the biblical instruction in its original context?
2. Is there a principle behind the given instruction and if so, what is it?
3. Is this instruction or concept timeless or time-bound or transcultural or for a specific culture?
4. How is the new context the same and how is it different?
5. How can this concept be developed to be understood in the new culture?
6. How can this instruction function analogously in the new context?

Different texts and interpretive situations may use only some of these questions that are relevant rather than all in every situation. These questions are given as a guide for this science and art of application or moving the message into a new context.

Conclusion

In essence, the researcher needs to become somewhat of an expert in communications, theology, linguistics, philosophy, anthropology, history, religion, and interpretation. The good news is that much of this expertise is developed in the process of doing biblical study. All good hypotheses must get in the data, do so with simplicity, and shed light beyond its own borders (Wright, 1992). Getting in the data and moving to propositions for application is the goal. Then once these propositions are proposed, they can be developed, tested, and nuanced with further study. However, this process takes intentionality, persistence, and creativity. Who is up to such a task? You are as a believer and follower of Jesus Christ. He set the path for us to follow so that we can indeed follow in His steps. The most common title for Jesus while on the earth was Lord but the most common human title was that of Rabbi or teacher. He was the ultimate teacher. He is divine. However, the results of his depth in Scripture are seen clearly in His earthly ministry. He opened the Scripture to them because they first were open to Him. Believers are to be the deep people, the profound people on the earth. In sharing the parables in the gospels, Jesus tells His disciples that to him who has been given more will be given but to him who does not have even what he has will be taken from him. He was not talking about economics He was talking about truth. The Kingdom or the rule of God does not belong to the casual observer but to the one who passionately pursues God and His truth, which is found in Scripture.

Chapter Twelve Reflective Exercises

1. Develop a research question based upon an analysis of 1 Peter 5:1–8. This research question needs to be focused on leadership. Then explain how you would revisit this question in the final interpretive phase.
2. Show and explain how you would see and note your own bias on the issue of husbands and wives in their relationships in the interpretation of this text of Scripture in 1 Peter 3:1–7.
3. Describe the process and the results of moving from interpretation to application from the text of 1 Peter 5:1–8 concerning leadership. How would you move from interpretation to application to the modern context? What are some of the results from this move? Finally, how does this move to application confirm, challenge, or nuance contemporary leadership theory?

Part 5
Ending with the "Now Whats"

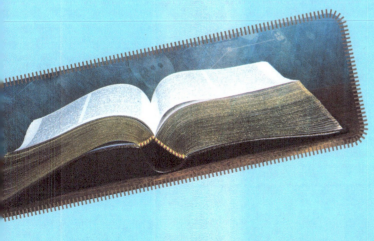

Chapter 13

The Potential for Future Research to Bridge Theory and Practice

Where does all of this leave us for the future of Christian influence on the fields of the social sciences? On the one hand, it requires that Christian scientists be aware of both a biblical approach to the sciences while embracing scientific methodology that is appropriate for each field. This book is purposely designed to assist Christian researchers in identifying biblical approaches to a variety of social sciences. On the other hand, it requires that Christian researchers allow the biblical data to drive them to answers that might be less than acceptable or even anathema to their cultural context. This is what we see in the ministry of Jesus. While not purposely degrading valid and reliable data, at the same time, Christian approaches to social sciences admit their bias that they believe the world works in a particular manner. While this admission to bias may not be embraced by the cultural context, it is a more honest approach to research and necessary to maintain integrity.

Ultimately, since Christianity is a follower-based movement, it is expected that leaders will develop from followers (Huizing, 2011). What this means is that the Christian theorist, researcher, and practitioner must necessarily subsume their leadership under the discipleship of Christ. To become like Christ in every sphere of influence is the goal of the Christian disciple. Thus, in every field of influence, the Christian asks how Christ would most be represented in this field based on the biblical evidence as it intersects with valid and reliable research. This is how the faith is passed on from generation to generation. Leaders from the last generation pass on the biblical research to the next generation of followers who then become leaders for the future generation. In this way, Christian research is built on a solid history of experience that recognizes the changes in cultural contexts. This would suggest not only the need for a future-based analysis of data but an understanding of the historical perspectives that might contribute to our contemporary experiences.

Theory and Theology

Ultimately, there should be a development of both a researched theory as well as a biblically-based theology. Since Christianity recognizes a connection between the reality of theology and the reality of the sciences, the two ought to find some kind of common ground. This requires something more than just Christian perspectives on the social sciences. It compels Christian researchers to test and retest their theories in both qualitative and quantitative forms that provide evidence for their theological underpinnings. Of course, a Christian perspective of the world recognizes that sin causes a brokenness in everything and therefore nothing will ultimately completely represent the biblical expectations. Still, with the "desired" theory before us and the measured reality guiding us, we can pursue a truly Christian answer to each of the social sciences.

It has been said that, "In theory, there is no difference between theory and practice. In practice, there is" (Savitch, 1987). Such is the difficulty of connecting theory and practice. This is further complicated by the range of fields within the social sciences. This work's focus on exegetical analysis necessarily presumes a unique Christian iteration of each of these fields that will likely overlap in some manner with secular research. However, once we find that unique iteration, the complications multiply with a whole gamut of diverse presuppositions, varying traditions, preferred interpretive methodologies, and distinctive consummations based on the different nuances of Christian theologies. In short, it would be impossible to lay out one pathway from theory to practice. Thus, what follows is less of a road map as much as it is a "web of webs" (Smith, 2019, p. 34) where each element has its own internal relationships while being intricately connected with the other elements.

The Chicken or the Egg?

Which comes first—theory or practice? In most conversations, it is presumed that theory has a linear relationship to practice, much like Figure 13.1. This probably has more to do with the process of writing, which is almost necessarily a linear experience. So, most writers move from theory to practice. The relationship, though, is probably a bit more complex.

Figure 13.1 Theory and Practice
Source: Russell Huizing

Chapter 13: The Potential for Future Research to Bridge Theory and Practice

More likely, most theory is not directly connected with practice. Rather, research usually bridges the gap between theory and practice. However, these relationships are not simply linear. Rather, theory leads to research, the results of which refine the theory. This eventually leads to practice, the results of which also lead to a refinement of the theory with the cycle repeating itself (Figure 13.2).

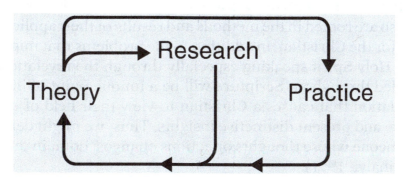

Figure 13.2 Theory, Research, and Practice
Source: Russell Huizing

If this were the whole process, then scholars would never leave their offices and practitioners would have all theoretical possibilities at their fingertips. However, more often than not, theories drop off the apple tree and must be accepted by the masses. In other words, theorists do not work in a vacuum. There must be creativity to the theory that is, paradoxically, often drawn from practice on a small scale. Additionally, irrespective of the validity and reliability of any theory, it must be adopted on a large scale to truly be tested in practice. Thus, Figure 13.3 seems to capture the web that is necessary for a relationship between theory and practice. Ultimately, the relationship must include a combination of creatively immersive experiences that test the rigorously studied theories.

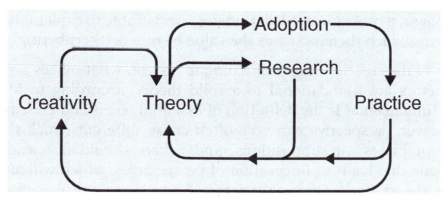

Figure 13.3 The Complexities of Theory and Practice
Source: Russell Huizing

Creative Theory

Creativity nearly always starts with a problem. Whether it is confronting a dead end in research or encountering a hurdle in the field, usually, it is these types of setbacks and hindrances that stoke the fire of inventiveness. The confrontation of these obstacles requires the development of original, practical, adaptable, and resourceful ideas (Choi, Hanh, Tran, & Park, 2015; Zubair & Kamal, 2015) that go beyond just individual application but also are rooted in the methods and results of their application (Kandiko, 2012). Of course, for the Christian, in addition to the problems that might be faced, it is expected that the Holy Spirit speaking especially through the revelation of the Father in Jesus as recorded throughout Scripture will be a unique point of illumination. It is through this revelation that causes a Christian to view their field of expertise from a unique perspective and present distinctive insights. Thus, we might define creativity as coming from "someone whose thoughts or actions change a domain or establish a new one" (Csikszentmihalyi, 1997).

While certainly there are nuanced differences between creativity, innovation, novelty, imagination, and genius (Kandiko, 2012), for the sake of our discussion, we will batch them all together and use them synonymously. Even a cursory look at the history of innovation shows that at times the speed of change can be revolutionary and other times incremental (Kandiko). Creativity can occur through the individual, through an environment that promotes creativity, or through the encouragement of creativity in others (Kandiko).

Since the status quo is embraced by society at large, it is not uncommon for inspiring ideas to be rejected as bothersome or offensive and reason enough to be ignored (Sternberg, 2005). Creativity is especially likely to occur in environments that encourage ingenuity. These are places where disagreement is allowed, outside the box thinking is cultivated, and there is no fear of reprisal when things are done differently (Jung, 2011). If the idea were a stock, it is simply too speculative and too undervalued to see the wisdom of investing in it (Sternberg). As will be discussed as we move into the adoption phase, a broker is needed: someone who is able to explain the theoretical in practical terms which then increases the value by others (Sternberg).

In addition to the creative nature of a unique insight, what makes a good theory? Several key factors are foundational to a solid theory, according to Malek (2018). Perhaps most fundamental is the definition of essential terms and classifying specific variables. However, perspective can very often cause different conclusions. So, the researcher's own biases, presuppositions, and beliefs should be clearly identified allowing dialogue that leads to integration of perspectives, which will almost always strengthen the theory itself. Often theorists will use hypothetical scenarios to both test and indicate the relevance of the theory, which can then assist practitioners to apply the theory to their own conclusions. These scenarios also assist the theorist to anticipate potential concerns that may be raised and thus show a respect for the diverse perspectives that the theory may be applicable toward.

However, theorists must be careful that their theory is not so abstract as to provide no real-world questions (Malek, 2018). This is not to say that there is no place for philosophical or conceptual theorizing; only that such theorizing must continue to rely upon the theory/research cycle until the theory has been developed to a point of applicability. Additionally, theorists must beware that the nuancing of variables and semantics does not become such small degrees of separation as to be meaningless in practice (Malek). Going down either of these pathways rightly breeds skepticism about the significance of the theory and whether it has value (Malek). Thus, it is worthwhile for theorists to make sure that they are always building toward a theory that has an *answer* to it rather than something that will simply remain unknown (Malek).

Smith (2019) and Zahle (2017) suggested that there were four types of theories that could be derived: descriptive–explanatory, action, ends–means, or stakeholder. A descriptive–explanatory theory explains what is happening and why. Action theories recommend an appropriate response to what is happening by advocating for a specific methodology. Ends–means theories recommend particular procedures to accomplish a valued end. Finally, stakeholder theories identify manners in which stakeholders may have different perspectives on a particular focus of research. While nuancing the types of theories may seem superfluous, its importance is seen in understanding what a theory is advocating by those who embrace it.

Scrutinizing Theory

Once the theory has been inspired, it needs to be researched. This is typically done in one of three ways: qualitatively, quantitatively, or a mixture of these approaches. Much of the qualitative material has already been covered in the chapter 11. As was developed there, qualitative analysis is designed to understand data from the perception of the informant (Minichiello, Aroni, Timewell, & Alexander, 1990). Due to the nature of these sources, it is expected that data will be largely anecdotal and inductive in nature (Minichiello et al., 1990; Southern & Devlin, 2010). This is because qualitative analysis is dependent on observation of the data in its original context (Southern & Devlin). Exegetical analysis clearly falls within this method of research. This does not mean that the researched data remains as such. However, nor does qualitative analysis seek to stay in its dependency on experience. The development of qualitative analysis should eventually move toward a measurable, quantitative result.

Quantitative analysis is the deductive method of research. This requires building off an accumulation of established knowledge, identifying a gap or new insight, defining the variables that impact a hypothesis to be researched and replicated, and applying the results for practical application (Southern & Devlin, 2010). Often these results are quantified and statistically analyzed to understand the normative significant results that can be expected. Since much, if not all of life, is a bell curve, it is expected that every theory will have its weaknesses and its effectiveness be contextualized in some manner. Due to this, the development of quantitative analysis should eventually be enhanced through understanding the outliers of the bell curve. This often requires qualitative analysis.

The strongest forms of analysis are mixed methods approaches that seek to enhance results of analysis by combining multiple forms of research. A sequential explanatory design will build from quantitative data collection and analysis to qualitative collection and analysis resulting in an interpretation of the whole research (Creswell, 2009). A sequential exploratory design follows a similar sequence but instead begins with qualitative collection and analysis, moves to quantitative collection and analysis resulting in an interpretation. A third type of mixed method is the concurrent triangulation design. In this research, quantitative and qualitative collections and analyses are done separately and the results are compared to each other. Finally, a concurrent embedded design embeds, on the one hand, qualitative analysis within quantitative (e.g., open-ended questions in a survey) and, on the other hand, embeds quantitative within qualitative (e.g., quantifying number of uses themes) and separately analyzes the results.

Making the Jump

Returning to Figure 13.3, once a theory has been imagined and sufficiently researched, it is time to put it into practice. According to Gardner (2011), for research to be accessible to practitioners, it must be "accessible, relevant, persuasive, credible, and authoritative" (p. 555). Still, it is unlikely for theories to make a large-scale impact unless there is a broker that assists the process (Sternberg, 2005). These brokers are the resource that makes the theory available to a larger audience than simply the sphere of influence of the theorist and/or researcher(s). Typically, then, theory brokers are not part of the research team and may not even be in the same field that the theory is anchored. Even as creativity was needed in the development of the theory, so also it is needed through the extended network of the broker. It is in this way that those who seem the least connected or the greatest irritant can often be the person most responsible for assisting researchers to expand the influence of the theory.

Of course, the wider the social and/or spatial gap between theorists/researchers and practitioners will make the adoption of the theory less likely (Neal, Watling Neal, Lawlor, & Mills, 2015). The broker dissemination may be intentional, like a publication, or unintentional, like getting into news media (Neal et al.). As can be surmised, the more the gap between researchers and practitioners is narrowed and/or the number of brokers is reduced, the more likely that researched theories will be adopted by practitioners (Neal et al.). Additionally, people newer to their research or practitioner field will not have a sufficient network to obtain meaningful brokers (Neal et al., 182).

According to Neal et al. (2015), several different types of networks can occur. On one end of the spectrum is the closed network consisting of theorists, researchers, and practitioners who only speak to one another. Given that this causes groupthink, this is the least desired type of network. On the other side of the spectrum, is a group of theorists, researchers, and practitioners who make utterly random communications with anyone that they come in contact with. While this may seem idea to allow the most creative theories, such a network does not adequately foster community among its participants and as such loses all of the benefits of team. Better is a combination of the closed–open network in which there is a clearly defined parameter of community similar to the parameters of a team that purposefully seeks random interactions that allow the development of brokers as well as bringing in creative material.

From all of this, Neal et al. (2015) provides several lessons to narrow the gap and maximize brokers. First, the most effective broker is not one that knows a lot of people but rather brokers that know people that are clearly outside the social–cultural influence of the theorist/researcher group. This also suggests that brokers are going to be less like theorists/practitioners than like them—this is particularly challenging since most people would prefer colleagues who fit nicely within the existing team.

Much of the applicability of theories for practitioners requires the perception that the theory is appropriate and/or effective (Zahle, 2017). Appropriateness is understood as the action that ought to be done and effectiveness is understood as an action that is likely to accomplish goals (Zahle). Additionally, applicable theories will have a wide social component. The theories will advocate some form of community involvement, behavior that effective practitioners should practice irrespective of others, or a model for others to replicate (Zahle). Applicable theories will also provide the opportunity to test its appropriateness and/or effectiveness (Zahle). While perfection is not to be expected in any activity, still, those who are more likely to appropriately and effectively apply the theory more often than not (Zahle). Thus, it is presumed that at some level, researched theory will need to be acquired (Zahle)—thus, the broker who increases the value of the theory to those outside the sphere of influence of the researchers.

Conclusion

The Christian social scientist, then, is one who is keenly aware of the theoretical underpinnings of their field and how Scripture informs, transforms, or discards aspects of that theory. Additionally, the Christian social scientist will be testing the practical application—the fruit—of that theory to make sure that it aligns with the fruit of the Spirit that followers of Jesus are to produce. Through the repetitive analysis and honing of these theories and practices through research, adoption, and new insights, the Christian can bring another portion of our world under the influence of the King of Kings.

Chapter Thirteen Reflective Exercises

1. Describe a time when theory contributed to your understanding of practice. How much of the theory worked in practice?
2. Describe a time when you felt like you needed to change a working theory based on experience. How were you able to stick with those changes or did you find that you had to keep tweaking theory based on practice?
3. Describe a time when you had an inspired idea that developed from practice. How were you able to work through the theoretical to the new practice? Or what hindrances kept you from developing your inspiration?

Appendices

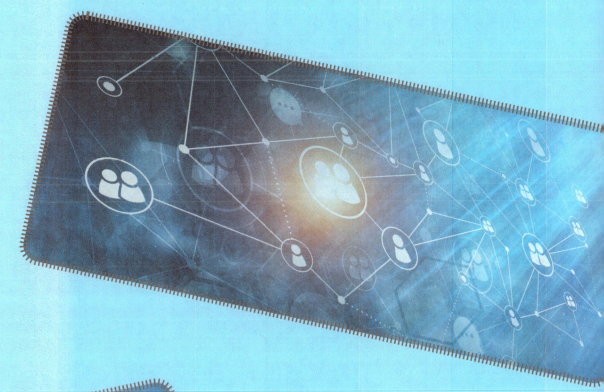
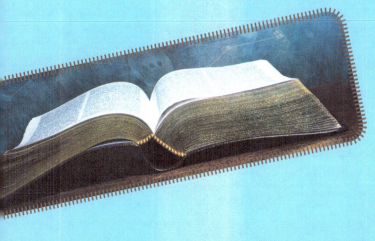

Appendix A

Choosing What to Study

The following contains excerpts from the dissertation of Dr. Joshua Henson. Henson (2015) sought to explore the role of Christian spirituality on the moral and ethical development of authentic leadership from the socio-rhetorical analysis of Paul's letter to Titus.

	Narrowing the Literature
Broad Topic	**Authentic Leadership Theory**
Argument	Authentic leadership is largely defined by the presence of morality (Hannah, Lester, & Vogelgesang, 2005).
	There are six core virtues by which moral development occurs: wisdom, courage, humanity, justice, temperance, and transcendence (Hannah et al., 2005; Park, Peterson, & Seligman, 2004).
	Park et al. (2004) pose that these character virtues are grounded in biology through an evolutionary process.
Potential Problem	**Hannah et al. (2005) conceptualize moral development from a biological, or evolutionary, perspective but does not consider other ways that morality may be developed.**
Argument	Klenke (2007) posed that spiritual identity is at the core of authentic leadership.
Identified Problem	**Missing in the construct of authentic leadership is an understanding of how spirituality and spiritual identity help guide moral development (Henson, 2015).**
	Why is the Bible a good source of data for identified problem?

(Continued)

(*Continued*)

	Narrowing the Literature
Argument	Dent, Higgins, and Wharff (2005) extended spirituality in organizational settings to include religion in the workplace and defined religion as a codified set of beliefs.
	Kretzschmar (2002) connected religious authority to spiritual growth.
	Gibbons (2000) argued that spirituality cannot be separated from ancient religious traditions.
	Kriger and Hanson (1999) posed that the world's major religions hold inherent values that are relevant to contemporary organizations.
	From a Christian perspective, the Bible provides a way to discover new insights into leadership development (Ali, Camp, & Gibbs, 2000).
Assertion	**Therefore, the Bible is a valuable source of data to research moral development from a Christian worldview.**
	Why is the specific author qualified to speak to the problem?
Argument	Bruce (2000) stated that Paul has remained unsurpassed in his insight of the mind of Christ.
	deSilva (2004) wrote that Paul's spiritual journey demonstrated "a level of authenticity in his experience of God that surpassed by far what had been bequeathed to him by his heritage" (p. 486).
	Paul was a supreme example of an authorized servant (Genade, 2011).
	Paul's Christ-centered theology established him and his writings as both credible and authoritative (deSilva, 2004).
Assertion	**Therefore, the writings of the Apostle Paul are a vital resource for those seeking to research the spiritual development from a Christian worldview.**
	Why is the specific book a good source of data for the problem?
Argument	The epistle of Titus is Paul's *mandata principis* to Titus and is thus his orders to be carried by his delegate (deSilva, 2004).
	Martin Luther regarded the letter to Titus as a model of Christian doctrine.

	Narrowing the Literature
Assertion	The letter was primarily concerned about the spiritual progress of the faith community and the necessity of quality leadership (Genade, 2011).
	Paul was concerned about developing virtuous and ethical behaviors among his followers (deSilva, 2004).
	Therefore, the epistle of Titus potentially provides insight into the moral, ethical, and authentic leadership development from a biblical perspective.
	Why is the specific passage a good source of data for the problem?
Argument	[*Note: Henson (2015) conducted an exegetical analysis of the entire epistle of Titus. However, the same types of arguments can now be applied to individual passages*]
	The salutation in chapter 1 identified a threefold perspective of development in the *ekklesia*: spiritual (faith), cognitive (truth), and behavioral (godliness).
	Chapter 1 juxtaposes the trustworthiness of godly leaders and the deceiving rebels.
	Chapter 1 identifies virtues that are to be cultivated (Witherington, 2006).
	Paul configured his list as a reconfiguration of Hellenistic virtues: prudence, temperance, fortitude, justice, and piety (Witherington, 2006).
	Chapter 1 identifies six virtues: hospitable, lover of good, self-controlled, upright, holy, and disciplined (1:8).
Assertion	**Therefore, Titus 1 a potential source of data to research the role of virtues in the development of leadership from a biblical perspective.**
RQ1	What leadership values and practices did Paul express in his letter to Titus?
RQ2	How do these values and practices support or negate the moral development processes of the contemporary model of authentic leadership theory?

Appendix B

Example of Inductive Bible Analysis

This is an example of an Inductive Bible Analysis on Mark 4:35–6:6a

Survey Outline

4:35–41 Jesus calms the storm
5:1–20 Jesus casts out Legion
5:21–34 Jesus heals—Object lessons of faith
     5:21–24; 5:35–43 Jesus heals Jairus' daughter
     5:25–34 Jesus heals woman with issue of blood
6:1–6a Unbelief in Jesus' hometown

Significant Observations

1. *Conceptual contrast*: Faith and unbelief is significant in this pericope—4:40 Jesus' statement about the disciples unbelief and his expectation of their faith; 5:17 the people implore Jesus to leave—unbelief and 5:18–19 the formerly possessed man's desire to go with Jesus, which is an act of faith; 5:23 Jairus' faith for his daughter's healing and 5:39–40 the people who were weeping then laughed at Jesus—unbelief; the woman who was healed 5:34—faith and 5:31 the disciples—unbelief. Finally 6:6a Jesus commented on their unbelief in his hometown but he wondered at it as well. This contrast is in every story in this section and every section involves some miraculous event or healing.
2. *Verbal repetition*:
   a. Be afraid—Mark 4:41, 5:15,33,36
   b. Boat or by boat—Mark 4:36 (2×), 37 (2×), 5:2,18,21
   c. Earnestly ask for, implore, beg—5:10,12,17,18,23
   d. Sea—Mark 4:39,41, 5:1,13 (2×),21

e. Daughter—Mark 5:23,34,35
   f. Healed—Mark 5:23,28,34
   g. Crowd—Mark 4:36, 5:21,24,27,30,31
   h. Miracle—Mark 5:30, 6:2,5
3. *Conceptual repetition*: Amazement or wonder—Mark 4:41 (implied), amazed 5:20, astounded 5:42, astonished 6:2, He wondered
4. *Contrast*:
   a. In the storm
      i. Jesus—asleep, peace
      ii. Disciples—agitated, fearful
   b. Fear and faith (rhetorical questions)
      i. Why are you afraid?
      ii. Do you still have no faith?
5. *Cause and effect*: The storm came up the disciples became fearful and woke Jesus from sleep
6. Movement from fear of the storm to fear of the unknown identity of Jesus
7. *Problem–Solution*: 4:41—Who then is this? 5:7 demons cry out—Jesus, Son of the Most-high God
8. *Substantiation*: Man with unclean spirit because he had often been bound—of the powerful forces at work in the man
9. *Chiasm*:
   A—What business do we have–Son of God–I implore you! Do not torment me 5:7
      B—The demons implored him—go into the swine 5:12 vs. 15, 16
         C—People frightened by Jesus' power
      B'—The people implored him to leave from story of demons and swine 16, 17
   A'—The man imploring him to accompany them–Lord–business of the Lord 18, 19
10. *Adversative*: 5:17 And he did not let him, *but* He said to him
11. *Generalization*: Summary statement of the man's obedience 5:20
12. *Repetition of dark images in this episode*: 5:1–20
    a. Tombs—3×
    b. Chains, shackles—4×
    c. Swine—3×
    d. Unclean spirit, legion, demons—9× (1 is implied)
13. *Chiasm*:
    A 5:23—my daughter is at the point of death—lay hands on her
       B 5:24—crowd pressing in on him
          C 5:34—Daughter your faith made you well (12-year infirmity)
       B' 5:38–40—crowd laughed at him
    A' 5:41 took her by the hand and said - Little girl get up (12 years old)

14. *Result*—come and lay your hands on her *so that* she will get well and live 5:23
15. *Adversative*—Your daughter has died; why trouble the teacher anymore? *But* Jesus . . . said to the official
16. *Repetition*—Jesus referred to as Teacher twice—both were in a question about perishing/dying. First instance of Peter James and John as inner circle
17. *Repetition*—immediately in the context of this section only—(4×)
18. *Conditional*—If I just touch his garments, I will get well
19. *Contrast*—endured spent and grown worse with touch immediately healed
20. *Causation*—Jesus perceived power had gone from him (so) he asked who touched my garments?
21. *Repetition in this section*—fell down before him—5:22,33
22. *Cause and Effect*—your *faith* has made you *well*
23. *Repetition of questions by Jesus*—4:40,5:9,30,39
24. *Particularization*—went to his hometown and disciples followed—then a particular event in the synagogue

Major Structural Observations

1. *Cruciality*—Jesus calms the storm and the disciples ask who he is—then the rest of this section is an answer to that question through deliverances and healing finally with his hometown rejecting him and his disciples following him—they have begun to answer the question properly. It is a crucial change.
2. *Recurrences*—common elements in each story.
   a. Begins with a person or persons in need manifest in asking a question or imploring for help
   b. Then Jesus miraculously meets the need—all involve a miracle or healing
   c. Jesus concludes by giving final instructions
   d. Each story centers around faith versus unbelief
3. *Inclusion*: This section begins by Jesus questioning the disciples about their faith and concludes by Jesus wondering at the unbelief of his hometown as his disciples are with him.

Interpretive Questions

1. What are the implications of Jesus' two rhetorical questions to the disciples concerning faith and fear?
2. What is the significance of the lengthy description of the demon-possessed man?
3. What are the implications of Jesus being amazed at the unbelief of the people in his hometown?

4. How is it significant that he told them not to tell anyone about the girl being raised from the dead when it would be obvious to all that a miracle had happened when Jesus was there?
5. What is the significance of the story of the woman healed of the issue of blood being interjected in the middle of the story of the young girl being raised from the dead?
6. What are the implications of the demons being sent into the swine in the country of the Gerasenes, that there were 2,000 of them and they drowned in the sea?
7. What is the significance of Jairus being a synagogue official and yet appealing to Jesus for the healing of his daughter?
8. What are the implications of the woman touching Jesus' garments and that her sickness involved a flow of blood?
9. What are the implications that Jesus taught in the synagogue in his hometown and yet was met with astonishment and unbelief?

Initial Answer

For the interpretive answers sometimes background information is needed and following is an example.

1. What are the implications of the woman touching Jesus' garments and that her sickness involved a flow of blood?
2. Synagogues—Jesus' Relation to Synagogues by B. Chilton and E. Yamauchi (*Dictionary of the New Testament background*) p. 1150.
3. Purity is one of the issues addressed by Jesus in relation to synagogues that are underscored by Jesus healing the woman with the issue of blood on his way to heal Jairus' daughter both of which were ceremonially unclean.
4. Blood, Flow of—by F. D. Wulf (*Eerdman's dictionary of the Bible*) pp. 193–194. A woman is considered unclean during this time and this impurity is transmitted to anyone she touches. When she touches Jesus' garment, he should have become unclean or she should have been destroyed—instead, the power of his holiness cleansed her.
5. Purity by L. H. Schiffman, PhD (*HarperCollins Bible dictionary*) pp. 854–855. One of the causes of impurity—involuntary flow of fluids from the sexual organs. Early conceptions of impurity saw aspects of the demonic involved. The Hebrew Bible understands moral impurity to be the underlying cause of physical impurity. The moral imperfection represented a defilement from within, a rebellion against God's law. The physical symptoms of impurity were seen as the symptoms of this perfection. This impurity was contagious.

Then the interpretive answer can follow from the analysis of the text and the background research. The woman with the issue of blood was healed in the midst of the story of Jairus' daughter and was significant in that they both had to do with purity issues, which would have been understood by the original readers. Part of the Kingdom message is that of cleansing even the impossible cases. When she touched Jesus' garments, he should have been made unclean and she should have been judged but instead she was cleansed/healed, and he proclaimed blessing on her because of her faith. Through faith there is cleansing but in this case the person had to seek out the object of her faith—Jesus. It was understood that her physical ailment was the result of her moral impurity, but this was a cultural prejudice but Jesus by blessing her touch of him challenged this connection between moral and physical impurity in individual cases. His power was more powerful than the power of defilement so instead of defilement being transferred to Him, which was the expected scenario; His power was transferred to her. This is a powerful picture of God's power through Jesus to cleanse from impurity and to show God's compassion and power that is accessed through faith. Mercy triumphing over judgment is shown in a very real personal sense to those in need, whatever their status.

In this story, this woman is physically healed but it does not stop there in that she was ceremonially unclean and was in a state of undue shame due to the moral implications of this physical ailment. Jesus cleansed here of her impurity physically, socially, and ceremonially. Her life was totally changed. As a Rabbi Jesus should have been repulsed by her and brought judgment upon her but instead, He cleansed here. The power and purity of Jesus is greater than any power of impurity. He did not condemn her instead he encouraged here by telling her that her faith had made her whole. There were several factors at work in this healing, but Jesus chose to focus on this one aspect of her faith. The first issue here is that the power of Jesus is more powerful than any darkness or impurity in anyone's life even today. Seeking Him for healing and help has more power for change than we realize and even expect. Leaders today need to learn this lesson of the power of grace. The disciples wanted to ignore her, but Jesus focused on her and brought cleansing, freedom, and a new life with a simple touch. What power! What compassion! What attention to the individual! This is the power of supernatural grace available today that needs to be understood and taught. This type of grace needs to invade the life and teaching of modern Christian leaders. The disciples clearly misunderstood and could have easily missed the whole event if Jesus had not paused to explain it to them. Leaders today must not miss this important point and they must teach it to new developing leaders as well so that Christian leaders can learn to lead with grace in ways that are countercultural and counterintuitive.

Definition of Terms

Allusion: The reference to a cultural tradition without a direct or indirect attempt to recite any particular text on the part of an author.

Amanuensis: The literary practice in which a literary assistant takes dictation or copies manuscript under the direction of an author.

Anachronism: Attributing a contemporary value, ethic, custom, or item as part of the world of the past without evidence of its presence.

Appropriation: The act of setting apart or assigning to a particular use, it is taking a message that has been given to another and taking it to one's self.

Argument: A supported claim made by an author usually consisting of multiple explicit or implicit claims that provide evidence for a conclusion.

Bibliographical Saturation: The point in the review process that the researcher feels that any missing sources will have minimal effect upon what is known of a theoretical construct, or the researcher has exhausted the requisite resources to continue the literature review.

Chiasm: A literary structure where there are matching themes on opposite ends of the poem with the ideological emphasis of the poem being revealed in its middle.

Common Social and Cultural Topics: These are diverse topics that address the overall environment in a text.

Contextualization: The second part of the hermeneutical process; identifying the significance of text for contemporary society (contemporary context).

Contracultural Rhetoric: A rhetoric that is primarily a reaction to some form of dominant culture, subculture, or counterculture rhetoric and it reacts in a negative way. This is a reaction to existing issues in other cultures and the element of conflict is central in this rhetoric though the conflict need not be violent.

Conversionist: This special social topic can be characterized by a view that the world is corrupt and so are people and the world can be changed when people are changed by salvation.

Definition of Terms

Countercultural Rhetoric: This rhetoric promotes the creation of a better society through its rhetoric by providing an alternative with the hope that the dominant society will see this new way of life with the hope of voluntary reform of the culture.

Criticism: The science of studying Scripture with the intent of uncovering the truth of its development and meaning of its texts.

Dominant Cultural Rhetoric: This is a system of attitudes, values, and norms that the person presupposes are supported by social structures vested with power to impose its goals on people. These are the people in power or what is called the majority culture.

Echo: A word or phrase that evokes, or potentially evokes, a concept from a cultural tradition generally in a subtle, indirect way such that no words or phrases indisputably come from only one cultural tradition.

Editing: A common practice in ancient times in which copies of ancient manuscripts were transcribed by hand.

Eisegesis: To bring one's own presuppositions or biases into the interpretative process; to read into a text.

Exegesis: To pull out the meaning of a text; derived from the Greek word meaning to interpret.

Exegetical Analysis: A scientific, or systematic, approach to the Scriptures with the interpretive intent of exploring biblical texts in their original context for application to contemporary society.

Final Cultural Categories: Rhetoric of those topics that most decisively identify one's cultural location and these locations show the particular group that the person or group belongs to and how they think in distinction to others.

Foretelling: Prophets primarily looking into the distant future.

Forthtelling: Prophets primarily drawing upon the past to describe the present and near future.

Genre, Literary: Written texts that share common forms, styles, and/or subject matter.

Gloss Definition: Taking several definitions and making them shorter but merging them all together for one word.

Gnostic-Manipulationist: This worldview is focused on learning or knowledge in an effort to bring transformation in relationships or in overcoming the problem of evil.

Grammatical-Historical: The use of exegetical analysis to examine the words, the sentences, the paragraphs, and books of the text of Scripture to understand the meaning of the text. This includes the issues of historical background and contexts as well.

Hermeneutics: The overall term for interpreting an author's meaning; derived from the Greek word meaning to interpret. It involves a two-part process: exegesis and contextualization.

Historical-Cultural: The artifacts, values, and customs of a specific group in a particular time.

Ideological: A texture of socio-rhetorical analysis that explores the ancient, historical, and contemporary perspectives and their impact on the interpretation of the text.

Ideological, Individual Locations: Identification of specific topics (conversionist, revolutionist, introversionist, gnostic-manipulationist, thaumaturgic, reformist, and utopian topics) and final categories (dominant culture, subculture, counterculture, contraculture, and liminal culture) of ancient, historical, and contemporary interactors and the impact those locations have on interpretation.

Ideological, Modes of Intellectual Discourse: The presumed interpretive approach that ancient, historical, and contemporary interactors have analyzed Scripture with, including historical-critical, social-scientific, history-of-religions, new historical, and postmodern deconstructive.

Ideological, Relation to Groups: The type of group that ancient, historical, and contemporary interactors belong to (including clique, gang/troop, action set, faction, corporate group, and historic tradition) and the impact those groups have on interpretation.

Ideological, Spheres of Ideology: Identification of individual locations, relation to groups, and modes of intellectual discourse for all possible interactors and the impact those spheres have on different interpretations.

Illumination: The application of inspired revelation to new contexts.

Implied Audience: The reader or audience whom the interpreter infers from the text itself.

Implied Author: The author whom the interpreter infers from the text itself; never completely identical to the flesh-in-blood author.

Implied Purpose: The purpose or occasion of a text whom the interpreter infers from the text itself.

Inductive Biblical Analysis: A method doing exegetical study that is fiercely text centered and based upon inductive thinking in its interaction with the text. The three building blocks of this method are observation, interpretation, and appropriation.

Inner Texture: A texture of socio-rhetorical analysis that explores the parts, structure, and internal message using six filters: textual unit, repetitive patterns, progressive patterns, opening-middle-closing patterns, argumentative patterns, and sensory-aesthetic patterns.

Inner Texture, Argumentative Patterns: Purposeful use of thesis, rationale, contrary, restatement, analogy, example/testimony of antiquity, and conclusion to support authorial conclusion and/or lessons.

Inner Texture, Opening-Middle-Closing Patterns: Purposeful structuring of the text and/or its units to have meta- or mini-plot developments.

Inner Texture, Progressive Patterns: Purposeful developments within the text that assist in identifying authorial intention or lessons.

Inner Texture, Repetitive Patterns: Purposeful reiteration within the text that assist in identifying authorial emphases.

Inner Texture, Sensory-Aesthetic Patterns: Purposeful connection of thinking, feeling, communicating, and activity within the text explicitly or through the use of body-related idioms.

Inner Texture, Textual Unit: Purposeful divisions within the text that mark blocks of meaning identified by common markers including time indicators, a shift of focus within the text, a shift from narrative to commentary, conjunctions, and/or conjunctive adverbs.

Inspiration: The initial revelation of God and His will within a specific context.

Interactors: All individuals that impact the text either ancient, historical, or contemporary.

Intertexture: A texture of socio-rhetorical analysis that explores the relationship of a text being interpreted with the world outside: oral-scribal, cultural, social, historical, and reciprocal intertexture.

Intertexture, Cultural: A subtexture of intertexture that explores the cultural knowledge of the people represented in a text; how meaning and memory are conveyed through a text: references, allusions, and echoes.

Intertexture, Historical: A subtexture of intertexture that researches specific events that are referenced or alluded to in a text.

Intertexture, Oral-Scribal: A subtexture of intertexture that explores how a text configures outside texts or bardic traditions: recitation, recontextualization, reconfiguration, narrative amplification, and thematic elaboration.

Intertexture, Reciprocal: A subtexture of intertexture that allows the interpreter to move forward and backward through Scripture to better understand the location of a given text in the canon of Scripture.

Intertexture, Social: A subtexture of intertexture that explores the social knowledge commonly held by all people of a region: social roles, social identities, social institutions, social codes, and social relationships.

Introversionist: This worldview sees the world as evil with no human solution available. The answer for those with this view is withdrawal from the world and renouncing the world system.

Liminal Cultural Rhetoric: This exists in the language appears as people transition from one cultural identity to another or with groups who have never been able to establish a clear cultural identity in their setting.

Location, Social and Cultural: The social and cultural world that the text describes and in which the implied audience lives.

Narrative Amplification: A form of oral-scribal intertexture that utilizes recitation, recontextualization, and reconfiguration of source texts to amplify an argument.

Pericope: A passage of text from the Bible; the plural form being pericopae.

Primary Sources: Firsthand accounts, artifacts, original works, empirical research, or original theoretical works.

Problem of Distance: Refers to the separation that exists between the interpreter and the original author and audience: time, culture, language, and geography.

Qualitative Analysis: Research methodologies that allow the researcher to understand recorded experiences and apply the descriptions of those experiences to contemporary fields of study.

Qualitative Research: A method of inquiry that extracts research questions from literature and then seeks to answer the research questions through direct observation and interviews and/or the content analysis of texts.

Quantitative Research: The empirical investigation that seeks to quantify a problem by establishing hypotheses based on the literature and then statistically testing the hypotheses with data collected from a sample of people or relevant data source.

Recitation: When a biblical text relies upon other written texts (biblical or otherwise) or oral traditions to evoke meaning. Can present as exact phrases, minor differences, or substantially change, but must contain a direct or indirect attribution to an outside source.

Reconfiguration: When a text utilizes the recitation or recontextualization of outside written or oral traditions to establish a new event, and this new event outshines, foreshadows, or replaces the previous event.

Recontextualization: When a text relies upon other written or oral traditions to evoke meaning; however, it does not provide a direct or indirect attribution of an outside source.

Reference: A word or phrase that points to a personage or tradition known to the people on the basis of tradition.

Reformist: This worldview sees the world as evil due to its social systems therefore the solution is through changing the social systems.

Research Problem: A statement that arises from a literature review that identifies a potential problem, gap, or opportunity to extend the existing body of knowledge.

Research Question(s): A qualitative questions designed to explore a problem found in the literature and generally has four criteria: (a) begins with why, what, or how; (b) identifies the problem from the literature; (c) identifies the selected pericope, and (d) references the methodology.

Revolutionist: This special social topic rhetoric declares that only the destruction of the world in the natural and social order will save people and supernatural powers perform the destruction though people can assist in the process, the central issues here are about the ultimate destruction of the world.

Rhetography: The pictures that represent our perception of the world and their identification based on ideology within the text.

Rhetoric: The quality in discourse by which a speaker or writer seeks to accomplish his or her purposes, refers to the way language is used as a means of communication.

Sacred Texture: This analysis looks deeply into the issues of God in who He is and what He says to humans in the text.

Secondary Sources: Sources that offer a once-removed account of an event or comments upon, analyzes, or interprets information from a primary source.

Social and Cultural Texture: This aspect of interpretation explores the social and cultural location of the language and the type of world the language evokes, and it deals with the impact of society and culture on the text just as society and culture impacts a person.

Social Codes: Written or unwritten rules for behavior, relationships, and appearance that are widely understood by the people of a region.

Social Institutions: An organization or system of organizations; a structure of differentiated roles, functions, culture, and sanctions.

Social Relationships: The relational interactions between various groups, institutions, roles, and segments of society.

Social Roles: The social functions and requisite expectations of those functions such as slave, shepherd, and king.

Social-Scientific Criticism: A hermeneutical method that utilizes sociological and anthropological information to exegete biblical passages.

Socio-Rhetorical Analysis: A hermeneutical method that explores the values, beliefs, and relationships of the people of a text and the textual arguments made by the author through inner texture, intertexture, social and cultural texture, ideological texture, and sacred texture.

Specific Social Topics: Ways of talking about the world can be seen in the text in the way life or spirituality, in essence these are different types of religious worldviews or worldviews that could be unique to Christians and people of other religious traditions.

Subculture Rhetoric: This imitates the attitudes, values, and norms of the dominant culture claiming to enact them better than the dominant culture whereas an ethnic subculture has its origins in a different language from the dominant group.

Tertiary Sources: Sources that provide an overview of a topic or rely heavily upon secondary sources in order to analyze, synthesize, or summarize any given topic in a user-friendly fashion.

Thaumaturgical: This worldview looks to relieve the results of evil in this world for individuals. It concerns issues of healing, comfort, restoration, or overcoming disaster. The concern is not in dealing with the force of evil but with the plights of individuals in this world.

Thematic Elaboration: Like narrative amplification, is a rhetorical technique that builds upon a theme, or chreia, at the beginning of unit through (a) argument from the opposite or contrary; (b) argument from analogy; (c) argument from example; or (d) argument from ancient testimony.

Theoretical Saturation: The point in ground theory research that any missed data will have little to no modifying effect on the theory.

Transhistorical Principle: A principle that can be understood and applied across time and cultures.

Utopian: This worldview sees the world in need of being totally rebuilt after a divine design, reform is not sufficient, and the system is the problem not the people. Therefore, there must be a totally new system and people must initiate and build this new perfect system.

Resources for Further Study

Biblical Research Methodology

Bauer, D. R., & Traina, R. A. (2011). *Inductive Bible study: A comprehensive guide to the practice of hermeneutics*. Grand Rapids, MI: Baker Academic.

Beale, G. K. (2011). *A New Testament biblical theology: The unfolding of the Old Testament in the new*. Grand Rapids, MI: Baker Academic.

Bradley, J. E., & Muller, R. A. (1995). *Church history: An introduction to research, reference works, and methods*. Grand Rapids, MI: William B. Eerdmans Publishing.

Bray, G. (1996). *Biblical interpretation: Past & present*. Downers Grove, IL: InterVarsity Press.

deSilva, D. A. (2004). *An introduction to the New Testament: Contexts, methods, and ministry formation*. Downers Grove, IL: IVP Academic.

Duvall, J. S., & Hays, J. D. (2012). *Grasping god's word: A hands-on approach to reading, interpreting, and applying the bible* (3rd ed.). Grand Rapids, MI: Zondervan.

Kibbe, M. (2016). *From topic to thesis: A guide to theological research*. Downers Grove, IL: InterVarsity Press.

Klein, W. W., Blomberg, C. L., & Hubbard, R. L., Jr. (2017). *Introduction to biblical interpretation*. Grand Rapids, MI: Zondervan.

Linnemann, W. (1990). *Historical criticism of the Bible: Methodology or ideology* (R. Yarbrough, Trans.). Grand Rapids, MI: Kregel Publications.

Malina, B. J. (2001). *The testament world: Insights from cultural anthropology*. Louisville, KY: Westminster John Knox Press.

Osborne, G. R. (2006). *The hermeneutical spiral: A comprehensive introduction to biblical interpretation*. Downers Grove, IL: InterVarsity Press.

Robbins, V. K. (1996a). *Exploring the texture of texts*. Harrisburg, PA: Trinity Press International.

Robbins, V. K. (1996b). *The tapestry of early Christian discourse: Rhetoric, society, and ideology*. New York, NY: Routledge.

Stone, H. W., & Duke, J. O. (2013). *How to think theologically*. Minneapolis, MN: Fortress Press.

Vyhmeister, N. J., & Robertson, T. D. (2014). *Your guide to writing quality research papers; for students of religion and theology* (3rd ed.). Grand Rapids, MI: Zondervan.

Witherington, B., III. (2009). *What's in the word: Rethinking the socio-rhetorical character of the New Testament*. Waco, TX: Baylor University Press.

Yamauchi. E. M., & Wilson, M. R. (2017). *Dictionary of daily Life in biblical and post biblical antiquity*. Peabody, MA: Hendrickson.

Social-Scientific Methodology

Creswell, J. W., & Creswell, J. D. (2018). *Research design: Qualitative, quantitative, and mixed methods approaches* (5th ed.). Thousand Oaks, CA: Sage Publications.

Glaser, B. G., & Strauss, A. L. (1967/1999). *The discovery of grounded theory: Strategies for qualitative research*. New Brunswick, NJ: Aldine Transaction.

Huberman, A. M., & Miles, M. B. (2002). *The qualitative researcher's companion*. Thousand Oaks, CA: Sage Publications.

Patton, M. Q. (2002). *Qualitative research & evaluation methods* (3rd ed.). Thousand Oaks, CA: Sage Publications.

Yin, R. K. (2003). *Case study research: Design and methods* (2nd ed.). Thousand Oaks, CA: Sage Publications.

Biblical/Theological Journals

Biblica
Biblical Interpretation
Currents in Biblical Research
Harvard Theological Review
Hervormde teologieses studies
Horizons in Biblical Theology
Journal of Applied Christian Leadership
Journal of Biblical Integration in Business
Journal of Biblical Literature
Journal of Biblical Perspectives in Leadership
Journal of Reformed Theology
Journal of Pentecostal Theology
Journal of the Evangelical Theological Society
Journal of Theological Studies
New Testament Studies
Novum Testamentum
Pneuma
Princeton Seminary Bulletin
Pro Ecclesia
Review of Religious Research
Theology of Leadership Journal

Biblical Commentaries

Anchor Bible
Ancient Christian Commentary on Scripture
Expositor's Bible Commentary
Interpretation: A Bible Commentary for Teaching and Preaching
New International Commentary on the New Testament
New International Commentary on the Old Testament
New International Greek Testament Commentary

List of References

Foreword

Arnold, D. W., & George Fry, C. (1988). *Francis: A call to conversion* (p. 25). Grand Rapids: Cantilever Books.

Deist F. E. (1992). *A concise dictionary of theological and related terms*. Pretoria: J. L. Van Schaik.

Duvall, J. S., & Hays, J. D. (2005). Grasping God's word: A hands-on approach to reading, interpreting, and applying the Bible (2nd ed.). Grand Rapids, MI: Zondervan.

Foster, R. J. (2008). *Life with God: Reading the Bible for spiritual transformation* (pp. 80–120). New York, NY: HarperCollins.

Kretzschmar, L. (2002). Authentic Christian leadership and spiritual formation in Africa. *Journal of Theology for Southern Africa, 113*, 41–60.

Kretzschmar, L. (2007). The formation of moral leaders in South Africa: A Christian-ethical analysis of some essential elements. *Journal of Theology for Southern Africa, 128*, 18–36.

Luther, M. (n.d.). *Es muss verderben, alles was nicht Gottes Wort ohn Unterlass treibt*. L. Opp. (L.) xvii.

Peterson, E. H. (2006). *Eat this book: A conversation in the art of spiritual reading*. Wm. B. Eerdmans Publishing.

Scaperlanda, M. R., & Scaperlanda, M. (2004). The journey: A guide for the modern pilgrim. Loyola Press.

Chapter One

Augustine, S. (n.d.). *De Doctrina Christiana*. (R. P. Green, Trans). (1997/1999). *On Christian Teaching: St Augustine*. New York, NY: Oxford University Press.

Beale, G. K. (2011). *A New Testament biblical theology: The unfolding of the Old Testament in the new*. Grand Rapids, MI: Baker Academic.

Bray, G. (1996). *Biblical interpretation: Past & present*. Downers Grove, IL: InterVarsity Press.

Calvin, J. (2008). *Institutes of the Christian Religion*. (H. Beveridge, Trans.). Peabody, MA: Hendrickson.

Duvall, J. S. & Hays, J. D. (2005). *Grasping God's Word: A Hands-On Approach to Reading, Interpreting, and Applying the Bible* (2nd ed.). Zondervan: Grand Rapids, MI.

Elliot, J. H. (1993). *What is Social-Scientific Criticism?*. Minneapolis, MN: Fortress Press.

González, J. L. (1971). *A history of Christian thought: From Augustine to the eve of the Reformation* (Revised ed., Vol. 2). Nashville, TN: Abingdon Press.

Klein, W. W., Blomberg, C. L., & Hubbard, R. L., Jr. (2017). *Introduction to biblical interpretation*. Grand Rapids, MI: Zondervan.

Linnemann, W. (1990). *Historical criticism of the Bible: Methodology or ideology* (R. Yarbrough, Trans.). Grand Rapids, MI: Kregel Publications.

Moynagh, M. (2018). *Church in life: Innovation, mission and ecclesiology*. Eugene, OR: Cascade Books.

Osborne, G. R. (2006). *The hermeneutical spiral: A comprehensive introduction to biblical interpretation*. Downers Grove, IL: InterVarsity Press.

Robbins, V. K. (1996). *Exploring the texture of texts*. Harrisburg, PA: Trinity Press International.

Stone, H. W., & Duke, J. O. (2013). *How to think theologically*. Minneapolis, MN: Fortress Press.

Vyhmeister, N. J., & Robertson, T. D. (2014). *Your guide to writing quality research papers; for students of religion and theology* (3rd ed.). Grand Rapids, MI: Zondervan.

Williams, J. R. (1996). *Renewal theology: Systematic theology from a Charismatic perspective*. Grand Rapids, MI: Zondervan.

Witherington, B., III. (2009). *What's in the word: Rethinking the socio-rhetorical character of the New Testament*. Waco, TX: Baylor University Press.

Chapter Two

Bradley, J. E., & Muller, R. A. (1995). *Church history: An introduction to research, reference works, and methods*. Grand Rapids, MI: William B. Eerdmans Publishing.

Creswell, J. W. (2009). *Research design: Qualitative, quantitative, and mixed methods approaches* (3rd ed.). Thousand Oaks, CA: Sage Publications.

Creswell, J. W., & Creswell, J. D. (2018). *Research design: Qualitative, quantitative, and mixed methods approaches* (5th ed.). Thousand Oaks, CA: Sage Publications.

Damer, T. E. (2009). *Attacking faulty reasoning: A practical guide to fallacy-free arguments* (6th ed.). Belmont, CA: Wadsworth Cengage Learning.

Gardner, W. L., Cogliser, C. C., Davis, K. M., & Dickens, M. P. (2011). Authentic leadership: A review of the literature and research agenda. *The Leadership Quarterly*, *22*(6), 1120–1145.

Glaser, B. G., & Strauss, A. L. (1967/1999). *The discovery of grounded theory: Strategies for qualitative research*. New Brunswick, NJ: Aldine Transaction.

Huberman, A. M., & Miles, M. B. (2002). *The qualitative researcher's companion*. Thousand Oaks, CA: Sage Publications.

Kibbe, M. (2016). *From topic to thesis: A guide to theological research*. Downers Grove, IL: InterVarsity Press.

Osborne, G. R. (2006). *The hermeneutical spiral: A comprehensive introduction to biblical interpretation*. Downers Grove, IL: InterVarsity Press.

Taylor, S. J., Bogdan, R., & DeVault, M. (2015). *Introduction to qualitative research methods: A guidebook and resource*. Hoboken, NJ: John Wiley & Sons. Retrieved from https://ebookcentral-proquest-com.ezproxy.regent.edu

Stone, H. W., & Duke, J. O. (2013). *How to think theologically*. Minneapolis, MN: Fortress Press.

Vyhmeister, N. J., & Robertson, T. D. (2014). *Your guide to writing quality research papers; for students of religion and theology* (3rd ed.). Grand Rapids, MI: Zondervan.

Chapter Three

Adams, G. A. (1999). Preaching from 1 & 2 chronicles. *The Fellowship for Reformation and Pastoral Studies, 27*(7), 1–15.

Allender, D. B. (2006). *To be told: God invites you to co-author your future*. Colorado Springs, CO: WaterBrook Press.

Anderson, Garwood (2003). *Book of Mark* [Class Notes, Asbury Theological Seminary, Orlando, FL].

Bauer, D. R., & Traina, R. A. (2011). *Inductive Bible study: A comprehensive guide to the practice of hermeneutics*. Grand Rapids, MI: Baker Academic.

Blomberg, C. L. (1990). *Interpreting the parables*. Downers Grove, IL: InterVarsity Press.

Bray, G. (1996). *Biblical interpretation: Past & present*. Downers Grove, IL: InterVarsity Press.

Carter, T. G., Duvall, J. S., & Hays, J. D. (2018). *Preaching God's word: A hands-on approach to preparing, developing, and delivering the sermon* (2nd ed.). Grand Rapids, MI: Zondervan.

Corly, B., Lemke, S., & Lovejoy, G. (2002). *Biblical hermeneutics: A comprehensive introduction to interpreting scripture*. Nashville, TN: Broadman and Holman.

Duvall, J. S., & Hays, J. D. (2012). *Grasping God's word: A hands-on approach to reading, interpreting, and applying the Bible* (3rd ed.). Grand Rapids, MI: Zondervan.

Fee, G. D. (2002). *New testament exegesis: A handbook for students and pastors*. Louisville, KY: Westminster John Knox Press.

Fee, G., & Stuart, D. (2014). *How to read the Bible for all its worth: A guide to understanding the Bible*. Grand Rapids, MI: Zondervan.

Mickelson, A. B. (1972). *Interpreting the Bible*. Grand Rapids, MI: William B. Eerdmans Publishing.

Osborne, G. R. (2006). *The hermeneutical spiral: A comprehensive introduction to biblical interpretation*. Downers Grove, IL: InterVarsity Press.

Vanhoozer, K. J. (1998). *Is there a meaning in this text? The Bible, the reader and the morality of literary knowledge*. Grand Rapids, MI: Zondervan.

Virkler, H. A., & Ayayo, K. G. (2007). *Hermeneutics: Principles and process of biblical interpretation*. Grand Rapids, MI: Baker Academic.

Witherington, B. (2009). *New Testament rhetoric: An introductory guide to the art of persuasion in and of the New Testament*. Eugene, OR: Wipf and Stock.

Chapter Four

Austin, S. A., Franz, G. W., & Frost, E. G. (2000). Amos's earthquake: An extraordinary Middle East seismic event of 750 B.C. *International Geology Review, 42*(7), 657–671.

Bauer, D. R., & Traina, R. A. (2011). *Inductive Bible study: A comprehensive guide to the practice of hermeneutics.* Grand Rapids, MI: Baker Academic.

Bruce, F. F. (1981). *The New Testament documents: Are they reliable?* (6th ed.). Grand Rapids, MI: William B. Eerdmans Publishing.

Creswell, J. W. (2009). *Research design: Qualitative, quantitative, and mixed methods approaches* (3rd ed.). Thousand Oaks, CA: Sage Publications.

Damer, T. E. (2009). *Attacking faulty reasoning: A practical guide to fallacy-free arguments* (6th ed.). Belmont, CA: Wadsworth Cengage Learning.

deSilva, D. A. (2004). *An introduction to the New Testament: Contexts, methods, and ministry formation.* Downers Grove, IL: IVP Academic.

Fee, G. D. (2011). 1&2 Timothy, Titus. In W. W. Gasque, R. L. Hubbard Jr., & R. K. Johnston (Eds.), *Understanding the Bible commentary series* (Revised ed.), Grand Rapids, MI: Baker Books.

Henson, J. D. (2015). *An examination of the role of spirituality in the development of the moral component of authentic leadership through a sociorhetorical analysis of Paul's letter to Titus.* Unpublished doctoral dissertation. Regent University, Virginia Beach, VA.

Huberman, A. M., & Miles, M. B. (2002). *The qualitative researcher's companion.* Thousand Oaks, CA: Sage Publications.

Klein, W. W., Blomberg, C. L., & Hubbard, R. L., Jr. (2017). *Introduction to biblical interpretation.* Grand Rapids, MI: Zondervan.

Lakey, M. J. (2010). *Image and glory of God: 1 Corinthians 11: 2-16 as a case study in Bible, gender and hermeneutics. Library of New Testament studies.* New York, NY: T&T Clark International.

Longman, T., III., & Dillard, R. B. (2006). *An introduction to the Old Testament* (2nd ed.). Grand Rapids, MI: Zondervan.

Osborne, G. R. (2006). *The hermeneutical spiral: A comprehensive introduction to biblical interpretation.* Downers Grove, IL: InterVarsity Press.

Quinn, J. D. (1990). *The letter to Titus: A new translation with notes and commentary and an introduction to Titus, 1 and 2 Timothy, the pastoral epistles.* New York, NY: Doubleday.

Robbins, V. K. (1996). *The tapestry of early Christian discourse: Rhetoric, society, and ideology.* New York, NY: Routledge.

Thomas, D. W. (Ed.). (1967). *Archaeology and the Old Testament study.* London: Oxford University Press.

Witherington, B. (2006). *Letters and Homilies for Hellenized Christians: A socio-rhetorical commentary on Titus, 1-2 Timothy, and 1-3 John.* Downers Grove, IL: InterVarsity Press.

Yin, R. K. (2003). *Case study research: Design and methods* (2nd ed.). Thousand Oaks, CA: Sage Publications.

Chapter Five

Cotterell, P., & Turner, M. (1989). *Linguistics and biblical interpretation.* Downers Grove, IL: InterVarsity Press.

DeWeese, G. J., & Moreland, J. P. (2005). *Philosophy made slightly less difficult.* Downers Grove, IL: InterVarsity Press.

Fee, G. D. (2002). *New Testament exegesis: A handbook for students and pastors.* Louisville, KY: Westminster John Knox Press.

Fee, G., & Stuart, D. (2014). *How to read the Bible for all its worth: A guide to understanding the Bible.* Grand Rapids, MI: Zondervan

Kennedy, G. A. (1984). *New Testament interpretation through rhetorical criticism.* Chapel Hill, NC: University of North Carolina Press.

Ong, W. J. (2002). *Orality and literacy.* New York, NY, Routledge.

Polkinghorne, J. (2007). *Quantum physics and theology: An unexpected kinship.* New Haven, CT: Yale University Press.

Robbins, V. K. (1996). *Exploring the texture of texts.* Harrisburg, PA: Trinity Press International.

Vanhoozer, K. J. (1998). *Is there a meaning in this text? The Bible, the reader and the morality of literary knowledge.* Grand Rapids, MI: Zondervan.

Witherington, B. (2009). *New Testament rhetoric: An introductory guide to the art of persuasion in and of the New Testament.* Eugene, OR: Wipf and Stock.

Chapter Six

Allender, D. B. (2005). *To be told: Know your story, shape your future.* Colorado Springs, CO: Waterbrook Press.

Bledstein, A. J. (1977). Genesis of humans: The Garden of Eden revisited. *Judaism, 26*(2), 187–200.

Bray, G. (1996). *Biblical interpretation: Past & present.* Downers Grove, IL: InterVarsity Press.

Loubser, J. A. (2005). Invoking the ancestors: Some socio-rhetorical aspects of the genealogies in the gospels of Matthew and Luke. *Neotestamentica, 39*(1), 127–140.

Robbins, V. K. (1996a). *Exploring the texture of texts.* Harrisburg, PA: Trinity Press International.

Robbins, V. K. (1996b). *The tapestry of early Christian discourse: Rhetoric, society and ideology.* New York, NY: Routledge.

Chapter Seven

Bauer, D. R., & Traina, R. A. (2011). *Inductive Bible study: A comprehensive guide to the practice of hermeneutics.* Grand Rapids, MI: Baker Academic.

Creswell, J. W. (2009). *Research design: Qualitative, quantitative, and mixed methods approaches* (3rd ed.). Thousand Oaks, CA: Sage Publications.

Fusch, P. I., & Ness, L. R. (2015). Are we there yet? Data saturation in qualitative research. *The Qualitative Report, 20*(9), 1408–1416.

Gowler, D. B. (2010). Socio-rhetorical interpretation: Textures of a text and its reception. *Journal for the Study of the New Testament, 33*(2), 191–206. doi:10.1177/0142064X10385857

Jaeger, W. (1939). *Paideia: The ideals of Greek culture* (G. Highet, Trans.). *Archaic Greece—The Mind of Athens* (Vol. 1). New York, NY: Oxford University Press.

Klein, W. W., Blomberg, C. L., & Hubbard, R. L., Jr. (2017). *Introduction to biblical interpretation*. Grand Rapids, MI: Zondervan.

Mayan, M. J. (2016). *Essentials of qualitative inquiry*. New York, NY: Routledge. (Originally published in 2009). Retrieved from https://ebookcentral-proquest-com.ezproxy.regent.edu

McConville, J. G. (2002). *Exploring the Old Testament: A guide to the prophets*: Vol. 4. *A guide to the prophets*. Downers Grove, IL: InterVarsity Press.

Miller, S. (2010). *The moral foundations of social institutions: A philosophical study*. Cambridge: Cambridge University Press.

Noegel, S. B., & Wheeler, B. M. (2002). *Historical dictionary of prophets in Islam and Judaism*. Lanham, MD: Scarecrow Press.

Osborne, G. R. (2006). *The hermeneutical spiral: A comprehensive introduction to biblical interpretation*. Downers Grove, IL: InterVarsity Press.

Robbins, V. K. (1996a). *Exploring the texture of texts: A guide to socio-rhetorical interpretation*. Harrisburg, PA: Bloomsbury Academic.

Robbins, V. K. (1996b). *The tapestry of early Christian discourse: Rhetoric, society, and ideology*. New York, NY: Routledge.

Robbins, V. K. (2010). Socio-rhetorical interpretation. In D. E. Aune (Ed.), *The Blackwell companion to the New Testament* (pp. 192–219). Chichester, West Sussex: Blackwell Publishing Ltd.

Witherington, B. (2006). *Letters and homilies for Hellenized Christians: A socio-rhetorical commentary on Titus, 1-2 Timothy, and 1-3 John*. Downers Grove, IL: InterVarsity Press.

Wright, N. T. (2013). *Paul and the faithfulness of God*. Minneapolis, MN: Fortress Press.

Chapter Eight

Alexander, J. C., & Siedman, S. (1990). *Culture and society: Contemporary debates*. New York, NY: Cambridge University Press.

Bekker, C. J. (2007). *Sharing the incarnation: Towards a model of mimetic Christological leadership. Servant leadership research roundtable*. Virginia Beach, VA: Regent University.

Bekker, C. J. (2008). Leading with your head bowed down: Lesson in leadership humility from St. Benedict of Nursia. *Inner Resources for Leaders, 1*(3), 1–10.

Eisenberg, R. L. (2005). The 613 Mitzvot: A Contemporary Guide to the Commandments of Judaism. Schreiber Publishing: Rockville, MD. ISBN:978-0884003335

Grunlan, S. A., & Mayers, M. K. (1988). *Cultural anthropology: Christian perspective*. Grand Rapids, MI: Zondervan.

Heddendorf, R., & Vos, M. (2010). *Hidden threads: A Christian critique of sociological theory*. Lanham, MD: University Press of America.

Kennedy, G. A. (1984). *New Testament interpretation through rhetorical criticism*. Chapel Hill, NC: University of North Carolina Press.

Malina, B. J. (2001). *The testament world: Insights from cultural anthropology*. Louisville, KY: Westminster John Knox Press.

Nanda, S., & Warms, R. L. (2018). *Culture counts: A concise introduction to cultural anthropology*. Boston, MA: Cengage Learning.

Phillips, T. (2015). *Liminal fictions in postmodern culture: The politics of self-development*. New York, NY: Palgrave MacMillan.

Robbins, V. K. (1996a). *Exploring the texture of texts*. Harrisburg, PA: Trinity Press International.

Robbins, V. K. (1996b). *The tapestry of early Christian discourse: Rhetoric, society and ideology*. New York, NY: Routledge.

Virkler, H. A., & Ayayo, K. G. (2007). *Hermeneutics: Principles and processes of biblical interpretation*. Grand Rapids, MI: Baker Academic

Wilson, B. R. (1973). *Magic and the millennium: A sociological study of religious movements of protest among tribal and third-world peoples*. New York, NY: Harper and Row.

Witherington, B. (2009). *New Testament rhetoric: An introductory guide to the art of persuasion in and of the New Testament*. Eugene, OR: Wipf and Stock.

Wright, N. T. (1992). *The New Testament and the people of God*. Minneapolis, MN: Fortress Press.

Yamauchi, E. M., & Wilson, M. R. (2017). *Dictionary of daily life in biblical and post biblical antiquity*. Peabody, MA: Hendrickson.

Chapter Nine

deSilva, D. A. (2008). Seeing things John's way: Rhetography and conceptual blending in revelation 14:6–13. *Bulletin for Biblical Research, 18*(2), 271–298.

Erfani, S. M., Iranmehr, A., & Davari, H. (2011). Deepening ESP reading comprehension through visualization. *Journal of Language Teaching and Research, 2*(1), 270–273. doi:10.4304/jltr.2.1.270-273

Gowler, D. B. (2010). Socio-rhetorical interpretation: Textures of a text and its reception. *Journal for the Study of the New Testament, 33*(2), 191–206.

Malina, B. (2001). *The New Testament world: Insights from cultural anthropology* (3rd ed.). Louisville, KY: Westminster John Knox Press.

Robbins, V. K. (1996a). *Exploring the texture of texts*. Harrisburg, PA: Trinity Press International.

Robbins, V. K. (1996b). *The tapestry of early Christian discourse: Rhetoric, society and ideology*. New York, NY: Routledge.

Robbins, V. K., von Thaden, R. H., Jr., & Bruehler, B. B. (Eds.). (2016). *Foundations for sociorhetorical exploration: A rhetoric of religious antiquity reader*. Atlanta, GA: SBL Press.

Vogt, S., & Magnussen, S. (2007). Expertise in pictorial perception: Eye-movement patterns and visual memory in artists and laymen. *Perception, 36*(1), 91–100.

Chapter Ten

deSilva, D. A. (2000). *Perseverance in gratitude: A socio-rhetorical commentary on the Epistle to the Hebrews*. Grand Rapids, MI: William B. Eerdmans Publishing.

Duvall, J. S., & Hays, J. D. (2012). *Grasping God's Word*. Grand Rapids, MI: Zondervan Publishing.

Fee, G., & Stuart, D. (2014). *How to read the Bible for all its worth: A guide to understanding the Bible*. Grand Rapids, MI: Zondervan.

Grudem, W. (1994). *Systematic theology*. Grand Rapids, MI: Zondervan Publishing.

Osborne, G. R. (2006). *The hermeneutical spiral: A comprehensive introduction to biblical interpretation*. Downers Grove, IL: InterVarsity Press.

Ramm, B. (1999). *Protestant biblical interpretation*. Grand Rapids, MI: Baker Books.

Robbins, V. K. (1996). *Exploring the texture of texts*. Harrisburg, PA: Trinity Press International.

Chapter Eleven

Breck, J. (1983). Exegesis and interpretation: Orthodox reflections on the "hermeneutic problem." *St Vladimir's Theological Quarterly, 27*(2), 75–92.

Creswell, J. W. (2009). *Research design: Qualitative, quantitative, and mixed methods approaches* (3rd ed.). Thousand Oaks, CA: Sage Publications.

Denzin, N. K. (2002). The interpretive process. In A. Michael Huberman & M. B. Miles (Eds.), *The qualitative researcher's companion*. Thousand Oaks, CA: Sage Publications.

Denzin, N. K., & Lincoln, Y. S. (2000). Introduction: The discipline and practice of qualitative research. In Denzin & Lincoln (Eds.), *Handbook of qualitative research* (2nd ed.). Thousand Oaks, CA: Sage Publications.

Dorman, T. M. (1998). Holy Spirit, history, hermeneutics and theology: Toward an evangelical/catholic consensus. *Journal of the Evangelical Theological Society, 41*(3), 427–438.

Duvall, J. S., & Hays, J. D. (2012). *Grasping God's word: A hands-on approach to reading, interpreting, and applying the Bible* (3rd ed.). Grand Rapids, MI: Zondervan Academic.

Hart, L. (1987). Hermeneutics, theology, and the Holy Spirit. *Perspectives in Religious Studies, 14*(4), 53–64.

Huizing, R. L., & James, K. (2018). Apprentices or pupils? An analysis of teaching in the New Testament. *Evangelical Review of Theology, 42*(2), 157–170.

Keener, C. S. (2016) *Spirit hermeneutics: Reading scripture in light of Pentecost*. Grand Rapids, MI: William B. Eerdmans Publishing.

Krippendorff, K. (1980). *Content analysis: An introduction to its methodology* (Vol. 5). Beverly Hills, CA: Sage Publications.

Maxwell, J. A. (2002). Understanding and validity in qualitative research. In A. Michael Huberman & M. B. Miles (Eds.), *The qualitative researcher's companion*. Thousand Oaks, CA: Sage Publications.

Nebeker, G. L. (2003). The Holy Spirit, hermeneutics, and transformation: From present to future glory. *Evangelical Review of Theology, 27*(1), 47–54.

Neuendorf, K. A. (2002). *The content analysis guidebook*. Thousand Oaks, CA: Sage Publications.

Noblit, G. W., & Hare, R. D. (1988). *Meta-ethnography: Synthesizing qualitative studies. In qualitative research methods* (Vol. 11). Thousand Oaks, CA: Sage Publications.

Patton, M. Q. (2002). *Qualitative research & evaluation* methods (3rd ed.). Thousand Oaks, CA: Sage Publications.

Pinnock, C. H. (1993). The work of the Holy Spirit in hermeneutics. *Journal of Pentecostal Theology, 1*(2), 3–23.

Seale, C. (1999). *The quality of qualitative research*. Thousand Oaks, CA: Sage Publications.

Strauss, A. L. (1987). *Qualitative analysis for social scientists*. New York, NY: Cambridge University Press.

Timulak, L., & Creaner, M. (2013). Experiences of conducting qualitative meta-analysis. *Counseling Psychology Review, 28*(4), 94–104.

Zuck, R. B. (1984). The role of the Holy Spirit in hermeneutics. *Bibliotheca Sacra, 141*(562), 120–130.

Chapter Twelve

Cotterell, P., & Turner, M. (1989). *Linguistics and biblical interpretation*. Downers Grove, IL: InterVarsity Press.

Creswell, J. W. (2014). *Research design: Qualitative, quantitative and mixed methods approaches*. Thousand Oaks, CA: Sage Publications.

Crowther, S. S. (2012). *Peter on leadership: A contemporary exegetical analysis*. Fayetteville, NC: Ontos Zoe Publishing.

Duvall, J. S., & Hays, J. D. (2012). *Grasping God's word*. Grand Rapids, MI: Zondervan Publishing.

Fee, G., & Stuart, D. (2014). *How to read the Bible for all its worth: A guide to understanding the Bible*. Grand Rapids, MI: Zondervan

Flick, U. (2009). *An introduction to qualitative research*. Thousand Oaks, CA: Sage Publications.

Kraft, C. H. (2007). *Anthropology for Christian witness*. Maryknoll, NY: Orbis Books.

Osborne, G. R. (2006). *The hermeneutical spiral: A comprehensive introduction to biblical interpretation*. Downers Grove, IL: InterVarsity Press.

Vanhoozer, K. J. (1998). *Is there a meaning in this text? The Bible, the reader and the morality of literary knowledge.* Grand Rapids, MI: Zondervan.

Virkler, H. A., & Ayayo, K. G. (2007). *Hermeneutics: Principles and process of biblical interpretation.* Grand Rapids, MI: Baker Academic

Wright, N. T. (1992). *The New Testament and the people of God.* Minneapolis, MN: Fortress Press.

Chapter Thirteen

Choi, S. B., Hanh Tran, T. B., & Park, B. I. (2015). Inclusive leadership and work engagement: Mediating roles of affective organizational commitment and creativity. *Social Behavior & Personality: An International Journal, 43*(6), 931–943.

Creswell, J. W. (2009). *Research design: Qualitative, quantitative, and mixed methods approaches* (3rd ed.). Los Angeles: SAGE.

Csikszentmihalyi, M. (1997). *Creativity: Flow and the psychology of discovery and invention* (p. 28). New York, NY: HarperCollins.

Gardner, J. (2011, August). Educational research: What (a) to do about impact! *British Educational Research Journal, 37*(4), 543–561.

Huizing, R. L. (2011). Leaders from disciples: The church's contribution to leadership development. *Evangelical Review of Theology, 35*(4), 333–344.

Jung, D. I. (2001). Transformational and transactional leadership and their effects on creativity in groups. *Creativity Research Journal, 13*(2), 186.

Kandiko, C. B. (2012). Leadership and creativity in higher education: The role of interdisciplinarity. *London Review of Education, 10*(2), 191.

Malek, J. (2018). Bridging the gap between theory and practice: Philosophy through a wide-angle lens. *Journal of Medicine & Philosophy, 43*(1), 1–7.

Minichiello, V., Aroni, R., Timewell, E., & Alexander, L. (1990). *In-depth interviewing: Researching people.* Hong Kong: Longman Cheshire.

Neal, Z. P., Watling Neal, J., Lawlor, J. A., & Mills, K. J. (2015). Small worlds or worlds apart? Using network theory to understand the research-practice gap. *Psychosocial Intervention, 24*(3), 177–184. doi:10.1016/j.psi.2015.07.006

Savitch, W. J. (1987). *Pascal, an introduction to the art and science of programming* (2nd ed.). San Francisco, CA: Benjamin Cummings.

Smith, C. (2019). Education theory and practice: A "web of webs" of theories? *Psychology of Education Review, 43*(1), 34–38.

Sternberg, R. H. (2005). WICS: A model of positive educational leadership comprising wisdom, intelligence, and creativity synthesized. *Educational Psychology Review, 17*(3), 228.

Southern, S., & Devlin, J. (2010). Theory development: A bridge between practice and research. *Family Journal, 18*(1), 84–87. doi:10.1177/1066480709358422

Zubair, A., & Kamal, A. (2015). Authentic leadership and creativity: Mediating role of work-related flow and psychological capital. *Journal of Behavioural Sciences, 25*(1), 151.

Zahle, J. (2017). Ability theories of practice and Turner's criticism of Bourdieu. *Journal for General Philosophy of Science, 48*(4), 553–567.

Appendix A

Ali, A. J., Camp, R. C., & Gibbs, M. (2000). The ten commandments perspective on power and authority in organizations. *Journal of Business Ethics, 26*(4), 351–361.

Bruce, F. F. (2000). *Paul: Apostle of the heart set free*. Grand Rapids, MI: William B. Eerdmans.

Dent, E. B., Higgins, M. E., & Wharff, D. M. (2005). Spirituality and leadership: An empirical review of definitions, distinctions, and embedded assumptions. *The Leadership Quarterly, 16*(5), 625–653.

deSilva, D. A. (2004). *An introduction to the New Testament: Contexts, methods, and ministry formation*. Downers Grove, IL: IVP Academic.

Genade, A. A. (2011). *Persuading the Cretans: A text-generated persuasion analysis of the letter to Titus*. Eugene, OR: Wipf and Stock.

Gibbons, P. (2000). *Spirituality at work: Definitions, measures, assumptions, and validity claims*. Proceedings of the Academy of Management, USA. Retrieved from http://www.paulgibbons.net/sites/default/files/field/image/Spirituality%20at%20Work%20-%20MASTER.doc

Hannah, S. T., Lester, P. B., & Vogelgesang, G. R. (2005). Moral leadership: Explicating the moral component of authentic leadership. In W. Gardner, B. Avolio, & F. Walumbwa (Eds.), *Authentic leadership theory and practice: Origins, effects, and development* (pp. 43–81). San Diego, CA: Elsevier.

Henson, J. D. (2015). *An examination of the role of spirituality in the development of the moral component of authentic leadership through a sociorhetorical analysis of Paul's letter to Titus*. Unpublished doctoral dissertation. Regent University, Virginia Beach, VA.

Klenke, K. (2007). Authentic leadership: A self, leader, and spiritual identity perspective. *International Journal of Leadership Studies, 3*(1), 68–97.

Kretzschmar, L. (2002, July). Authentic Christian leadership and spiritual formation in Africa. *Journal of Theology for Southern Africa, 113*, 41–60.

Kriger, M. P., & Hanson, B. J. (1999). A value-based paradigm for creating truly healthy organizations. *Journal of Organizational Change Management, 12*(4), 302–317.

Park, N., Peterson, C., & Seligman, M. E. (2004). Strengths of character and well-being. *Journal of Social and Clinical Psychology, 23*(5), 603–619.

Witherington, B. (2006). *Letters and homilies for Hellenized Christians: A socio-rhetorical commentary on Titus, 1-2 Timothy, and 1-3 John*. Downers Grove, IL: InterVarsity Press.

Appendix B

Chilton, B., & Yamauchi, E. (2000). Jesus' relation to synagogues. In C. Evans & S. Porter, Jr. (Eds.), *Dictionary of the New Testament background* (p. 1150). Downers Grove, IL: Intervarsity Press.

Schiffman, L. H. (2011). Purity. In M. A. Powell (Ed.), *Harper Collins Bible dictionary* (pp. 854–855). New York, NY: Society of Biblical Literature.

Wulf, F. D. (2000). Blood. In D. N. Freedman (Ed.), *Eerdman's dictionary of the Bible* (pp. 193–194). Grand Rapids, MI: William B. Eerdmans Publishing.

List of Scripture References

1

1 Corinthians
- 1:18-25 169
- 1:18-31 95
- 2:13-14 10
- 2:6-16 95
- 3:18 170
- 3:18-22 170
- 6 170
- 6:19 48
- 8 170
- 9:8-10 170
- 10:1-5 170
- 11:2-16 69
- 11-14 170
- 12:15-31 94
- 13 .... 95, 169, 172, 173
- 14:5 95
- 15 169

1 John
- 1:9 48

1 Peter
- 1:1-12 177
- 1:13-19 183
- 2:1-12 159
- 3 .... 133, 134, 154
- 3:1-7 213
- 4:7 181
- 4:12-19 137
- 5 141
- 5:1-11 189
- 5:1-8 213

1 Samuel
- 17 49

2

2 Chronicles
- 36:20-21 148

2 Corinthians
- 2:5-11 172
- 5:17 169
- 5:20 169
- 7 173

2 Peter
- 1:21 .... 39, 121
- 3 133
- 3:10-12 155

2 Samuel
- 7:11-13 116

2 Timothy
- 2:15 73
- 3:7 9
- 3:16-17 .... 7, 65

A

Acts
- 1:8 156
- 2 118
- 2:11 118

Acts (*Continued*)
- 2:14 ... 118
- 2:16-21 ... 111
- 2:22 ... 118
- 2:24 ... 119
- 2:25-28 ... 65
- 2:29 ... 118
- 2:29-31 ... 115
- 2:29-36 ... 118
- 2:30 ... 118
- 2:31 ... 111
- 2:34 ... 118
- 2:34-35 ... 111
- 2:36 ... 118
- 3:22 ... 109
- 7 ... 121
- 7:38 ... 183
- 7:58 ... 115, 122
- 8:3 ... 119
- 15:1-35 ... 174
- 15:4-21 ... 119
- 16 ... 169
- 22 ... 169

Amos
- 1:1 ... 67
- 9 ... 134

D

Daniel
- 1:8-15 ... 154

Deuteronomy
- 18:15 ... 109
- 34 ... 64

E

Ephesians
- 4:25 ... 47
- 6:14 ... 169

Exodus
- 13:3-16 ... 182
- 17:1-7 ... 162

- 19 ... 121
- 19:16-19 ... 121
- 20:2 ... 51
- 24:6-8 ... 182

G

Galatians
- 1:13 ... 119
- 1:18 ... 119
- 2:1 ... 119
- 2:11-14 ... 119
- 5:19-21 ... 198

Genesis
- 1-2 ... 94
- 3 ... 49
- 5 ... 86
- 9:5-6 ... 86
- 12 ... 51, 130
- 22 ... 181
- 37:1–11 ... 92

H

Hebrews
- 1:1 ... 66
- 9:18-23 ... 182
- 10:4 ... 48
- 13:8 ... 10

I

Isaiah
- 7:10-25 ... 55
- 65:7 ... 134

J

James
- 1:17 ... 10
- 3:9 ... 86

Jeremiah
- 25:11-12 ... 148
- 31:31-34 ... 119, 121

List of Scripture References

Joel
- 2:28-32 .... 111, 120

John
- 1:1-18 91
- 1:42 96
- 1:45 65
- 3 56
- 3:1-21 19
- 3:16 19
- 4 .... 28, 56
- 5:39 197
- 5:46 65
- 8:1-5 115
- 8:7 115
- 10 96
- 11 85
- 12 141
- 13 142
- 14:26 8
- 15:26 8
- 17:14-17 9
- 18:1-21:25 24
- 19:10 153
- 21 96
- 21:24-25 50
- 21:25 93

Joshua
- 7:25 115

Judges
- 4 28
- 6:11 156
- 15:15-20 155

L

Leviticus
- 1:5 182
- 1-7 166
- 5:2-6 47
- 9:12-15 182
- 11:44 183
- 20:10 115
- 25:3-7 148
- 26:32-35 148

Luke
- 2:1-3 119
- 3:37 66
- 5:2-11 100
- 5:17-39 168
- 6:15 155
- 20:28 65
- 22:15-20 182
- 22:20 121
- 22:47-53 24
- 24 156
- 24:27 197

M

Mark
- 2 .... 144, 146
- 2:23-24 145
- 5:21-43 .... 147, 159
- 10:17 157
- 12:13-17 93
- 12:19 65
- 14:43-16:20 24

Matthew
- 1 52
- 1:18 47
- 1:19 47
- 1:26-27 154
- 5 85
- 15:11 9
- 17:27 146
- 19:23 137
- 21:12-17 195
- 23:1-12 195
- 26:28 119
- 26:36-28:20 24
- 27:27-37 56
- 28 102

N

Numbers
- 5:2 147
- 15:36 115

P

Philippians
- 1:1-11 189
- 2:5-11 144
- 2:6 208
- 3:6 51

Proverbs
- 22:6 54
- 25:2 .... 73, 80

Psalms
- 14:13 109
- 16 65
- 16:10 .... 111, 115
- 23 .... 26, 132
- 53:1-3 109
- 110 65
- 110:1 111
- 119:11 9
- 142 122

R

Revelation
- 1:4 66
- 2:29 10
- 3:18 10
- 22 179

Romans
- 3:1 112
- 3:10-12 109
- 3:10-18 .... 109, 112
- 8:9 180
- 14:20 117

Ruth
- 2:2-3 146

T

Titus
- 1:5-16 112–113
- 1:15 117

About the Authors

Joshua D. Henson, PhD

Joshua currently serves Regent University as an adjunct professor in the School of Business & Leadership lending his expertise in the fields of exegetical analysis and ecclesial leadership to the PhD in Organizational Leadership and Doctor of Strategic Leadership programs as instructor and dissertation chair in the ecclesial leadership concentration. For the past 14 years, he has served as senior pastor, regional overseer, and conference speaker. He has published and presented exegetical research on contemporary leadership at several academic conferences. He has edited and contributed to three academic books. He teaches at multiple institutions throughout the United States and South America having students on five continents. He serves as the Editor of the *Journal of Biblical Perspectives in Leadership* and Chair of Regent University's Regent Roundtables Biblical Studies Roundtable. His research interests include biblical leadership, the Pastoral Epistles, Christian spirituality, moral and ethical development, authentic leadership, and developing ethical organizational mission and vision.

Steven S. Crowther, PhD

Steven is the President of Grace College of Divinity in Fayetteville, North Carolina. He teaches undergraduate and graduate courses in theology, leadership, and practical ministry. He is also an adjunct professor in Regent University's DSL program. Prior to this, he had 23 years of experience in ecclesial leadership as a pastor. In addition, he has worked in the area of missions establishing leadership training centers in different countries from Latin America to Eastern Europe. His research has been in the areas of exegetical analysis, organizational leadership, biblical leadership, servant leadership, church history, oral cultures, ethics, and church development. He has written two books on Christian leadership and has written several journal articles. These journal articles have included Organizational Learning and Organizational Leadership: Some Paramount Considerations for the Global CEO, Integral Biblical Leadership and The Spirit of Service: Reexamining Servant Leadership in the Gospel of Mark. His dissertation was recognized as "Outstanding Dissertation of the Year" by Regent University in 2012.

Russell L. Huizing, PhD

Russell is an associate professor of Pastoral Ministries at Toccoa Falls College in Georgia. He is also an instructor in Regent University's online PhD, DSL, and undergraduate programs. Prior to entering the academic field, he acquired nearly 15 years of experience in ecclesial leadership. Prior to that, he had nearly 15 years of leadership experience as a corporate trainer and a small business owner. His research has spanned the topics of exegetical analysis, organizational leadership, follower development, mentoring, development of ritual translation, and discipleship. He has contributed chapters to multiple books on Christian leadership. Journal publications have included, among others, *Mentoring and Tutoring*, *Downside Review*, *Evangelical Review of Theology*, *Journal of Applied Christian Leadership*, and *Great Commission Research Journal*. His dissertation was recognized by Regent University as "Outstanding Dissertation of the Year, 2013." He has received the Vulcan Teaching Excellence Award (2015), TFC Faculty Scholar of the Year Award (2018), and TFC Faculty of Impact Award (2019). He is the Editor of the Theology of Leadership Journal.